D0620931

Bloom's Modern Critical Interpretations

Bloom's Modern Critical Interpretations

Bloom's Modern Critical Interpretations

Nathaniel Hawthorne's
Young Goodman Brown

Edited and with an introduction by
Harold Bloom
Sterling Professor of the Humanities
Yale University

CHELSEA HOUSE
P U B L I S H E R S
A Haights Cross Communications Company
Philadelphia

A Haights Cross Communications ⋔ Company

http://www.chelseahouse.com

Printed and bound in the United States of America.

10 9 8 7 6 5 4 3 2 1

Library of Congress Cataloging-in-Publication Data applied for.

Library of Congress Cataloging-in-Publication Data

Young Goodman Brown / [edited by] Harold Bloom.
     p. cm. — (Modern critical interpretations)
  Includes bibliographical references and index.
  ISBN 0-7910-8124-9 (alk. paper)
  1. Hawthorne, Nathaniel, 1804-1864. Young Goodman Brown. 2. Satanism in
literature. 3. Puritans in literature. 4. Devil in literature. I. Bloom, Harold. II. Series.
  PS1872.Y63Y68 2004
  813'.3—dc22
                              2004022351

Contributing Editor: Janyce Marson

Cover designed by Keith Trego

Layout by EJB Publishing Services

Contents

Editor's Note

My Introduction finds in Hawthorne's superb tale some aspects of its author's vexed relationship to the Emersonian dialectic of self and society.

The ambiguity of the story is viewed through the spectacles of Lévi-Strauss by Harold F. Mosher, Jr., while Jane Donahue Eberwein finds the equivocal patterns of Puritan conversion a basis for the plot.

John S. Hardt considers the ideals of paradise as presented in Irving's "Rip Van Winkel," Hawthorne's "Young Goodman Brown," and Poe's "The Fall of the House of Ushe," after which Jules Zanger contrasts "Young Goodman Brown" to Sarah Orne Jewett's wonderful story, "The White Heron," which also centers upon moral choice.

Joan Elizabeth Easterly explicates the imagery of tears in Hawthorne's symbolism, after which Walter Shear, seeking versions of the American self, juxtaposes Henry James's "The Jolly Corner" and Washington Irving's "Rip Van Winkle" to Hawthorne's story.

Benjamin Franklin V ponders the use by Hawthorne of a Puritan catechism of John Cotton's, while James C. Keil uncovers the sexual anxieties of Brown.

Debra Johanyak returns us to the fallen Eden as the background of the tale after which Edward Jayne diagnosis paranoia as Brown's ailment.

This volume concludes with its most distinguished critical essay, in which David Bromwich places "Young Goodman Brown" in the context of a more individual American psychosis, once induced by the death of Calvinism.

Introduction

There is no single way to characterize Nathaniel Hawthorne's complex vision of the American self. I think I have learned some of the intricacies of the Emersonian self in the Sage of Concord's work, and in its further developments (and departures) in Thoreau, Whitman, Dickinson, and Melville, all of whom would have been very different had Emerson never existed. Hawthorne's relationship to Emerson is far more difficult to perceive and describe. They were unlikely but fairly frequent walking-companions, with the essayist probably carrying most of the desultory discourse along. Except for his wife Lidian and daughter Ellen, Emerson really needed no one, though he found the taciturn Hawthorne pleasant enough company, if of little interest as a writer. But then, our national sage did not much enjoy prose fiction. The *Moralia* of Plutarch, Montaigne's essays, Dante, and Shakespeare were Emerson's preferred reading. He searched for wit and wisdom, not for moral perplexity. Right and wrong were unambiguous for the prophet of self-reliance, at home with the God within, the best and oldest part of his being. Hawthorne, uneasy with Emerson, nevertheless could never quite evade him. Hester Prynne, like Henry James's Isabel Archer, is the American Eve, and both are Emersonian, even as Whitman and Thoreau are versions of Emerson's American Adam, always early in the morning. Emerson, satirized by a defensive Melville in *Pierre* and in *The Confidence Man*, nevertheless is the American Plato who informs the Gnostic cosmos of

Moby Dick, despite itself as profoundly Emerson as is the original 1855 *Leaves of Grass*. Captain Ahab refuses a role as American Adam, but his Promethean rebellion against the Creation-Fall of his catastrophic maiming by the snowy Leviathan allies him to the grim sublimity of Emerson's masterwork, *The Conduct of Life*. Hawthorne, of all the titans of the American Renaissance, has the subtlest and most surprising relationship to the inescapable Emersonian self.

"Young Goodman Brown" (1835) is early Hawthorne, composed when he was about thirty, and just beginning to fully find his mode as a writer. Poor Brown is not at all self-reliant, but a rather pathetic instance of societal over-conditioning. Hawthorne neither wants to be or is an Emersonian, yet he gives us a young "goodman" who badly needs a blood-transfusion from Hester Prynne, or some other fictive apostle of Emerson. One of many implicit Hawthornian ironies is that the strong self's cost of confirmation comes too high, while society's conformities are hopelessly low, and are not worth even the smallest price. Hawthorne never satirizes Emersonianism, because he agrees with its dialectic of self-reliance against societal repression, but he also shudders at Emerson's casual stance towards antinomianism. Still, Hawthorne has made his choice: he will not join Emerson's Party of Hope, but he has no use whatever for the Party of Memory. Like his more capable readers, Hawthone falls in love with Hester Prynne, and consigns the wretched Brown to a silent death-in-life:

> Had Goodman Brown fallen asleep in the forest, and only dreamed a wild dream of a witch-meeting?
>
> Be it so, if you will. But, alas! it was a dream of evil omen for young Goodman Brown. A stern, a sad, a darkly meditative, a distrustful, if not a desperate man, did he become, from the night of that fearful dream. On the Sabbath-day, when the congregation were singing a holy psalm, he could not listen, because an anthem of sin rushed loudly upon his ear, and drowned all the blessed strain. When the minister spoke from the pulpit, with power and fervid eloquence, and, with his hand on the open Bible, of the sacred truths of our religion, and of saint-like lives and triumphant deaths, and of future bliss or misery unutterable, then did Goodman Brown turn pale, dreading, lest the roof should thunder down upon the gray blasphemer and his hearers. Often, awakening suddenly at midnight, he shrank from the bosom of Faith, and at morning or eventide, when the family knelt down at prayer, he scowled, and muttered to himself, and gazed sternly at his wife, and turned away. And when he had lived

long, and was borne to his grave, a hoary corpse, followed by
Faith, an aged woman, and his children and grand-children, a
goodly procession, besides neighbors, not a few, they carved no
hopeful verse upon his tomb-stone; for his dying hour was gloom.

Self-damnation could hardly go further, even in a tale by Hawthorne.
What precisely has destroyed Brown? Is it the American Psychosis, as
analyzed in a powerful essay of David Bromwich's (reprinted in this volume)?
The living death of Brown would thus be another instance of the extinction
of American radical Protestantism, the failed transformation of John Calvin
to these shores. Jonathan Edwards is no longer even a ghostly presence,
while Ralph Waldo Emerson lives on (except for the South). Perhaps
Emerson is even too lively, since we are ruled by Emersonians of the Right,
even as Emersonians of the Left go on destroying our universities in the
name of sacred Resentment, determined to expiate, whatever it costs in
humanistic culture. There are no young Goodman Browns among my
current students, and only a few Hester Prynnes.

HAROLD F. MOSHER, JR.

The Sources of Ambiguity in Hawthorne's "Young Goodman Brown": A Structuralist Approach

As Jonathan Culler has observed, the structuralist method, based on the linguistic model, should "account for our judgments about meaning and ambiguity, well-formedness and deviance." The structuralist critic studies the conventions of any system that enables its signs to produce meaning or certain effects. He does not primarily study meaning or seek to formulate new interpretations; rather he examines how meaning or effects are achieved.[1] In such analyses, of course, consideration of meaning cannot be ignored. Thus, Claude Lévi-Strauss, by a method that consists of "dividing the syntagmatic sequence into superposable segments, and in proving that they constitute variations on one and the same theme," studies patterns of opposition that produce meaning in myths.[2] A.J. Greimas has developed the "semiotic square" to account for even more complex relations governed by the principles of contradiction and contrariness.[3] Similarly, a structuralist reading of Hawthorne's "Young Goodman Brown," rather than revealing new meaning, concentrates on how the story produces its ambiguities as well as how it suggests an unambiguous meaning. Using Lévi-Strauss' method, I propose to examine the structure of oppositions in the syntagmatic chain, and adapting other structuralist methods suggested by Gérard Genette, Gerald Prince, and Seymour Chatman,[4] I shall study the contradictions of meaning between and within the unmediated and mediated elements of the

From *ESQ: A Journal of the American Renaissance* 26, 1st quarter. ©1980 ESQ.

discourse, essentially involving the reader's relationship with the narrator and the characters.

Certainly the ambiguity that has created so much critical debate, resulting most obviously from the narrator's refusal to answer his own question about Brown's dream, is real. "Young Goodman Brown" is not unique in this respect in Hawthorne's *corpus*, sharing at least its moral ambiguity with that in such other major works as "My Kinsman, Major Molineux" and *The Scarlet Letter*.[5] In "Young Goodman Brown," Hawthorne, like his admirer Henry James, tries to create in his readers the same moral ambiguity that confronts his characters while suggesting, often very subtly, the implied author's judgments. Contradictions abound, leading in the imperfect reader (the "narratee" in Gerald Prince's terms)[6] to a confusion similar to the one Brown feels, but at the same time much evidence indicates the implied author's condemnation of Brown's final behavior.

In making these conclusions, I am, of course, not alone. Many critics have pointed out that the ambiguities of the story make a judgment about Brown's condemnation of his fellow villagers virtually impossible.[7] On the other hand, while some think that Brown did experience the forest events and is right in his condemnation of the villagers, still others believe that Brown dreamed or imagined the forest events and is wrong in his condemnation. Sheldon W. Liebman's 1975 article on the story, with which I am basically in agreement, provides a succinct classification of the studies subscribing to these three views and then, while recognizing the story's "diverting ambiguities" on unresolvable and relatively unimportant issues, argues that the story is unambiguous, if one attends closely to point of view, in showing Brown to be a victim of his own thoughts.[8] Liebman, however, provides no clear basis for distinguishing the narrator's point of view from Brown's, claiming that by the principle of "dissimulated point of view" the focus shifts "imperceptibly from narrator to character so that the reader sees through the character's eyes even when he thinks he is seeing through the narrator's" (p. 158). Though Liebman is right in pointing out the many verbs indicating Brown's perception of the action after he leaves Faith, his generalization that thenceforth Hawthorne reports subjective action as if it were objectively happening is open to question and is in fact contradicted, as shall be seen, by Liebman himself. One might, for example, agree with Liebman that the adjective "excellent" describing Brown's "resolve" as he hurries into the forest could represent Brown's interest point of view[9] (or it could, as Richard H. Fogle claims,[10] express the narrator's irony), but the following remark about the solitary traveller is evidently the narrator's editorial, identified by its generalizing sense and use of the present tense:

"and there is this peculiarity in such a solitude, that the traveller knows not who may be concealed by the innumerable trunks and the thick boughs overhead; so that with lonely footsteps he may yet be passing through an unseen multitude."[11]

A similar claim to Liebman's that the action of the central part of the story is seen exclusively from Brown's point of view is made by Thomas F. Walsh, Jr., who believes, however, that a study of point of view throws no light on the ambiguities.[12] But Walsh mistakenly identifies the narrator's editorial on man's instinct for evil as Brown's thought and then contradicts his claim for the consistency of Brown's point of view by ascribing to "Hawthorne" the judgment of Brown as "the chief horror" (pp. 334–335). Likewise, David Levin identifies the point of view as Brown's in the paragraph describing the baptism preparations where a shift to the narrator's point of view at least temporarily occurs in the description of Brown's and Faith's hesitating on the verge of evil. Levin argues from the assumption of consistency in point of view, but even a Jamesian consistency involves switches from the central consciousness to the narrator.[13] Agreeing with Levin, Darrel Abel compares Brown's sole authority to the governess' in James' *The Turn of the Screw*, "verifiable by no other observer or 'control'"[14] But *The Turn of the Screw* is told in the first person, not in the third-person selective omniscient mode of "Young Goodman Brown." Furthermore, if the action is viewed exclusively from Brown's point of view, we have to accept such contradictions as his revering his father while picturing him in the devil's guise, as E. Arthur Robinson observes.[15] Although in dreams such contradictions can occur, the text does not clearly set off the real world from the dream world. Even if we were to accept the forest episode as the dream, the narrator's voice and focus are still present periodically throughout the discourse and are distinguishable, at least in many places, from Brown's.

To neglect the switches in point of view which can reveal the narrator's presence and interpretation is to ignore what Leo Levy describes as the mixed realistic/objective and allegorical/subjective nature of the tale whose narrator "moves into Brown's state of mind and then outward" elusively.[16] Although many of these critics' conclusions about the tale's meaning are not invalid, often their analyses of Hawthorne's techniques would benefit from more attention to detail. To examine these techniques in greater depth, I plan to analyze not only the story's structure but also its point of view and particularly what Genette calls "paralipses," omissions by the omniscient narrator (p. 212). Agreeing with much recent criticism, I assume that the implied author intends certain ambiguities because he allows his narrator to leave them unresolved, especially the one on the nature of the action in the forest. I shall also argue that the condemnation of Brown is relatively unambiguous. What I propose to study are the methods by which both the ambiguities and the condemnation are conveyed to the reader.

I will begin with probably the greatest source of ambiguity in "Young Goodman Brown"—the unmediated or nonnarrated parts, what characters say and think about themselves and each other and what characters do, as recorded by a relatively "absent" narrator. In Chatman's terminology, the narrator may be either "overt"—describing, summarizing, characterizing, judging, generalizing, and commenting on the discourse (pp. 219–253)—or "covert"—reporting characters' words and thoughts in indirect discourse and its variations (pp. 196–219)—or "absent"—reporting characters' words and thoughts in indirect discourse and its variations. This last is considered unmediated narration whereas the first two are mediated (pp. 146–194). The story's beginning emphasizes by dramatic (unmediated) interpretation or characterization the moods of Faith, Brown's wife. The message that the narratee receives directly from her speech is that she is "troubled" and "afeared of herself" for this "of all nights in the year," and her parting husband also analyzes directly her mood in his thoughts as "melancholy" and troubled by the warnings of her dreams. Furthermore, Brown characterizes Faith as an "angel," in contrast to himself, whom he dramatically and indirectly characterizes as temporarily belonging to another persuasion, at least until the morrow (pp. 74–75).[17] This portrait of the wife concerned for her husband seems to accord with the vision of Faith joyfully welcoming Brown the next morning on his return, but her concern for her own steadfastness might just as well be indirectly conveyed by these remarks and especially by her caution to Brown, "may you find all well when you come back" (p. 74). These stasis statements not only expose ambiguous traits and moods of existents (characters), but at the same time project by implied prolepsis (flashforward) events in the future of the plot and thus create suspense, another form of uncertainty.[18] Of what is Faith afraid? What will possibly change the next day's situation?

Brown's character traits are even more evidently self-contradictory, paradigmatically, and are presented, at least dramatically, in the syntagmatic pattern of alternating oppositions, typical of the story's plot.[19] Early he characterizes himself as eliciting doubt from Faith, as being a "wretch," and as having "scruples" for this "one night" after which he will follow Faith "to heaven" (p. 75). In contrast, Brown describes himself to the figure in the forest as one of a "race of honest men and good Christians," who "abide no such wickedness" and vows to return to Faith to avoid this "wickedly" spent night and his feeling of guilt (pp. 77, 81). Despite these professions of goodness, Brown continues deeper into the forest, and, confronted with various spectacles of temptation to pursue evil, he embraces the opportunity to follow the call of the wilderness and identifies with the brotherhood of the wicked, having found his true nature, as the witch minister tells him, inherited from his grandfather and father. The last macro-episode or large segment in the syntagmatic chain shows Brown again resisting evil, or what he considers to be evil, in the form of his fellow citizens, including Faith.

The flat characters, who tend to be part of the setting in accordance with Chatman's distinction between bona fide characters and named but unimportant ones (p. 141), are also characterized contradictorily by unmediated or dramatic means. Brown calls Deacon Gookin and the minister "holy" and Goody Cloyse "pious and exemplary" (pp. 82, 78). Again, however, in the typical pattern of alternating contrasts, this portrait of the villagers is contradicted by framing sets of dramatic characterizations, which picture Cloyse's and Brown's ancestors as friends of the devil in the earlier part of the plot and, in the final part, the deacon and minister as involved in "deviltry" and the whole village as steeped in sin.[20] Finally, the devil is somewhat less ambiguously characterized, the syntagmatic pattern being a simple two-part opposition between his first appearance in "grave and decent attire" in the person of Brown's grandfather (as is learned later from Goody Cloyse) and his gradual identification as the devil until he is directly named so by Cloyse. By such contradictory dramatic characterizations, the story and discourse involve the narratee in the moral ambiguities confronting Brown.

According to the conventions of most nineteenth-century fiction, the implied reader could usually count on the omniscient reliable narrator to convey overtly through the narratee the "truth" of the narrative, as the implied author intends it. This is not entirely the case in Hawthorne's tale, beginning with the overtly mediated interpretation of Faith, who is "aptly named." The narratee might accept this trait only up to certain point in the plot; after the cloud, which seems to Brown to contain Faith's voice, has passed overhead, something flutters down, and Brown "beheld a pink ribbon." The mystery is resolved for Brown, who decides on the basis of this ocular evidence that his "Faith is gone" (p. 83). To the narratee caught up in the excitement of this discovery, the evidence of Faith's guilt might also be convincing, but a narratee closer to the implied reader might look more analytically at the point of view and decide that this token of Faith's infidelity is perceived through Brown's interest point of view and therefore is not evidence for a "fact" of the ribbon's existence. The narrator has only reported that "something fluttered lightly down."[21] This more perceptive narratee might take the description of the ribbon as the narrator's report of what Brown thinks he sees; that is, the narrator is reliable in characterizing Faith as "aptly named" and in reporting strictly what happens in Brown's mind, though the narrator does not comment on the "truth" of those thoughts. A sort of paralipsis has occurred.[22]

Thus the contradictions that seem to abound in the narrator's characterizations and judgments of the Salem villagers may turn out not to be his self-contradictions at all when the point of view is scrutinized. For example, Goody Cloyse is judged to be "pious" (p. 78) and an "excellent old Christian" (p. 89); the "good old minister" is characterized as a "venerable saint" (p. 88). When elsewhere these citizens are called "fiend worshippers" (pp. 87, 88), point of view plays an ambiguous role. Although the judgment of Cloyse as "pious" might very well be Brown's, these other characterizations could be either Brown's or the narrator's. Likewise, during the witches' sabbath episode, it is sometimes not clear whether the action is seen through Brown's eyes or the narrator's. By the omnitemporal analeptic (Genette's term for flashback, p. 82) and proleptic description of these very faces' devout and benign looks, the point of view seems to be the narrator's, but if so, he is describing only the appearance of faces, not necessarily character. Even the presence of the governor's wife is qualified by the narrator's dubious "Some affirm" (p. 85). After the narrator asserts the presence of other Salem villagers including "high dames" and "church members of ... especial sanctity," he leaves their attendance at the ceremony open to question by switching to Brown's "bedazzled" (p. 85) point of view. The physical, metaphysical, and moral confusions continue as the narratee must reconcile the presence of these people at a witches' sabbath with the narrator's characterization of them as "grave, reputable, and pious" (p. 85). Moreover, in this passage, the narrator uses the very terms—"Good old Deacon Gookin" and "venerable saint"—in which he describes the same characters as they appear in Salem the next day (pp. 88–89). Such a contradiction may indicated the narrator's ironic stance or his unreliability, or it may suggest disagreement between his judgment of the villagers' piety and Brown's conception of their wickedness, or an identification of his language with Brown's in reporting Brown's point of view.

In addition to this manipulation of point of view, the narratee is also subjected to other paralipses. Some minor examples include the narrator's hesitant description of the minister of the witches' sabbath as one who "bore no slight similitude ... to some grave divine" (p. 86) and whose "once angelic nature could yet mourn for our miserable race" (pp. 87–88). The narratee will probably recognize him as the devil in yet another disguise. The narrator also hesitates in this episode to identify the contents of the communion cup as being either "water, reddened by the lurid light" or "blood" or "liquid flame" (p. 88). Earlier the narrator had analyzed Goody Cloyse's mutterings as "a prayer, doubtless" (p. 79), as if he were not sure, just as he is not certain about the dark figure's staff: that it could "almost be seen to twist and wriggle itself like a living serpent" "must have been an ocular deception" (p. 76). It is certainly difficult at this point in the tale for the narratee to decide if the narrator is speaking ironically (describing indirectly or implicitly), implying that the staff is actually a snake, or describing directly what is the "truth"— that the form of the staff and the light were deceptive. As Victor Vitanza points out,[23] from the point in the plot at which Brown passes "a crook of the road" and sees a "figure of a man" (p. 75), the rest of the action might be recuperated, in Jonathan Culler's term, as a delusion, except that the narrator does seem to assert the objective existence of "these two," Brown and the figure (p.76).

In contrast, these paralipses and apparent contradictions yield to the narrator's consistency in his characterization and judgments of Brown, who is pictured as "evil" (p.75), a "horror" (p. 83), "frightful" (p. 83), "demoniac" (p. 84), and a "polluted" wretch (p. 88). One of the major ironies of the tale should be mentioned. As opposed to Brown's and the narrator's paraliptic ignorance about the outcome of Faith's indoctrination into the knowledge of evil, the implied reader must observe what apparently is Brown's awareness of evil by the end of the plot when he sees evil or thinks he sees it everywhere, fulfilling the promise of the "sable form." The narratee might be tempted to conclude that Brown's successful quest for evil turns him into evil, as Brown's own identification with the wicked brotherhood and the wilderness attests. At any rate, the result is, as the narrator characterizes Brown at the end of the story, a "stern, a sad, a darkly meditative, a distrustful, if not a desperate man" (p. 89), suffering the effects of his search. Does the implied author intend the implied reader to conclude that in a tale of conflicting binary oppositions in the characterizations and judgments of all the other characters, where these oppositions do not exist, the "truth" of the fiction lies? One of the narrator's few generalizations would seem to support this conclusion about Brown's evil nature and consequently mistaken opinion about the evil of life (one delusion leads to another): "The fiend in his own shape is less hideous than when he rages in the breast of man" (p. 84).

But before deciding this matter, I want to look at some of the events, in addition to the existents, both narrated and nonnarrated (Chatman's synonyms for mediated and unmediated). Actually the mutterings of Goody Cloyse and the incident of the staff may be considered not only as integrative indices (signs) of character but also as satellites (minor events), or part of the distributive chain of functions (actions).[24] As already noted, the discourse treated them paraliptically. Paralipsis is a mark of this discourse's narrating other events as well and would therefore seem to be, in turn, an indirect dramatic index of the narrator's unreliability or else his manipulation of the narratee, effected by the narrator's inability, on one hand, or his refusal, on the other, to tell what "really" happened. Thus the narrator's discourse is filled with expressions of doubt. For example, when the dark figure gives his staff to Goody Cloyse, the narrator observes that "perhaps, it assumed life, being one of the rods which its owner had formerly lent to the Egyptian Magi" (p. 79). At first, such an indirect authorial identification of the figure with the devil seems clear, but the "perhaps" modifies not only the "fact" of the transformation of the rod into life but also the reason for that transformation. The narrator might be said to be speculating ironically on a popular explanation of the transformation, if, indeed, a transformation occurred. Or again the narrator tells the narratee that the minister and Deacon Gookin "appeared to pass along the road ... ; but owing doubtless to the depth of the gloom at that particular spot, neither ... were visible" (p. 81). The narrator ambiguously both asserts the existence of the "hoof tramps and the voices of the riders" and "their figures" and seems to deny their reality with the qualifiers "appeared" and "neither ... were visible."[25] Although the point of view here is not always the narrator's, it might well be argued that the narrator is attempting to "naturalize" supernatural events by physical or historical explanations to assure the narratee, at least in this second example, that the figures are people who are there but invisible because of the dark, not apparitions or delusions in Brown's mind. But such reassurances are contradicted paradigmatically by the pervading atmosphere of the supernatural: the miracle of Satan's staff and the "haunted" forest, for instance. Of course, one could argue also that the narrator is ironic and only pretending to convince the narratee that the rod assumed living form or that the people are "real," while expecting the implied reader to realize that the narration is indirect and that these are phantoms of evil or appearances only to Brown. Or, again, the position that the point of view is partly Brown's, at least in the vision of the minister and deacon, can also be argued.[26]

Similar to this trait of the narrator's to imply that supernatural appearance might be explained realistically is the "seems" expression. After describing what to Brown is convincing evidence of Faith's guilt in the form of the ribbon, the narrator says that Brown "seemed to fly along the forest-path rather than to walk or run" (p. 83). Here the narrator's incompetence to report what "really" occurred would appear clear because the point of view can only be his. Later he narrates the hesitancy of Faith and Brown before the baptismal font—"there they stood, the only pair, as it seemed, who were yet hesitating on the verge of wickedness" (p.88)—as if the narrator did not know how many other pairs might also be hesitating.[27] But these expressions of appearance could also be interpreted simply as common exaggerations which the narrator expects the implied reader to detect. By far the most often repeated expression of paralipsis is "as if." The devil, after Goody Cloyse's disappearance, waits "calmly as if nothing had happened" (p. 80). He disappears "as if he had vanished" (p. 80). Sounds are heard, "as if from the depths of the cloud" (p. 82); their echoes mock "as if bewildered wretches were seeking" Faith (p. 83). Again, though, the doubt could be ascribed to the ambiguity of point of view: these observations might be Brown's.

Other paraliptic measures serve the same purpose of confusing the narratee by either contradicting or asserting and denying. As already noted, the narrator will switch point of view without warning. At the witches' sabbath the identifying of the congregation seems to be in the omniscient narrator's register, but this changes to a simple report of what, in an obscure prolepsis, "Some affirm" (p. 85). The same passage continues, "Either the sudden gleam of light ... bedazzled Goodman Brown, or he recognized a score of the church members" (p. 85). The narrator is not sure exactly whom Brown sees, if anybody. Such uncertainty might, however, again be ascribed to the narrator's "naturalizing" Brown's hallucination. Switching from Brown's view, the narrator then offers his own judgment of the hymn in the short generalization that it expresses what "our nature can conceive of sin" (p. 85; the first person is a sign of the narrator's voice), and concludes in another editorial, "Unfathomable to mere mortals is the lore of fiends" (p. 85). These two generalizations are somewhat self-contradictory in asserting both the common knowledge and the ignorance of sin. Further, the first one seems to contradict a conclusion about the exclusive evil to Brown. But because generalizations, though perhaps inspired by the fictional action, point outside that action, these are not necessarily commenting on this particular congregation. At the same time, however, the generalization about shared evil serves its contradictory purpose of ironically implicating others, including the narratee, in Brown's evil while seeming to place that evil exclusively in the congregation at the witches' sabbath. On the other hand, the narrator, earlier in the discourse, might seem to be asserting the morality of that congregation. With the same phrase, "In truth" (p. 83), he had used to judge Brown's frightfulness as he ran madly toward evil, the narrator replies to Brown's dramatic characterization of the congregation as a "grave and dark-clad company" by commenting, "In truth, they were such" (p. 84). But this is only a comment on the appearance of the multitude and is not necessarily making a character judgment. In the same episode the narrator might seem to naturalize the supernatural fire by describing it to be like one in a clearing where felled trees burn, but he immediately cancels this reassuring, realistic impression by saying that only the tops of the pines were burning, "like candles at an evening meeting" (p. 84). The narratee is continually made a victim of apparently reliable commentary that subsequently seems to be denied but seldom provides a firm basis for a definitive judgment.

Again, though, the narratee might conclude that these binary oppositions serve to emphasize the unambiguous theme that the narrator is only reporting the conflicting delusions of a fanatic's mind. Evidence for this view might include the description of the tempest that accompanies Brown's apparent conversion. When the cloud first appears hurrying across the sky, the narrator says that "no wind was stirring" (p. 82) and later that the sky was "clear and silent" (p. 83), but when Brown then accepts evil and hurries off to look for it, the narrator reports that the trees creaked and the "wind tolled" (p. 83), becoming a "tempest" (p. 84) swelling in the hymn at the Ceremony. After Brown calls on Faith to abandon wickedness, he finds himself in a calm, as the wind's roar dies away. The narrator might intend us to interpret the wind as an objective correlative of Brown's excited delusion or, less metacritically, as part of his delusion.[28] Of course, the most obvious paralipsis creating ambiguity is the narrator's raising the question addressed directly to narratee, suggesting that Brown might have just dreamed this action. On one hand, the narrator seems to answer his own question: "it was a dream of evil omen"; but on the other, this assertion is qualified by the preceding clause—"Be it so, if you will" (p. 89)—as if the identification of the experience as a dream depended on the narratee's decision and is therefore a subjective choice and relatively unimportant. According to the narrator, only the consequences of Brown's experience are significant, being "of evil omen" (p. 89), for the rest of his life and his death were "gloom" (p. 90).

The paradigmatic pattern of binary oppositions or contradictions for the existents is also evident in the syntagmatic structure of the plot's narremes or shorter events.[29] In most of the plot, the alternation between the assurance that life in the story is or can be normal, "real," or good and the doubt or suspicion that it is odd, supernatural, or evil is strikingly regular. For instance, the plot begins with a normal leave-taking, but this normalcy is immediately questioned by Faith's warnings. This is followed by Brown's recognition of the extraordinary errand. His prolepsis about following Faith to heaven after this particular night is undermined by the narrator's judgment of his "present evil purpose" (p. 75) and by the appearance in the forest of the suspicious dark figure. This regular alternation continues until the meeting with Goody Cloyse, during which several narremes elicit doubt about the goodness and normalcy of life. A similar span of unsettling narremes occurs after Brown discovers the pink ribbon, but the alternation resumes when Brown believes that the figure of his mother warns him away from the initiation ceremony. The pattern continues to the end of the plot with such reassuring narremes as Faith's and Brown's hesitation before the baptismal font, Brown's warning to Faith, the disappearance of the vision of the witches' sabbath, and the question from the narrator suggesting that Brown had only dreamed this experience. These narremes alternate with Brown's irresistible attraction to the ceremony, the dark form's description of evil pervading the world, the preparation for baptism, Brown's doubt in Faith's refusal of the baptism, his unusual behavior the next morning in Salem, and finally his ensuing darkened life.

Lévi-Strauss has warned that the oversimplification involved in establishing binary oppositions can result in the contrasting items being changed or distorted beyond recognition.[30] To try to avoid this error, I have multiplied the categories to cover different situations: normal, real, and good are opposed to odd, supernatural, and evil. One must also consider that the identification of this paradigmatic pattern of alternation depends on the recognition of the syntagmatic progress of the narremes that fulfill the pattern. Oversimplification results also from the narratee's failure to see the variations within this pattern. There is in Brown an increasing realization of and attraction to evil as the doubting narremes increase somewhat in quantity and, much more significantly, in importance, particularly in the witches' sabbath episode. Another subtle change that the pattern alone does not reveal is that Brown first denies, then accepts the existence of evil in others and eventually recognizes it also in himself. From a patient enduring happenings, Brown becomes an agent causing actions in his search for evil and then returns to being a patient enduring the evil in himself or ineffectively resisting the evil outside himself.[31] Ultimately we might say that the pattern of doubt and assurance and its subtle variations dramatize the insidious self-persuasion in Brown, and possibly in the narratee, of the prevalence of evil in the world. Brown, at any rate, comes to an assurance that the world is evil, not good, and at least one type of narratee might also be encouraged to doubt that it is entirely good, "real," and normal. Furthermore, because of the network of conflicting characterizations, the narrator's paralipses, contradictions, and ambiguous and switching points of view, as well as the pattern of alternating doubt and assurance, the narratee in the end may not be able to decide whether Brown's rejection of the world receives the author's commendation as a refusal of evil or his condemnation as a result of an immersion in the knowledge of evil. I have suggested that close analysis reveals that Brown is responsible for many questionable judgments which an undiscriminating narratee might assign to the narrator, and I have further argued that the narrator's consistently unfavorable judgment of Brown may reveal the implied author's preference for condemning Brown. Whether one accepts this conclusion or prefers, using Wayne Booth's principle of "unstable irony,"[32] the interpretation accepting the story's ultimate ambiguity, the structuralist critic has learned, by studying the story's pattern and the discourse's manipulation of point of view, something about the sources and effects of that ambiguity.

NOTES

1. *Structuralist Poetics* (Ithaca: Cornell Univ. Press, 1975), p. 31.

2. *The Raw and the Cooked*, trans. John and Doreen Weightman (New York: Harper and Row, 1969), p. 307.

3. *Du Sens* (Paris: Seuil, 1970).

4. Genette, "Discourse du récit" in *Figures III* (Paris: Seuil, 1972), pp. 65–273; Prince, "Introductiion à l'étude du narrataire," *Poétique*, 14 (1973), 178–196; Chatman, *Story and Discourse* (Ithaca: Cornell Univ. Press, 1978).

5. Regarding this problem of ambiguity, and more specifically its source, Edgar A. Dryden, *Nathaniel Hawthorne: The Poetics of Enchantment* (Ithaca: Cornell Univ. Press, 1977), p. 138, notes that in "*The Scarlet Letter* and *The House of the Seven Gables* it is difficult to distinguish between fiction and history, imagination and perception."

6. Wayne Booth, *The Rhetoric of Fiction* (Chicago: Univ. of Chicago Press, 1961), pp. 70–71, is, of course, responsible for the term "implied author," the real author's other self, invented as the moving principle for the fiction. Gerald Prince, "Introduction," pp. 179–187, makes careful distinctions among types of readers and narratees. See also Chatman, pp. 33; 147–151; 253–262, on narratee, narrator, implied author, and implied reader.

7. Referring to the realistic and the fantastic readings of the story, Charles Child Walcutt, *Man's Changing Mask* (Minneapolis: Univ. of Minnesota Press, 1966), p. 126, remarks that "Hawthorne ... has interwoven these two possibilities so tightly that it is impossible to show that either one represents the accurate reading of the story."

8. "The Reader in 'Young Goodman Brown,'" *The Nathaniel Hawthorne Journal* 1975, ed. C.E. Frazer Clark, Jr. (Englewood, Colo.: Microcard Editions Books, 1975), pp. 156–169. See Liebman's review of some of the scholarship, p. 157, and also Robert J. Stanton, "Secondary Studies on Hawthorne's 'Young Goodman Brown,' 1845–1975: A Bibliography," *Bulletin of Bibliography*, 33 (1976), 32–44, 52.

9. Chatman, *Story and Discourse*, p. 162, defines interest point of view as the concerns of a character, if not actually his vision or thought.

10. *Hawthorne's Fiction: The Light and the Dark* (Norman: Univ. of Oklahoma Press, 1952), p. 31.

11. Nathaniel Hawthorne, "Young Goodman Brown" in *Mosses from an Old Manse*, ed. William Charvat, Roy Harvey Pearce, and Claude M. Simpson, The Centenary Edition of the Works of Nathaniel Hawthorne, X (Columbus: Ohio State Univ. Press, 1974), p. 75. Further references to this edition will be noted in the text.

12. "The Bedeviling of Young Goodman Brown," *Modern Language Quarterly*, 19 (1958), 331.

13. "Shadows of Doubt: Specter Evidence in Hawthorne's 'Young Goodman Brown,'" *American Literature*, 34 (1962), 350.

14. "Black Glove and Pink Ribbon: Hawthorne's Metonymic Symbols," *New England Quarterly*, 42 (1969), 180.

15. "The Vision of Goodman Brown: A Source and Interpretation," *American Literature*, 35 (1963), 222.

16. "The Problem of Faith in 'Young Goodman Brown,'" *Journal of English and Germanic Philology*, 74 (1975), 375.

17. My terms "indirect" and "direct" correspond to Chatman's implicit (ironic) and explicit commentary respectively, p. 228.

18. For more complete definitions of "stasis statement," "exposing," "projecting," and "events," see Chatman, p. 32–33. "Prolepsis" is Genette's term, p. 82.

19. I am using "paradigmatic" and "syntagmatic" in the usual Saussurean, structuralist way to mean, respectively, the reserve of meaning (particularly character traits and settings) available for the discourse's use and the sequence of actions occurring "linearly" throughout the story.

20. Joseph T. McCullen, "Young Goodman Brown: Presumption and Despair," *Discourse*, 2 (1959), 149 and 156, n. 13, notices these contradictions but attributes them to Hawthorne's belief in the mixture of good and evil in people. On the other hand, without taking contradictory evidence into consideration, D.M. McKeithan, "Hawthorne's 'Young Goodman Brown': An Interpretation," *Modern Language Notes*, 67 (1952), 96, asserts the goodness of the Salem villagers.

21. P. 83. L. Moffitt Cecil notes the correspondence between Brown's deluding eyesight and his faulty insight as typical of many of Hawthorne's characters in "Hawthorne's Optical Device," *American Quarterly*, 15 (1963), 82–83.

22. Liebman, "The Reader," pp. 161–162, points out many such instances of objective "facts" being actually only perceived by Brown who, for instance, "beheld the figure of a man," "recognized a very pious and exemplary dame," "heard the tramp of horses," "recognized the voices," "sees" a black cloud and a fire, thinks he sees his father and mother, and "beheld" Faith at the meeting. Many critics have, of course, discussed the famous pink ribbons, testing their reality or symbolic value. Leo Levy, "The Problem of Faith," p. 377, argues for their reality on the basis of the "tangible evidence" that Brown seizes and beholds, but Hawthorne's grammatical constructions typically do not allow such positive identification. What Brown seizes is referred to as "it," whose antecedent is the vague "something" that has fluttered down and which is seen only by Brown as a ribbon. Faith has her ribbons the next day. As for the symbolic significance of the ribbons, the ambiguity of the story has inspired much difference of opinion, as Levy points out, "The Problem," p. 382.

23. "Teaching Roland Barthes' Method of Textual Analysis, with an Example from Hawthorne," unpublished paper given at the Roland Barthes Special Session, Modern Language Association Convention, 1977.

24. Chatman's terminology, pp. 32–33, 53–56, is borrowed and adapted from Roland Barthes' as developed in his seminal article, "Introduction à l'analyse structurale des récits," *Communications*, 8 (1966), 1–27.

25. Taylor Stoehr, " 'Young Goodman Brown' and Hawthorne's Theory of Mimesis," *Nineteenth-Century Fiction*, 23 (1969), 402–403, points out Hawthorne's use of these qualifying expressions in his tales and claims that about thirty of them appear in "Young Goodman Brown." The purpose, according to Stoehr, is not to suggest allegorical meanings but rather to suspend "judgment on all apparent meanings, which are nonetheless offered as possibilities" (p. 403). This technique (and I agree) puts the reader in the same ambiguous situation as the characters but "with some additional hints" as to the solutions of the problem (p. 406). Stoehr, however, does not give any specific examples of these hints.

26. Misreading by critics like Leo B. Levy, "The Problem of Faith," p. 381, who on one hand seems to recognize the possibility of Brown's projection in hearing "a voice like Deacon Gookin's" but on the other claims that Gookin's words are not offered as "something Brown imagines," may very well result from a neglect of point of view. The

narrator emphasizes the subjective quality of Brown's perceptions by such qualifying words as "appeared," "without discerning," "were such a thing possible" (p. 81). Similarly, the other extreme of interpretation, like that of Paul J. Hurley, "Young Goodman Brown's 'Heart of Darkness,' " *American Literature*, 37 (1966), 415, which denies the possibility of the narrator's attesting to the objective existence of the minister and the deacon, is equally mistaken in neglecting the ambiguity and the shifting of point of view.

27. Liebman, p. 159, notices other examples of the "seems" expression: the figure's "snakelike staff actually seemed to wriggle in sympathy" and the figure touches Goody Cloyse's neck "with what seemed the serpent's tail." But Liebman claims that the comment about the couple's hesitation is Brown's, not the narrator's (p. 162), while identifying the following comments on the contents of the baptismal font to be "Hawthorne's (p. 159), a contradiction of his principal of subjective action. As noted before, Liebman does not provide a clear basis for distinguishing between the narrator's and Brown's points of view.

28. Liebman, p. 163, also interprets the tempest as part of Brown's delusion.

29. Richard Harter Fogle, *Hawthorne's Fiction: The Light and the Dark*, rev. ed. (Norman: Univ. of Oklahoma Press, 1964), pp. 25–27, points out other contrasts like those between day and night, town and forest, red and black, serving as symbolic and stylistic balancing, as well as the thematic opposition between appearance and reality.

30. See Culler, p. 15.

31. The relation between patient and happening and agent and action is defined by Chatman, p. 32.

32. See *A. Rhetoric of Irony* (Chicago: Univ. of Chicago Press, 1974), p. 240. In unstable irony, "the author—insofar as we can discover him, and he is often very remote indeed— refuses to declare himself, however subtly, *for* any stable proposition."

JANE DONAHUE EBERWEIN

My Faith Is Gone!
"Young Goodman Brown"
and Puritan Conversion

Thy joy is groundless, Faith is false, thy Hope
Presumption, and Desire is almost broke.

—EDWARD TAYLOR,
"The Soul accused in its Serving God"

The writer who attempts to traverse the labyrinthine paths of scholarship
on "Young Goodman Brown" may properly feel the misgivings Hawthorne
imputed to travelers who "with lonely footsteps ... may yet be passing
through an unseen multitude" of critics and scholars,[1] a grave company,
dark-clad in academic gowns. A simple bibliography of interpretations the
story has elicited would be longer than the tale itself and almost as ironic.
"Young Goodman Brown" has been presented as an allegorical revelation of
human depravity, as a symbolic study of sexual initiation, as an inquiry into
generational conflict, as a demonstration of Puritan hypocrisy, as evidence of
Hawthorne's sympathy for Puritan values, and as an artfully designed short
story making no essential reference beyond itself. Is there really anything
more to say by way of choosing among these interpretations or synthesizing
them? I think that there is and that attention to the story's Puritan
background is essential if one is to develop a comprehensively satisfying
explanation of what happens to Goodman Brown in his forest encounter.[2] It
is the thesis of this essay that "Young Goodman Brown" is an allegory of the

From *Christianity & Literature* 32, no. 1 (Fall 1982). © 1982 CCL.

particular kind of maturation which occurs in the context of Calvinist conversion psychology and which imposed a distinctively difficult spiritual burden in the special historical circumstances of late seventeenth-century Massachusetts.

In focusing attention on Calvinist conversion, I agree with Michael J. Colacurcio's and Claudia G. Johnson's arguments that Puritan theology operates significantly in the story—not just the psychology and morality which emanated from the dogma. This drama of Everyman's crisis of faith takes place in the context of Calvin's *Institutes*, Perkins's analyses of faith, John Cotton's defenses of the New England churches, and numerous seventeenth-century sermons. But, whereas Johnson interprets "Young Goodman Brown" as Hawthorne's representation of a false conversion, a mock descent into confrontation with evil and a failure to achieve justification,[3] I locate Goodman Brown's position at a different point in the process—after the initial conversion has apparently occurred, when the newborn Christian attempts to come to terms with his changed spiritual state. Like Colacurcio, I read the tale as Hawthorne's probing of the moral and psychological aftereffects of a false conversion, although I do not share his conviction that Goodman Brown's misjudgment of his election amounts to the "unpardonable sin" of presumption.[4] Whether presumption or simply unfounded hope, however, Brown's spiritual crisis raises troubling questions. What happens to a man who thinks he has achieved saving grace but finds he has not, who discovers that the Faith he married three months ago cannot justify him and that the new life he began with her has awakened him to sin rather than salvation?

A brief review of Puritan theology seems in order here to provide useful background for further analysis. Although I acknowledge the caveats of Nina Baym against viewing Hawthorne as a theological writer[5] and am persuaded by Waggoner's and Ziff's observations that Hawthorne's interest in the Puritans focused on the psychological issues that resulted from the Puritans' view of life as moral and spiritual dramas,[6] I agree with Colacurcio that religious issues are so fundamental to the central conflict of "Young Goodman Brown" as to require attentive study of the story in the context of Calvinist doctrine and practice insofar as Hawthorne seems to have understood them. The work directly confronts the basic Christian issues of faith and justification. It does so, however, in the specific framework of Calvinism, which emphasizes the Pauline tradition of converting grace. Man, in his natural condition, is depraved, even if he behaves responsibly and is thought of, by himself and others, as a good person. Without grace, a person deserves nothing but damnation from God and is incapable of performing any meritorious action; the best he can do by way of helping himself spiritually is to recognize his worthlessness, confront his sin, and attempt to atone—always inadequately—for his evil condition. Since Adam's fall, no human being can hope to satisfy God's anger against sin. Salvation, for the few predestined as the elect, comes through Christ's redemptive sufferings, which are imputed to the saints through the covenant of faith. Faith reaches the sinner through the action of irresistible sanctifying grace, by which the natural man is reborn to supernatural life, with his depraved condition changed to one of sanctification. The central questions in life, then, are those of conversion. Has the sinner been saved? Is he in a state of grace? Does he have redemptive faith?

As Edmund S. Morgan has shown in his book *Visible Saints*, these questions assumed special importance in Puritan New England, where the churches actively attempted to restrict membership to those who could give satisfactory evidence of their conversion.[7] The community called on each member to give a public accounting for the state of his or her soul, and it rewarded those who could meet its exacting standards of sanctification with admission to the Lord's Supper, church membership, and the civic privileges attendant upon such status. Frequent experience in examining prospective members for evidence of visible sanctity had led by the middle of the seventeenth century to a highly codified morphology of conversion, which represented the usual, although not the only, stages of Christian development. Typically, the person would acquire intellectual knowledge of dogma by listening to sermons and studying religious lessons suitable to his intellectual level, as Goodman Brown had learned the catechism from Goody Cloyse, and had received more advanced instruction from Deacon Gookin and the minister. He would, next, experience a profound conviction of his sin, an awakening to his nothingness which would cause him to open his empty heart to God in fervent prayers for grace. If he had been justified by Christ, he would then find faith and accept the covenant of redemption. Far from being the triumphant conclusion of the saint's salvation history, however, the experience of faith would be an introduction to a long period of strenuous combat with sinfulness. Jonathan Edwards, for example, reported in his "Personal Narrative" that grace gave him a more profound sense of his worthlessness than he has known in his natural state, revealing his "extreme feebleness and impotence, every manner of way; and the bottomless depths of secret corruption and deceit, there was in my heart."[8] With time, the converted Christian might reach a sense of assurance about his spiritual condition, but the assurance would always be imperfect. Agonizing spiritual self-scrutiny, then, was the lot of the Puritan saint. An easy experience of grace was almost inevitably deceptive.

But how could one tell whether one had been saved? In New England, the judgment the church congregations came to seem almost definitive, imposing a special relationship between the searching Christian and his community. When, from the middle of the seventeenth century, it became apparent that most young New Englanders, even children of visible saints, were unable to give satisfactory evidence of grace, the churches faced a spiritual crisis only temporarily mitigated by the Halfway Covenant of 1662, which offered baptism but not the Lord's Supper to the babies of those who, baptized as infants themselves on the assumption that children of saints would probably experience grace, had never been able to align themselves conclusively with the covenant of faith. Young Goodman Brown would have been a member of that first Halfway generation, and his story reflects Hawthorne's sensitivity to the unique spiritual pressures that these young people faced on reaching adulthood in a community which demanded much of them by way of spiritual maturity but which had practically branded them from birth as people who would need to find an easy road to heaven. [9]

As in *The Scarlet Letter*, Hawthorne starts this story after the central spiritual or moral event has occurred. "Young Goodman Brown" takes place three months after the protagonist's marriage to Faith, or his conversion and admission to the church. He has established himself publicly as her husband. We know little about his life between the time he studied the catechism and the time of his conversion. That he had experienced the normative conviction of sin seems unlikely, in view of later events, but he may have thought he had as a prelude to his courtship. He is evidently a dutiful member of the Salem village community and seems to have obeyed all its rules and regulations. Hawthorne presents him here as he encounters the first real test of his conversion, the experience that will indicate whether he has really achieved faith and experienced grace or whether he has simply undergone one of those seasons of awakening, which even Edwards found so difficult to distinguish from true conversion except by the test of perseverance. Only if the convert could sustain his hope of salvation until death, despite periods of trial, would he be known to be saved; and only if the joyful sense of his unmerited acceptance by God should bear fruit in a sanctified life of Christian benevolence could the conversion be validated; even then both the convert and the church might be mistaken in their interpretation of the signs.

One could never be sure of salvation, but one could discover that an apparent experience of grace had been delusory. That, I believe, is the subject of this tale: the awful revelation that Goodman Brown's marriage to Faith has brought temporary happiness but not a sanctifying transformation of the natural man. Brown's discovery allows Hawthorne to explore the psychological dynamic of a particularly rigid, naïve personality confronting the most agonizing spiritual crisis imaginable for a Puritan, while the uses Brown makes of his discovery offer profound insight into the failures of Puritan morality.

As the tale opens, Young Goodman Brown stands at the threshold of his honeymoon cottage in Salem village and bids farewell to his anxious Faith as he leaves for a night's appointed journey into the forest. I take this journey to be an allegorical representation of the Christian's necessary self-exploration after conversion, the probing for the results of the assumed change from a natural to a sanctified condition. After three months in his new state of life, Goodman Brown feels confident of his ability to confront whatever challenges he may find within his soul: a mysterious forest into which he has never before ventured at night. He has arranged to meet a diabolical guide whose weird resemblance to Brown himself and to his grandfather shows him to be the self-projection of one whose recent maturation has awakened a complex sense of identity. Taking him beyond the conscious defenses of his ego, the journey exposes Brown to nonrational associations of spiritually symbolic images. Whether the journey Brown undertakes be viewed as actual encounter or as nightmare, Hawthorne clearly intends it as a real spiritual trial, having definitive consequences for his remaining life and a probable bearing on his eschatological condition. Even if the happenings in the forest may be taken as spectral evidence, as David Levin argues,[10] they have internal reality as lasting influences on Brown's sense of himself within the Christian community. The new convert meets temptation and is overcome by it.

Goodman Brown's exploration of the hitherto concealed recesses of his soul would have come eventually as a test of his new birth, whenever he felt confident enough of his intimacy with Faith to risk brief separation from her protective embrace. If he needed a specific reason to venture away from her this one night of the year, it may well relate to the communion imagery running through the tale until the climactic inversion of Puritan worship. Married three months, he would be a new church member and might well be approaching the first Lord's Supper in which he would actively participate. Communion services occurred no more than once a month in the New England churches, generally much less frequently; and, as the one sacrament restricted to the visible saints, the Lord's Supper took on an extraordinary weight of spiritual importance as a sign of maturation within the worshiping community.

An analogue to Brown's situation may be found in Samuel Sewall's March 1677 note for his diary, recounting his psychological ordeal when, a twenty-five-year-old married man expecting his first child, he prepared for his first communion service as a member of Boston's South Church.

Reporting that "I have been of a long time loth to enter into strict Bonds with God," he admitted that he applied for church membership after recognizing the sinfulness and hypocrisy of his hesitation. His decision exposed him, however, to scruples about the South Church itself, and he told how he turned unsuccessfully for help to two senior members of the congregation. Having overcome his anxieties enough to offer himself as a church member and read his public account of the spiritual pilgrimage which had brought him to a sense of grace, Sewall was accepted into the church and admitted to the Lord's Supper. But the communion service itself turned out to be the most disturbing test of his newly asserted faith:

> And now that Scruple of the Church vanished, and I began to be more afraid of myself. And on Saturday Goodman Walker came in, who used to be very familiar with me. But he said nothing of my coming into the Church, nor wished God to show me grace therein, at which I was almost overwhelmed, as thinking that he deemed me unfit for it. And I could hardly sit down to the Lord's Table. But I feared that if I went away I might be less fit next time, and thought that it would be strange for me who was just then joined to the Church, to withdraw, wherefore I stayed. But I never experienced more unbelief. I feared at least that I did not believe there was such an one as Jesus Xt., and yet was afraid that because I came to the ordinance without belief, that for the abuse of Xt. I should be stricken dead; yet I had some earnest desires that Xt. would, before the ordinance were done, though it were when he was just going away, give me some glimpse of himself; but I perceived none. Yet I seemed then to desire the coming of the next Sacrament day, that I might do better, and was stirred up hereby dreadfully to seek God who many times before had touched my heart by Mr. Thacher's praying and preaching more than now.[11]

As modern readers know from Edward Taylor's "Preparatory Meditations," the review of the Christian's spiritual condition and reenactment of the stages of conversion from reflection on scripture, through conviction of sin, to affirmation of faith and celebration of grace could recur with every subsequent communion service. The prospect of the Lord's Supper might well confront Goodman Brown, then, with the need to reassure himself of his conversion, and he might encounter the self-doubt and scrupulosity which tortured Sewall—although with different results.

Whereas Sewall's authority figures and would-be comforters have been prevented from errands of spiritual mercy by worldly distractions, those to whom Goodman Brown looks for religious encouragement seem to be actively committed to the devil. As soon as he begins to penetrate into the recesses of his heart, acknowledging his curiosity about sin and his willingness to risk temptation—trusting to Faith to pull him back along the way of righteousness—he experiences devastating doubts of those family, church, and government leaders on whom he has relied for regulation of the natural impulses to sin occurring in his unconverted state. Having divided people too drastically into black and white moral categories, forgetting that good or bad behavior offers inconclusive evidence of salvation or reprobation, he readily succumbs to the temptation to reject prior spiritual models as hypocrites and to accept, on spectral evidence, the devil's parade of their sinfulness.[12] His faith has prepared him inadequately for this visual and auditory confrontation with the moral depravity still fermenting within his own soul and still tainting even the visible saints from whom he expects absolute moral purity. The revelations on this awful night recall those reported by seventeenth-century New Englanders in doubt of their election. Although Hawthorne could never have seen Edward Taylor's poems, his devil figure confronts the protagonist here with a spiritual temptation remarkably analogous to one Taylor described in *Gods Determinations touching his Elect* (composed at approximately the same time as Hawthorne sets "Young Goodman Brown" and addressed mainly to members of Brown's Halfway generation):

> Hence in their joy he straweth poyson on,
> Those Objects that their senses feed upon.
> By some odde straggling thought up poyson flies
> Into the heart: and through the Eares, and Eyes.
> Which sick, lies gasping: Other thoughts then high
> To hold its head; and Venom'd are thereby.
> Hence they are influenc't to selfe Ends: these darts
> Strike secret swelling Pride up in their hearts.
> > To which he fosters till the bladder flies
> > In pieces; then joy lies agast and dies.[13]

The correspondence between the authentically Puritan literary passage and Hawthorne's romantic tale indicates the extent of Hawthorne's empathy with Puritan habits of mind despite his conventionally nineteenth-century indifference to the theology which underlay such spiritual experience. It would take a strong faith to withstand such an assault on Christian hope, and what Goodman Brown discovers is that he does not have it. Nor does he benefit, like Taylor's characters, from the direct intervention of Christ's grace.

"With Heaven above, and Faith below, I will yet stand firm against the devil!" (82), Brown exclaims in his crisis of temptation. But, when he looks toward heaven for the sources of the murmurs, screams, and lamentations he hears above him, Faith's pink ribbons drift down and confirm his despairing commitment to evil: "My faith is gone! ... There is no good on earth; and sin is but a name. Come, devil! for to thee is this world given" (83). The pink ribbons have, of course, been variously interpreted by readers of this story. They demonstrate Faith's charm and joyfulness, even her healthy sexuality; but, as Hyatt Waggoner has noted, they also remind us of her immaturity.[14] When a soul is engaged in a mortal struggle for spiritual survival, it may look to heaven for the shield of faith and the helmet of salvation; it can neither protect itself nor attack the devil with pink ribbons.[15] What Goodman Brown discovers here, then, is that the Faith he has married is too frail and frivolous to save him. Whether she has fully committed herself to the devil or not, she is no longer his potential savior.[16] Yet, without reliance on her, he would never have ventured upon this ordeal. Recognizing that he has been deceived in his dependence on Faith, he abandons all hope of salvation and rushes demonically to the diabolical communion ritual. When a voice cries, "Bring forth the converts," he and his bride step forward to unite themselves with the "loathful brotherhood" of sin (86). Having thought himself redeemed by Faith from membership in the universal community of evil to which all men in their natural state belong, he finds himself from absolute damnation.

The communion scene in the forest would be a direct inversion of the communion ritual Goodman Brown might anticipate in Salem village, were it not for his resistance to the diabolical sacrament. Crying, "Faith! Faith! ... Look up to Heaven, and resist the Wicked One!" (88), he breaks the enchantment and finds himself alone in the chill, damp forest: not in bed with Faith but safe from the lurid scene of his temptation. Has he been saved by his refusal to accept Satan's covenant? Not unless a man can consciously will salvation or earn it by the righteous act of looking up to heaven. Nothing in Calvinist conversion theology suggests such probabilities. The sinner must certainly resist Satan to the best of his inadequate natural power, and he must implore Christ for help, but he can do nothing whatever to cause or even facilitate his salvation, and the thought that a conscious decision to reject Satan could earn redemption would be itself a sin. Grace is the missing figure in this allegory of a man's disillusionment with his weak Faith. Whether Brown ever attains it, we cannot know; but at the end of the ordeal his soul seems to be as chill and damp as the forest which has symbolized it. Returning to the village the next morning, he cynically judges the people he thinks he encountered in the forest, and he rejects Faith's affectionate welcome, probably feeling disgust at her obvious childishness. He has lost all belief in human goodness by losing his sense of personal conversion, and he shows no disposition to support or strengthen his fragile Faith.

If he is not saved by his decision in the forest to reject the hidden knowledge of evil he would gain from Satan's communion, is he then damned? Not necessarily, at least in terms of Calvinist theology. He has discovered that his premature marriage to an undeveloped Faith has been a season of awakening though not yet a conversion, but he does not know for sure that he has been rejected. He finds himself still in an unconverted state, with a heightened conviction of sin. In *Gods Determinations touching his Elect*, Edward Taylor had tried to calm the panic of those believers whose hopes of election kept colliding against experience of their persistent sin and who felt overwhelmed by Satan's charges that "Thy joy is groundless, Faith is false." In reply to Satan's strategies to unsettle the anxious coverts—his temptations of self-doubt, contempt for still imperfect saints, and general cynicism which parallel the devil's manipulation of Young Goodman Brown—Taylor's Christ offers reassurance:

> Although thy sins increase their race,
> And though when thou hast sought for Grace,
>   Thou fallst more than before
> If thou by true Repentence Rise,
> And Faith makes me thy Sacrifice,
>   I'l pardon all, though more.[17]

If honest with himself and the community, then, Goodman Brown might dismiss his premature claim to justification through marriage to his Faith without necessarily falling into despair. He needs to start over again, undertaking a new spiritual journey with increased awareness of the risks involved.

The catch is, of course, that he must be honest with the community of Salem village. Instead of protecting his own vulnerable self-image behind projections of his neighbors' sins, he must stop presenting himself as a visible saint. That the Puritans made public acknowledgment of failures and sins—even those they originally imagined to be righteous acts indicative of their sanctification—we know from many sources, most memorably Samuel Sewall's recantation of his part in the Salem witch trials, desiring "to take the Blame and Shame of it, Asking pardon of Men, And especially desiring prayers that God, who has an Unlimited Authority, would pardon that Sin and all other his Sins; personal and Relative: And according to his infinite

Benignity, and Soveraignty, Not visit the Sin of him, or any other, upon himself or any of his, nor upon the Land....[18] But Brown has lost confidence in the community even more than in himself and has mentally imposed upon his neighbors the sinfulness he should have come to terms with in his own soul. By ignoring this alternative of seeking the community's spiritual assistance and choosing instead to live in a joyless, unloving union with the Faith he has privately rejected, raising children by her, who will themselves have an added load of paternal sin to bear, and playing the role of a visible saint in the community, although he knows himself still unconverted, Brown closes off the opportunities he might normally enjoy for spiritual growth and becomes that quintessential Puritan sinner: the hypocrite. The excessive value he has consistently placed on authority and public respect deters Brown from the humiliation he must suffer in order to renew his chance of salvation, while the tendency toward hiding which has characterized his behavior in the forest makes it easy for him to acquire the habit of concealment.

Here, ironically, authentic Puritan theology would have offered more hope for Goodman Brown than Hawthorne does. False awakenings and mistaken conversions do not preclude true conversion later, as witness Edwards's "Personal Narrative." Grace could still come through Christ. But Hawthorne's Goodman Brown inhabited a fictively Puritan world which seems, at base, not really Christian. Faith, hope, love, communion, covenant, God, and the devil, but neither Christ nor grace, find mention in this story. Although Brown claims to come of "a race of honest men and good Christians" (77), he places more reliance on his fathers than on the Son. No saving power in this tale contravenes the force of evil which Goodman Brown experiences in the forest and apparently senses throughout his subsequent life. Nor does Brown experience the secular equivalent of grace, which Hawthorne groped toward with Kenyon in *The Marble Faun* as a possible substitute for the miraculous salvation in which he himself found it difficult to believe. Hawthorne would have looked for the means of spiritual healing in Brown's opportunity to humble his pride, to acknowledge his part in the general community of human imperfection, to forgive others and ask their forgiveness, and to struggle forward in life's pilgrimage doing the best he could and helping other men and women along the same path to hoped-for acceptance by God. Goodman Brown, however, never perceives the salvific potential of a struggling Christian life in an uncertain world. Expecting all or nothing by way of conversion, he winds up with nothing—both in Hawthorne's terms and in those of the seventeenth-century New England Puritans his character represents.

Were this only one man's tragedy, the tale would be sobering enough, but Hawthorne apparently intended Goodman Brown as an Everyman figure, typical of his community. His misplaced dependence first on an inadequate Faith and later on a self-justifying rejection of human community suggests the thwarted spiritual development Hawthorne found in other Puritan characters like Richard Digby in "The Man of Adamant" and the persecuting crowds of "The Gentle Boy" and *The Scarlet Letter*. The qualities of rigidity, gravity and sternness Brown exhibits upon his return from the forest are those which Hawthorne attributed to most of his Puritan characters—even more to the crowds of common goodmen and goodwives in his historical fiction than to the principal characters who, at least in the first generation, occasionally demonstrated the confident, forceful, even zealous personalities which might be expected in Christians sure of their election. But Perry Miller's statement that "It is impossible to conceive of a disillusioned Puritan"[19] applies only to those who had undergone the whole process of conversion, who had confronted the blackness of their own souls and survived the ordeal to accept themselves and celebrate their faith. It is not the passengers sweetly singing in Taylor's coach of the elect, however, nor the reborn Christians who, like Edwards, could kneel in the forest to experience a vision "of the glory of the Son of God, as Mediator between God and man, and his wonderful, great, full, pure and sweet grace and love, and meek and gentle condescension"[20] who populate Hawthorne's Puritan tales and romances. He gives us, instead, the gloomy, repressed, and repressive personalities of those who, like Young Goodman Brown, got lost halfway in the conversion process, emerging profoundly disillusioned with themselves, their neighbors, the church, and the faith, yet who continued hypocritically to maintain the facade of sanctification. Whether Goodman Brown's discoveries that awful night were true or false with respect to the personages he thought he saw in the forest, they must have been valid with regard to the church itself. No doubt there were many hypocrites among the visible saints, including some who deceived even themselves about their possession of grace.

The psychological pressures imposed by a schematically defined conversion theology had destructive personal and communal effects, then, especially on the younger generations faced with increasingly exacting standards of piety in a community which grew, each decade, more narrow and provincial. Although conspicuous sinners might escape from such repression by way of free thinking and licentious living, the ostensibly dutiful young New Englanders would grow more authoritarian as they came to identify piety with external behavior rather than internal awakening. It was Young Goodman Brown's generation, we must recall, children of the most godly families, who accused the witches at Salem.

NOTES

1. "Young Goodman Brown," *Mosses From an Old Manse*, Centenary Edition (Columbus: Ohio State University Press, 1974), p. 75. Further citations from the tale refer to this edition and will be annotated in the text.

2. Critics who have accorded serious attention to the religious aspects of this tale include: John E. Becker, *Hawthorne's Historical Allegory: An Examination of the American Conscience* (Port Washington, N.Y.: Kennikat Press, 1971); Michael J. Colacurcio, "Visible Sanctity and Specter Evidence: The Moral World of Hawthorne's 'Young Goodman Brown,' *Essex Institute Historical Collection*, 110 (1974), 259–99; Thomas E. Connolly, "Hawthorne's 'Young Goodman Brown': An Attack on Puritanic Calvinism," *American Literature*, 28 (1957), 370–75; Richard Harter Fogle, *Hawthorne's Fiction: The Light and the Dark*, rev. ed. (Norman: University of Oklahoma Press, 1964); Paul J. Hurley, "Young Goodman Brown's 'Heart of Darkness,' " *American Literature*, 37 (1966), 410–19; Claudia G. Johnson," 'Young Goodman Brown' and Puritan Justification," *Studies in Short Fiction*, 11 (1974), 200–203; Leo B. Levy, "The Problem of Faith in 'Young Goodman Brown,' " *Journal of English and Germanic Philology*, 74 (1975), 375–87; Barton Levi St. Armand, " 'Young Goodman Brown' as Historical Allegory," *The Nathaniel Hawthorne Journal* (1973), pp. 183–97; Joseph Schwartz, "Three Aspects of Hawthorne's Puritanism," *New England Quarterly*, 36, (1963), 192–208; John Caldwell Stubbs, *The Pursuit of Form: A Study of Hawthorne and the Romance* (Urbana: University of Illinois Press, 1970); and Hyatt H. Waggoner, *Hawthorne: A Critical Study*, rev. ed. (Cambridge, Mass.: The Belknap Press of Harvard University Press.1963). Both Michael Davitt Bell in *Hawthorne and the Historical Romance of New England* (Princeton, N.J.: Princeton University Press, 1971) and David Levin in "Shadows of Doubt: Specter Evidence in Hawthorne's 'Young Goodman Brown,'" *American Literature*, 34 (1962), 344–52, examine the cultural and historical background of seventeenth-century Massachusetts as a key to interpretation, as does James W. Clark, Jr., in "Hawthorne's Use of Evidence in 'Young Goodman Brown,'" *Essex Institute Historical Collections*, 111 (1975), 12–34. Among the critics who consider Puritanism neither theologically nor historically important in reading "Young Goodman Brown" are Nina Baym, *The Shape of Hawthorne's Career* (Ithaca, N.Y.: Cornell University Press, 1976); Frederick C. Crews, *The Sins of the Fathers: Hawthorne's Psychological Themes* (New York: Oxford University Press, 1966); Edward J. Gallagher, "The Concluding Paragraph of 'Young Goodman Brown,'" *Studies in Short Fiction*, 12 (1975), 29–30; and Roy R. Male, *Hawthorne's Tragic Vision* (New York: W.W. Norton & Co., 1957).

3. " 'Young Goodman Brown' and Puritan Justification," *Studies in Short Fiction*, 11 (1974), 200–203.

4. "Visible Sanctity and Specter Evidence: The Moral World of Hawthorne's 'Young Goodman Brown, ' "*Essex Institute Historical Collections*, 110 (1974), 259–99.

5. *The Shape of Hawthorne's Career* (Ithaca, N.Y.: Cornell University Press, 1976), pp.68–69.

6. Larzer Ziff, "The Artist and Puritanism," *Hawthorne Centenary Essays* (Columbus: Ohio State University Press, 1964), pp. 245–49; and Hyatt H. Waggoner, "Art and Belief," *Hawthorne Centenary Essays*, pp. 167–95.

7. Edmund S. Morgan, *Visible Saints: The History of a Puritan Idea* (Ithaca, N.Y.: Cornell University Press, 1963).

8. *Jonathan Edwards: Basic Writings*, ed. Ola Elizabeth Winslow (New York: New American Library, 1966), p. 86.

9. Colacurcio examines the psychological and theological problems of the Halfway

generation as historical background for this tale in "Visible Sanctity and Specter Evidence," where he argues that the story confronts the dilemma of Puritanism just before the witchcraft crisis at Salem demonstrated the church's inability to evaluate visible sanctity or damnation except on the inadmissible basic of spectral evidence. His thesis that "Goodman Brown's forest-education enfigures the ultimate breakdown of the Puritan attempt to define the human form of the Kingdom of God" offers an exceptionally revealing perspective on the allegory and demonstrates Hawthorne's extraordinary artistic sensitivity to the human experience underlying history.

10. "Shadows of Doubt: Specter Evidence in Hawthorne's 'Young Goodman Brown,'" *American Literature*, 34 (1962), 344–52.

11. *The Diary of Samuel Sewall*, ed. M. Halsey Thomas, (New York: Farrar, Straus & Giroux, 1973), 39–40.

12. See Levin, "Shadows of Doubt."

13. "The Effect of this Reply with a fresh Assault from Satan, " *The Poems of Edward Taylor*, ed. Donald E. Stanford (New Haven: Yale University Press, 1960), pp. 406–07.

14. *Hawthorne: A Critical Study* (Cambridge, Mass.: The Belknap Press of Harvard University Press, 1963), p. 210.

15. Paul's epistle to the Ephesians, the source of these familiar allusions of Christian armament, provides a comprehensive statement about the ideal relationship of converted Christians to themselves, their families, the community, and Christ. It provides a suggestive contrast with the development of "Young Goodman Brown."

16. Two quite different views of Faith's significance seem pertinent here. According to Leo B. Levy, Brown's dilemma is that his Faith mysteriously abandons him. "The Problem of Faith in 'Young Goodman Brown,' " *Journal of English and Germanic Philology*, 74 (1975), 375–97. Thomas E. Connolly argues, however, that the Puritan faith remains with Brown but is revealed to him as the source of his damnation rather than salvation. "Hawthorne's 'Young Goodman Brown': An Attack on Puritanic Calvinism," *American Literature*, 28 (1957), 370–75.

17. "Christs Reply," *Poems of Edward Taylor*, p. 416.

18. *Diary* (1 January 1696/7), I, 367. Hawthorne echoes this confession in a comic spirit in "The Custom House," where he offers to "take shame upon myself" for the sake of his Puritan ancestors and prays "that any curse incurred by them—as I have heard, and as the dreary and unprosperous condition of the race, for many a long year back, would argue to exist—may be now and henceforth removed." *The Scarlet Letter*, Centenary Edition (Columbus: Ohio State University Press, 1962), p. 10.

19. "Introduction" to *The Puritans: A Sourcebook of Their Writings* (New York: Harper & Row, 1963), I, 60.

20. "Personal Narrative," *Jonathan Edwards*, p. 93

JOHN S. HARDT

Doubts in the American Garden: Three Cases of Paradisal Skepticism

Knowledge is the knowing that we cannot know.
                    —Emerson, "Montaigne; or The Skeptic"[1]

Few works of early American short fiction have entered the nation's literary consciousness as profoundly as "Rip Van Winkle," "Young Goodman Brown," and "The Fall of the House of Usher." Individually, these stories by our first three masters of short fiction have long been interpreted as imaginative statements of the American experience. What has not been adequately recognized, though, is that each of these stories traces a remarkably similar pattern. Rip Van Winkle, Goodman Brown, and Poe's narrator journey into settings with paradisal associations, only to encounter doubts and uncertainties. Each of the three ultimately returns home with reduced confidence in what he can know about his world, a pattern clearly suggesting that the rural settings have become much less appealing than their paradisal associations would suggest.

This juxtaposition of a retreat from the paradisal ideal with a recognition of limits in human knowledge—a pattern which I will call here "paradisal skepticism"—modifies the usual formulation of the Edenic myth. In the usual interpretation, the fall moves mankind from ignorance to knowledge, but this pattern suggests that the fall (i.e., the loss of a paradise)

From *Studies in Short Fiction* 25, no. 3 (Summer 1988). © 1989 by *Studies in Short Fiction*, Inc.

occurs when humans encounter their own limits in knowledge. The fall moves them from a false confidence in their knowledge to a realization that full knowledge is in fact not possible, no matter how paradisal the environment seems. The implication is that the apparent paradise can only seem such so long as its inhabitants maintain their unacknowledged illusions about it and about their own abilities in it. Once they realize their limited knowledge, the setting's paradisal dimensions disappear. Ironically, then, the innocence usually associated with paradise brings with it, in these three American classics, an inherent ignorance which prevents the realization of the setting's paradisal possibilities.

Of course, the pattern described here does not altogether contradict the more usual interpretation of the fall, for the knowledge attained in the conventional interpretation might be an awareness of one's limited knowledge. Even in the traditional account of Adam and Eve, their fall occurs partly because of their feelings of inadequate knowledge in paradise. After all, they would not have been tempted to eat from the Tree of Knowledge had they been satisfied with their existing knowledge. Consequently, one might wish to think of the present pattern as a shift in the emphasis of the conventional interpretation so that the fall's main lesson becomes an awareness of humanity's limited knowledge.

I

Although usually not attributed such dark meanings, "Rip Van Winkle" offers a useful beginning point from which to explore this pattern. Of course, Rip's sojourn in the mountains leaves no damaging psychological scars, but afterwards he seems less interested in spending his days in the rural retreats he had earlier found so inviting (obviously, too, the intervening demise of his wife further explains his newfound contentment with village life). At any rate, this story, like the others to be examined here, presents two versions of its rural setting, creating a tension between ideal and actual responses to the American landscape.

The opening panoramic paragraph of Irving's tale is all too familiar to require recounting here; suffice it to say that its emphasis is on the serene mountain setting toward which Rip subsequently escapes from the termagant Dame. As David J. Kann claims, "the story begins as a romantic pastoral,"[2] but what is specifically important here is the depiction of the mountains as "perfect barometers" of the changes in weather and seasons.[3] In other words, the mountains are presented as a place of increased knowledge of the world—at least they are so interpreted from the perspective of the village. After Rip has made his ascent, however, the perspective of the mountains reveals a rather different dimension of this setting. Looking toward the Hudson below him, Rip sees "many a mile of rich woodland," but in the opposite direction he finds "a deep mountain glen, wild, lonely, and shagged, and bottom filled with fragments from the impending cliffs, and scarcely lighted by the reflected rays of the setting sun" (58-59). This second view offers the first hint that the mountains are not merely "perfect barometers" but also a place of disorder and fragmentary meaning. It seems, then, more than coincidence that the strange voice beckoning Rip comes from the glen. Not yet recognizing this second dimension of the apparently idyllic setting, Rip, upon hearing the voice, thinks "his fancy must have deceived him" (59), but when he reaches the amphitheatre with the stranger, he realizes he is in a "strange and incomprehensible" world, a world of "the unknown that inspired awe and checked familiarity" (60). In contrast to the initial description of the mountains, which attributed to them powers of increased knowledge, the mountains now, at least their remoter parts, have become a place of wonder and uncertainty. In this setting, and with the help of the flagon's contents, Rip's senses are "overpowered," and he falls "into a deep sleep" (62).

Upon awaking, Rip continues to experience confusion in this setting which he had earlier considered so inviting, soothing and paradisal. After noticing, but not understanding, the rusting of his gun, the disappearance of Wolf, and the stiffness of his own body, he finds further confusion in the natural setting itself, as he is "sometimes tripped up or entangled by the wild grapevines that twisted their coils or tendrils from tree to tree, and spread a kind of network in his path" (64). Likewise, he finds the rocks "impenetrable" and a basin of water "black from the shadows of the surrounding forest" (64). Rip has clearly awakened to a world of confusion and obscured knowledge. Aware that his senses cannot explain his surroundings and perplexed by the contrast between his earlier view of the setting and his growing confusion in it, Rip quite justifiably begins "to doubt whether both he and the world around him were not bewitched" (65). This confusion about both his world and his own identity continues when he reaches his home village, but since his confusion translates there explicitly into political and social changes, it is to that extent less relevant to the present argument, which focuses on the rural natural setting and the increasing confusion within it.

What is relevant, however, is Irving's basically genial attitude toward the seemingly dark implications of Rip's tale. While Philip Young contends rightly that "Irving was groping darkly in a world of symbol, myth and dream for meanings beyond awareness,"[4] one must admit that Irving, much like Rip, ultimately recoils from such meanings. By ascribing Rip's experiences to

Dutch folklore, by maintaining his comic characterizations of the townspeople, by admitting that some villagers doubted Rip's story, and by having Geoffrey Crayton attribute the tale to Diedrich Knickerbocker, Irving allows himself and his readers to skirt the tale's darker implications. Moreover, through his use of alternative ending possibilities—a fictional technique Hawthorne was later to use as a means of emphasizing ambiguity and uncertainty—Irving finally shies away from the darker implications of Rip's mountain experiences. Like "Adventure of the German Student," which Irving attributes to the student himself in a Paris madhouse, "Rip Van Winkle" ends with details which allow a reader to dismiss the tale's supernatural dimensions. This lightening attitude seems partly a result of Irving's Knickerbocker sensibility, a tendency not to delve too deeply into philosophical questions, yet such an attitude occurs primarily in the tale's last third and does not totally extinguish the earlier dark implication about the American rural landscape.

Besides dramatizing conflicting attitudes towards this landscape (are the mountains "perfect barometers" or are they "entangled," "scarcely lighted," and "impenetrable"?), the tension in the tale between the two versions of the natural setting parallels a tension in Irving's own views of human knowledge. Hardly a philosopher, Rip is of course oblivious to such issues, for he quickly ignores the perplexities of his experience and settles back into village life. Likewise, Irving largely undercuts the apparent problems in knowledge through his comic tone. To transpose Hawthorne's famous description of Melville, Irving seems relatively comfortable in his unbelief, even if his tale plants the seeds of a paralyzing lack of confidence in the possibility of adequate human knowledge. His famous and representative tale, nonetheless, raises doubts, both about the American landscape's paradisal possibilities and about human knowledge, which other American fiction writers would explore more directly and centrally during the next several decades.

II

Unlike Irving, neither Hawthorne nor Poe could so easily dismiss these problems in knowledge. Of a later generation than Irving, these two writers demonstrated more directly the limits of knowledge impinging upon the American paradise. On first glance, though, neither "Young Goodman Brown" nor "The Fall of the House of Usher" seems to operate in an Edenic setting; after all, the darkness and gloom, not the radiance and serenity, of the natural setting are emphasized in each story. What one must realize, however, is that Hawthorne and Poe set up the paradisal framework of their stories less explicitly than does Irving in "Rip Van Winkle." Whereas Irving suggests the setting's paradisal associations through his descriptive landscapes, Hawthorne uses the allusive allegory so common throughout his fiction. On the descriptive level, he emphasizes the inscrutability of Goodman Brown's forest, but on the allegorical level, especially through his description of the stranger whom Brown meets in the forest and the association of this stranger with the serpent, Hawthorne implies that this forest is a version of the Garden of Eden, albeit a darkened one already controlled by the serpent. Indeed, this very tension between the descriptive and allegorical presentations of the forest, similar to the conflict between Rip's two visions from the mountain, suggests the two sides of paradisal skepticism. The present dark uncertainties which Brown encounters are all the darker because they occur in a setting which, at least allegorically, might have been a pristine paradise.

Like Rip's, Brown's retreat into nature is at least partially a retreat from his wife, but by naming Brown's wife "Faith," Hawthorne further presents his journey into the forest as a trip away from faith (both theological and epistemological) towards realms of uncertainly and doubt. As Rita K. Gollin observes, Brown is "uncertain about the reality of sights and sounds that seem to emerge from the forest,"[5] thus resembling Rip in his growing distrust in the accuracy of his senses. Distrusting his vision, he fears that "There may be a devilish Indian behind every tree."[6] Similarly, his perception that the stranger's staff resembles "a great black snake" is explained as "an ocular deception" (76), an explanation akin to those of Poe's narrator in "Usher." Like Poe, but unlike Irving, Hawthorne does not minimize these problems in sensory perceptions but leaves in tension the gaps between what Brown perceives and what really exists. As numerous scholars note, this intermixture of appearance and reality creates much of the tale's ambiguity.[7] Hawthorne also presents in tension two contrasting interpretations of Brown's uncertainties. On the one hand, his uncertainty results from the limited sensory abilities which he shares with all humans; on the other hand, his uncertainty comes from an over-reliance on his senses and a resultant misplaced trust in appearances. From the first perspective, Brown's uncertainty seems inherent in the human condition; from the second, his problems seem particular and self-induced.[8] While Irving's tale tends to discount both possibilities, Hawthorne's tale embraces both.

Of course, many of the allegorical dimensions, especially those implied by the name "Faith" and by the serpent-like staff, give these issues a theological slant not found in the comparable tales of Irving and Poe; nonetheless, the epistemological issues are by no means eclipsed by the theological ones. The ambiguous relationship between reality and dream suggested in Irving's tale is explicitly enunciated by Hawthorne's narrator, who asks, "Had Goodman Brown fallen asleep in the forest, and only dreamed a wild dream of witch-meeting?" (89). That neither Brown, nor the narrator, nor even the reader, can ever answer this question raises epistemological issues over and beyond the theological ones. In contrast to Irving's tale, which does not clearly affirm Rip's uncertainties, and in contrast to Poe's tale, which ascribes the uncertainties to a not-necessarily-reliable narrator, Hawthorne's tale offers even fewer hints at resolving the uncertainty, for his seemingly reasonable narrator shares Brown's limited vision. Throughout the story, this narrator explicitly expresses doubt about what is happening in the forest. As Neal Frank Doubleday puts it, "The narrator, with all his knowledge, yet does not fully understand the action he records."[9] Even through its narrative technique, Hawthorne's tale suggests the limitations in human knowledge.

Like Rip and Poe's narrator, then, Brown journeys into a rural setting which has paradisal associations, only to encounter doubts and uncertainties. Because he apparently shrugs them off, Rip is not greatly affected by such doubts, and Poe's tale never reveals how such doubts ultimately affect the narrator; but Hawthorne's Brown becomes paralyzed by them, undergoing what at least one critic calls "an unfortunate fall."[10] He can no longer trust himself or those around him; in particular, he no longer trusts the appearances which his sense offer him. His forest experience has caused Brown to perceive discrepancies between appearance and reality, between reputation and performance, between form and meaning, between action and intention, but he is not able to sort out these distinctions, perhaps because of his own simplistic faith in absolutes. Affirming this last possibility, Richard Fogle contends that Brown "is wrecked as a result of the disappearance of the fixed poles of belief."[11] As Jac Tharpe concludes, Brown's "former innocence derived from ignorance,"[12] an ignorance he realizes in the forest but which he cannot accept once he returns to town. Brown's (and the Puritan's) outlook is built upon black-white distinctions, but his night in the forest has blurred such distinctions for him, leaving him faithless, unknowing in a gray world, "A stern, a sad, a darkly meditative, a distrustful, if not a desperate man" (89). Not even partially is Brown able to accept the limitations in his own knowledge. Still, although it seems that his despair arises from his own failure, this view never totally eclipses the alternate interpretation, reinforced by the story's allegorical dimensions, that Brown's problems are inherent in the human condition.

"Young Goodman Brown" is finally not simply a tale depicting a traditional fall leading to increased knowledge, as numerous critics suggest,[13] but also a story revealing the ambiguities and uncertainties of existence, even if—and possibly because—that existence occurs in a paradisal setting. If Brown gains any knowledge in the forest, it is primarily a knowledge of how little he knows and can know, through his senses and his faith, of himself, his fellow villagers, and his world. Ultimately, his initiation is not so much into knowledge as into confusion and uncertainty. He gains, at best, "a partial knowledge," in Daniel Hoffman's words, "too incomplete to win him wisdom or happiness."[14] His fall, as Joseph T. McCullen contends, is a result of "deficient knowledge,"[15] and this knowledge is not increased by his forest experience. In all these ways, then, Hawthorne's story suggests through its plot, narrative form, and point of view how epistemological doubts prevent the realization of a truly paradisal existence.

III

A similar pattern of paradisal skepticism occurs in "The Fall of the House of Usher," where the emphasis is even more directly on the breakdown of rationality and the uncertainty of sensory perceptions. Even though Hawthorne's orientation is obviously more theological, both stories depict epistemological doubts darkening their once-paradisal settings.

As in "Goodman Brown," however, the paradisal dimensions of the setting in "Usher" are not immediately apparent; in fact, Poe's masterful first paragraph emphasizing the gloom, decay, and bleakness of the scene causes most readers to overlook subsequent hints of what this rural setting had once been. What the setting once was, however, is clearly implied by the poem "The Haunted Palace," which Poe attributes to Roderick Usher.[16] No one in the story has known this particular setting as thoroughly as Roderick, and he describes is as former paradise. Scholars who mention this poem often question its inclusion or related it to Roderick's aesthetic impulses or to his declining sanity.[17] At least as important, though, is the contrast the poem develops between the setting's past and present. The poem creates a tension between two contrasting views of the setting, particularly when one compares the first two-thirds of the poem to the opening paragraph of the story. The scene which is presently "dull," "dark," and "rank" (397) is described in the poem as having been a "happy valley," "The greenest of our valleys," a place of luminous colors with "Banners yellow, glorious, golden" and "with pearl and ruby glowing" (406–7); the currently "soundless" locale (397) had once echoed with "voices of surpassing beauty" (407). After thus describing the setting's former attractiveness, the poem's final third concedes the end of the paradisal alternative and returns us to the story's present: "the glory / That blushed and bloomed / Is but a dim-remembered story / Of the old time entombed" (407).

Some readers may, at this point, hesitate to accept this correlation between the story's setting and the poem's setting, yet the explicit contrasts in color and sound strongly suggest such a connection. Nor does it require a tremendous mental leap to grasp how a one-time "fair and stately palace" (406) could be transformed into a decaying Gothic mansion; that both edifices contain "red-litten windows" (401, 407) explicitly underscores their connection. Significant in a different way are the narrator's attribution of the poem to Roderick's "tottering ... reason" (406) and the poem's suggestion that the palace is governed by "Thought" (406); both of these associations imply that the setting's decay has paralleled a decline in the mental abilities of its inhabitants, even if it is not clear whether this decline was a cause or an effect of the decaying setting. Perhaps in Roderick's case his growing doubts about his own knowledge cause the setting to darken for him, bur for the narrator the darkened setting seems to have caused his own intellectual confidence to diminish. In either case, this poem offers a brief version of paradisal skepticism: a darkened, once-paradisal setting is presented in conjunction with increasing doubts about human mental capabilities.

To consider the causes of the mental decline in this setting, however, one must turn from the poem back to the story itself. If one is interested in Poe's aesthetic concerns, the frequent critical emphasis on Roderick is appropriate, but the present focus on the story's treatment of human knowledge shifts the primary attention to the unnamed narrator, whose journey into the formerly paradisal setting resembles the experiences of Rip and Goodman Brown. Like them, he sets out alone into a rural landscape where he encounters problems in perception almost immediately upon reaching his destination. He admits such problems even more directly than they, although he tries to rationalize his doubts away rather than allowing himself to be quickly transported to an imaginative, supernatural realm.

As the narrator approaches the Usher mansion, he is overwhelmed by "a sense of insufferable gloom" for which he cannot rationally account (397); to him sensory perceptions do not justify his present despair, and this discrepancy creates "a mystery all insoluble" (397). Yet this rationalistic narrator must explain the gap before he can advance toward the house, even if his explanation is an unsatisfactory one: "While, beyond doubt, there *are* combinations of very simple and natural objects which have the power of thus affecting us, still, the analysis of this power lies among considerations beyond our depth" (398). Such statements lead Joel Porte to describe the narrator at the story's beginning as "an eminently, even doggedly, reasonable person with a great need to make sense of experiences, or at least to believe that everything ultimately is capable of some rational explanation."[18] Yet even in the story's first paragraph, this narrator, thrust into a no-longer-paradisal setting, must admit limitations in his ability to understand his surroundings and his own thoughts. Almost immediately, though, he becomes uncomfortable with his initial admission and seeks another explanation. His subsequent claim that perhaps "a mere different arrangement of the particulars" might remove the mystery leads to his experiment of looking at the scene as it is reflected in the "black and lurid tarn," but this experiment only increases his confusion (398); he cannot, in David Ketterer's words, "distinguish between the illusive image in the tarn and the real form of the house."[19] He ultimately determines that his sensations "*must* have been a dream" (400). One will remember that Rip and Goodman Brown also experience this inability to distinguish between reality and dream, although Poe does not use this confusion as directly as Irving and Hawthorne to bring into question the basic events of the story. When the narrator finally enters the mansion itself, he retains the confusion caused by his perceptions of the setting; he cannot understand "how unfamiliar were the fancies which ordinary images were stirring up" (400–1).

Once the narrator is in the mansion, in fact, his confusion rapidly increases. Finding "an incoherence" in both Roderick's manner and appearance (402) and an inability "to account for such feelings" (404), he again tries to explain away such inconsistencies by claiming he is "in a dream" (404). Even on the story's climactic night, he continues to seek explanations for the discrepancies between his sensory perceptions and his rational thoughts, tentatively deciding that his "excited fancy had deceived" him (414). Yet, finally, upon the appearance of the revived Lady Madeline at the chamber door, he relinquishes his inadequate rationalism and flees "aghast" (417). Rather than being saved by his rationality, initiated into a new sense of unity, or transported to a higher level of understanding, as three critics have contended, [20] the narrator leaves the House of Usher stripped of his confidence in either empiricism or rationalism to explain the world around him. Reinforcing this interpretation, the last stanza of "The Haunted Palace" recounts the experience of travellers in the darkened valley who, like the narrator, find in it only "a discordant melody" and who "rush out forever, /And laugh—but smile no more" (407).

Clearly, this story is one of those Ketterer must have in mind when he says that Poe often "seeks to undermine man's confidence in his perception of 'reality,'"[21] but one must still consider what the story implies are the causes of mankind's inability to understand the world. Most basically, as already suggested, the story, especially through the experiences of the narrator, emphasizes the limits of rationalism. Much of the narrator's confusion, no doubt, results from an adherence to his faulty rationalistic constructs of the phenomena around him. He relics on his "sane" rationalism to discount too quickly his sensory experience in the house. At the same time, however, the story does not affirm unequivocally the powers of the human senses. At the beginning of the story, the narrator's senses do not accurately record the true condition of the house—he intuits the house's true condition more accurately than he understands it through his senses. Moreover, the story clearly suggests that large areas of human experience, especially those labelled "unconscious" or "irrational," simply cannot be explained by one's senses or rational mind: neither the narrator's senses nor his rationalism is adequate to understand the irrational world or mind of Roderick, which are dominated by the unconscious. Like Poe's detective fiction, this story seems to suggest that for full knowledge one must combine sensory perceptions, rational explanations of them, and the intuition of one's unconscious, yet clearly no one in "Usher" is able to achieve such a synthesis.[22] As Peter Obuchowski succinctly argues, Poe, through the narrator's sojourn, "has us experience the fact that once the mind abandons or is forced to abandon its ways of maintaining sanity it finds itself in a maze with little hope of getting out."[23] The one-time paradise described in Roderick's poem has become such a maze for both Roderick and the narrator.

The subjectivity of sensory experience, the lack of any standard by which to test one's perceptions, the recurring confusion between dream and reality, the frequent errors of rationalism, and the large part of human experience which can only be called "irrational" all account for the narrator's inability to understand this setting. He is unable to synthesize the data from all his sources of knowledge to produce a complete and satisfactory understanding of his world. Although the story does not reveal the long-term effects this rural sojourn has on the narrator, his confidence in his ability to know his world seems destroyed; he has fallen into the gaps between empiricism, rationalism, and intuition as the house has fallen into the tarn. Insofar as he learns anything from his visit to the House of Usher, he learns of the severe limitations of human knowledge—a lesson which makes Roderick's one-time "happy valley" of epistemological confidence "but a dim-remembered story."

To consider stories by Irving, Hawthorne, and Poe in a single essay may seem to overlook, or at least oversimplify, obvious major differences. After all, these three early masters of American short fiction were certainly quite different in philosophical outlook, narrative intention, and intellectual temperament, as well as regional and family background. Yet in these three representative stories, they reacted in similar ways to their era's dominant ideas. Unable to accept either the culture's widespread epistemological confidence (derived generally from the Enlightenment and specifically from the Scottish Common-Sense philosophers) or the pervasive paradisal view of

Americans and the American landscape, these three distinctive writers—a New Yorker, a New Englander, and a Southerner—expressed through a similar fictional pattern their objections to such optimistic interpretations of human existence. For them, problems in human knowledge were inescapable, no matter how paradisal the young American continent seemed to many of their contemporaries. Of course, the question of knowledge has always been a central one in interpretations of the fall, but for these American writers the fall seems to bring a recognition of limits more than an expansion of knowledge. Consequently, their stories show the ironies of a paradisal existence, rather than any possibility of its realization.

NOTES

1. *Selections from Ralph Waldo Emerson*, ed. Stephen E. Whicher (Boston: Houghton Mifflin, 1957), p. 295.

2. David J. Kann, "'Rip Van Winkle': Wheels Within Wheels," *American Imago*, 36 (1979) 179. Despite a totally different focus and context, Kann's reading resembles mine in his emphasis on the doubt and uncertainly which transform the opening "romantic pastoral."

3. Washington Irving, *Works* (New York: G.P. Putnam's Sons, 1880), XVI, 51. All further references to this story are from this volume and appear in the text.

4. Philip Young, "Fallen from Time: The Mythic Rip Van Winkle," *Kenyon Review*, 22 (1960), 567–68.

5. Rita K. Gollin, *Nathaniel Hawthorne and the Truth of Dreams* (Baton Rouge: Louisiana State Univ. Press, 1979), p. 127.

6. *The Centenary Edition of the Works of Nathaniel Hawthorne*, ed. William Charvat et al. (Columbus: Ohio State Univ. Press, 1962–80), X, 75. All further references to this story are from this volume and appear in the text.

7. Representative of such scholars are Richard H. Fogle, *Hawthorne's Fiction: The Light and the Dark* (Norman: Univ. of Oklahoma Press, 1952), pp. 11–27; Leon Howard, "Hawthorne's Fiction," *Nineteenth Century Fiction*, 7 (1953), 237–50; and Sheldon W. Liebman, "The Reader in 'Young Goodman Brown,'" *Nathaniel Hawthorne Journal*, 6 (1975), 156–69.

8. For a fuller articulation of these two possibilities, see Thomas F. Walsh, Jr., "The Bedeviling of Young Goodman Brown," *Modern Language Quarterly*, 19(1958), 331–36; and Leo B. Levy, "The Problem of Faith in 'Young Goodman Brown,'" *Journal of English and Germanic Philology*, 74 (1975), 376.

9. Neal Frank Doubleday, *Hawthorne's Early Tales, A Critical Study* (Durham: Duke Univ. Press. 1972), pp. 204–5. For another discussion of the narrator's role in creating the story's ambiguity and irony, see Norman H. Hostetler, "Narrative Structure and Theme in 'Young Goodman Brown,'" *Journal of Narrative Technique*, 12 (1982), 221–28.

10. Reginald Cook, "The Forest of Goodman Brown's Night: A Reading of Hawthorne's 'Young Goodman Brown,'" *New England Quarterly*, 43 (1970), 481. Similarly, in "*Paradise Lost* and 'Young Goodman Brown,'" *Essex Institute Historical Collections*, 94 (1958), 282, Bernard Cohen finds in Brown's forest experience "a reversal of the re-birth phase of the Adamic myth."

11. Fogle, *Hawthorne's Fiction: The Light and the Dark*, p. 21.

12. Jac Tharpe, *Nathaniel Hawthorne: Identity and Knowledge* (Carbondale: Southern Illinois Univ. Press, 1967), p. 77.

13. Representative of such critics are Arlin Turner, *Nathaniel Hawthorne: An Introduction and Interpretation* (New York: Barnes and Noble, 1961), p. 32; and Tharpe, pp. 75–77.

14. Daniel Hoffman, *Form and Fable in American Fiction* (New York: Oxford Univ. Press, 1965), p.156.

15. Joseph T. McCullen, "Young Goodman Brown: Presumption and Despair," *Discourse*, 2 (1959), 149. Other studies which stress the role of Brown's inadequate intellectual abilities include Gollin, p. 128; and E. Miller Budick, "The World as Specter: Hawthorne's Historical Art," *PMLA*, 101 (1986), 218–32.

16. *Collected Works of Edgar Allan Poe*, ed. Thomas Olive Mabbott (Cambridge: The Belknap Press of Harvard Univ. Press, 1969–78), II 406–7. All further references to this story are from this volume and appear in the text.

17. Charles Feidelson, Jr., *Symbolism and American Literature* (Chicago: Univ. of Chicago Press, 1953), p. 41; Daniel Hoffman, *Poe Poe Poe Poe Poe Poe Poe* (Garden City, N. Y.: Doubleday, 1972), pp. 310–12; and J.O. Bailey, "What Happens in 'The Fall of the House of Usher'?" *American Literature*, 35 (1964), 465. For another study of the poem's role in the story, to which I am generally indebted, see Michael J. Hoffman, "The House of Usher and Negative Romanticism," *Studies in Romanticism*, 4 (1965), 160–62.

18. Joel Porte, *The Romance in America* (Middleton, Conn.: Wesleyan Univ. Press, 1969), p. 62.

19. David Ketterer, *The Rationale of Deception in Poe* (Baton Rouge: Louisiana State Univ. Press, 1979), p. 193.

20. Donald A. Ringe, *American Gothic: Imagination and Reason in Nineteenth-Century Fiction* (Lexington: Univ. Press of Kentucky, 1982), p.147; Thomas J. Rountree, "Poe's Universe: The House of Usher and the Narrator," *Tulane Studies in English*, 20 (1972), 123–34; and E. Miller Budick, "The Fall of the House: A Re-Appraisal of Poe's Attitudes toward Life and Death," *Southern Literary Journal*, 9, No. 2 (1977), 30–50.

21. Ketterer, p.1.

22. From a different beginning point, Daniel Hoffman reaches a similar conclusion in *Poe Poe Poe Poe Poe Poe Poe Poe*, p. 319.

23. Peter Obuchowski, "Unity of Effect in Poe's 'The Fall of the House of Usher,'" *Studies in Short Fiction*, 12 (1975), 412.

JULES ZANGER

"Young Goodman Brown" and "A White Heron": Correspondences and Illuminations

It has become a commonplace of Sarah Orne Jewett criticism to observe, usually in passing, the parallels between her work and that of Nathaniel Hawthorne. Some critics find stylistic similarities, others thematic ones; there is general agreement about their shared concern with New England. Edward Garnett wrote that Jewett "ranked second only to Hawthorne in her interpretation of the spirit of New England Soil" (40–41). Van Wyck Brooks concluded his essay on Jewett in *New England: Indian Summer* by saying, "No one since Hawthorne had pictured this New England world with such exquisite freshness of feeling" (347–53). Other critics, notably Thompson (485–97), found traces of Hawthorne's influence in Jewett's "The Gray Man" and "The Landscape Chamber." More recently, Louis Renza makes a "bizarre" (his term) attempt to link Jewett's "A White Heron" to "The Minister's Black Veil" through the intermediary color coding of her "The Gray Man" and his "The Gray Champion" (142–52).

These adumbrations made, most critics have felt it unnecessary to identify, except in the most general and allusive ways, specific parallels, or influences, or variations linking one particular Hawthorne tale with one of Jewett's. I wish to demonstrate that such a detailed relationship does exist between what are probably two of the best known and most frequently anthologized stories of those writers: Jewett's "A White Heron" (1886) and

From *Papers on Language & Literature* 26, no. 3 (Summer 1990). © 1990 by The Board of Trustees, Southern Illinois University.

Hawthorne's "Young Goodman Brown" (1835). A comparison of these stories reveals a series of shared elements: themes, settings, narrative sequences, images, and dynamics—whose extensiveness suggests the possibility that in "A White Heron," at least, Jewett's indebtedness to Hawthorne, conscious or otherwise, extended well beyond the generalized relationships described above. The frequency and directness of these shared elements make it possible to read "A White Heron" as a personal variation upon the Hawthorne story: in the variations and transformations performed on "Young Goodman Brown" Jewett's particular vision is most fully revealed; at the same time, Jewett's story helps illuminate certain obscure elements in "Young Goodman Brown."

Both stories begin at sundown, Brown leaving Salem and Faith to walk upon a road "darkened by all the gloomiest trees of the forest." Sylvy, Jewett's protagonist, also first appears at sunset "going away from whatever light there was and striking deep into the woods." Almost immediately, both encounter the unnamed strangers with whom they will struggle. In both stories the strangers appear to be invoked by the fears of the characters. Brown, saying to himself, "What if the devil himself should be at my very elbow?" immediately afterward beholds the figure of the stranger with the staff. Sylvy, remembering the noisy town in which she lived before coming to her grandmother's farm, and recalling the great red-faced boy who used to chase and frighten her, is suddenly startled by the aggressive whistle of the young man with the gun. In both cases, the apprehension precedes the appearance.

Sylvy's stranger is linked to the "crowded manufacturing town" by the image of the red-faced boy who introduces him. Brown's stranger, he tells us in almost his first words, has just arrived from Boston. In the course of the stories, both these anonymous intruders are revealed to be hunters and tempters, offering knowledge, money, sexuality, a vision of the great world. Each potential victim accepts from his tempter his token, Satan giving Brown his staff, the hunter giving Sylvy his knife. Both protagonists, Brown and Sylvy, succumb to those temptations. Brown exclaims, "Come, devil, for to thee is this world given," and when the converts are called, "Goodman Brown stepped forth from the shadows of the trees and approached the congregation, with whom he felt a loathful brotherhood by the sympathy of all that was wicked in his heart" (86). Sylvy, after ascending to the pinnacle of the tree and "witnessing the wonderful sight and pageant of the world," descends fully committed to betraying the secret of the heron's nest to the hunter: "wondering over and over again what the stranger would say to her, and what he would think when she told him how to find his way straight to the heron's nest" (156).

Both, of course, change their minds, and they do this in ways which are remarkably similar. Brown, who until the moment of satanic baptism, has apparently acquiesced in the ritual, suddenly cries, "look up to heaven and resist the wicked one" (88). To this point we have been privy to Brown's thoughts through the medium of the omniscient narrator; from the moment in which he and Faith stand before the altar, we are rigorously excluded from them, so that his decision to reject Satan comes as an inexplicable surprise. Between his joining the satanic congregation and his rejecting it, no single incident or insight is provided to motivate or explain Brown's change of heart. Indeed, the final element which had convinced him to join the Devil's party—his conviction of Faith's sin as ambiguously evidenced by the pink ribbon—now appears to be absolutely confirmed by her presence at the altar. Brown's reversion to virtue, if that is what it is, remains a mystery.

Sylvy's decision to deny to the hunter and the grandmother the location of the heron's nest is just as surprising and inexplicable as Brown's change of heart. Employing an omniscient narrator, Jewett permits the reader to share Sylvy's thoughts all through the long climb to the top of the pine, the subsequent discovery of the heron's nest, and the dangerous descent. At the end of that descent, "well-satisfied," she remains fully determined to reveal to the hunter the location of the nest. At that point, Jewett shifts her focus to the grandmother and the hunter waiting at the farm for Sylvy's news. "But Sylvy does not speak after all, though the old grandmother fretfully rebukes her, and the young man's kind, appealing eyes are looking straight into her own ..." (157). That is, in the interval, marked appropriately by white space, between her descent from the tree and her arrival at the farm, something has happened to radically alter her intentions. We are told only after the fact the "the murmur of the pine's green branches is in her ears, she remembers how the white heron came flying through the golden air and how they watched the sea and the morning together, and Sylvy cannot speak...." But this is no adequate explanation of her change of heart, since it was immediately after this remembered experience that she was most committed to revealing the secret. As with Brown's decision to reject Satan, we are faced again with a mystery. Without speculating as to whether these reversals may be read as illustrations of the interventions of a mysterious providence, I would suggest that as dramatic strategies intended to manipulate the reader's sensibility they are remarkably like each other, moving the reader first to apprehension, then to an unexpected though desired resolution.

In the actual conclusions of both these stories, however, we discover that the apparent resolutions are no resolutions at all. Brown's denial of Satan is at best an equivocal act and his subsequent life one of desperation and gloom. Hawthorne's ending is doubly inconclusive, leaving the reader with at least two questions: "Was it a dream?" and, more seriously, was Brown's single act of recantation worth the profound dislocation and isolation of his subsequent life? In the same way, Sylvy's refusal to tell the heron's secret, which appears to be both triumphant and conclusive, is immediately called into question by the intrusive narrator: "Were the birds better friends than their hunter might have been,—who can tell?" And this uncertainty is emphasized in the narrator's final adjuration: "Whatever treasures were lost to her, woodlands and summertime, remember! Bring your gifts and graces and tell your secrets to this lonely country child" (158). This entreaty offers to the reader no positive resolution, formally balancing as it does "the treasures that were lost to her" against the gifts, graces, and secrets that Nature might bring. Both stories end in deliberate ambiguity, denying to the reader any easy moral or ideological closure or resolution.[1]

In the end, both characters return to communities with which they had enjoyed ties of affection and trust, ties now breached by their experiences in the forest. Brown's profound distrust of his wife and his townsfolk is echoed obliquely by Sylvy's unwillingness to trust the heron's secret to her grandmother and the hunter. As if to underline her isolation, the last words of the story are "this lonely country child."

All of these parallels—of settings, images, themes, strategies of rhetoric—link these otherwise quite different stories and suggest that Jewett wrote "A White Heron" out of profound familiarity with "Young Goodman Brown." Certainly the shared elements established connections between the two which make it legitimate to regard Jewett's story, written a half century later, as a variation upon what was perhaps Hawthorne's best-known tale. In the transformations her distinctive vision imposed, we can discover illuminations of both stories.

On the most general level, it is as if Jewett had translated Hawthorne's symbolic allegory into the realistic mode of post-Civil War fiction. Certainly Hawthorne's tale, though localized by history and myth, shows little evidence of the local color writer's concern with the particulars of regional landscape, dialect speech, or economy, all of which we find in "A White Heron." Jewett's work displays many other characteristics usually associated with the local color movement and especially with the contemporary fiction of New England women writers like H.B. Stowe, Rose Terry Cooke, and Mary Wilkes Freeman, all of whom depict life in rural or village New England, focusing often on lower-class women, spinsters, and widows, and the unromantic and often painful particulars of their lives. Despite these affinities, "A White Heron" deviates in several significant ways from such realistic models. First, of course, is the presence of an intrusive narrator, not unlike the narrator in "Young Goodman Brown," whose role as a high-relief commentator, adjuror, and enthusiastic partisan violates the illusion of realistic fiction as a direct transcription from life. Secondly, the intensely circumscribed scene and cast of characters in "A White Heron," the nameless hunter and the allegorically named sylvan child, the climactic uses of dusk and dawn, the opposition of wilderness and community, possess an immediately evident symbolic dimension, so that the story demands to be read on levels not normally appropriate to local color writing, thus linking it further to Hawthorne's model.

On the other hand, Jewett's wilderness is "real," as Hawthorne's never attempts to be, its reality continuously confirmed by particularizing details, including the unsentimental presence of a purring cat, "fat with young robins." Hawthorne's "wild beasts" never appear except as undifferentiated off-stage noises. Jewetts's woods are vividly populated with jaybirds and crows, squirrels and partridges, sparrows and robins, whippoorwills and thrushes, moths and toads.

Jewtt's wilderness, as has often been pointed out, is an essentially benevolent one with no suggestion of that lurking evil which haunts Hawthorne's postlapsarian forest. It is certainly possibly to read these contrasting visions of American nature as gender based, as has frequently been done,[2] but surely another possible explanation can be seen in the half century of historical change that separates them. In 1835 the New England wilderness was much closer to wildness than the settled, cutover, second growth woodlands of 1885: railroads and post roads had pretty well banished the last Indians and bears. Paradoxically, Jewett's "real" forest is, in 1885, much more a metaphorical stage than was Hawthorne's symbolic wilderness half a century before. Further, the moral nature of the wilderness in these stories is at least partially defined against a particular human community. In "Young Goodman Brown" that community which helps define the demonic wilderness is morning-lit Salem, offering at least the illusion of peace and order, virtue and love. In "A White Heron," fifty years later, the alternative community is a "noisy," "crowded manufacturing town," against which the tamed woodlands seem sanctuary-like. This was especially true in the last decades of the century when "noisy" and "crowded," applied to cities, had comes to be code words for the presence of undesirable ethnic types. That perception which opposed a beneficent, nurturing wilderness to an aggressive, noisy, dangerous city was one of the commonplaces of the last decades of the nineteenth century, being espoused by writers as various as Frederick Olmsted, Theodore Roosevelt, James Russell Lowell, and Mark Twain. By reversing Hawthorne's equation of community and nature, good and evil, Jewett was dramatizing that widely held perception which was publicly expressing itself in the Garden Cemetery and National Park movements. In the half century separating the stories, Hawthorne's wilderness had become Jewett's Nature, and that original sense of mission which had impelled the first settlers into the forest had turned on itself. Instead of that older vision in which civilization transformed wilderness, many Americans, taught by Thoreau and Emerson, and later by George Perkins Marsh, John Muir, Louis Agassiz, and others, had come to believe that civilization must somehow be redeemed by learning from and about Nature. In the opposition between these two perceptions dramatized by Jewett, the man with the gun is immediately recognizable as the dominant figure in the typology of wilderness central to the older vision. The child, on the other hand, might well be construed as emblematic of the new role in relation to Nature which the new vision required.[3]

Despite the differences between Jewett's presentation of Nature and Hawthorne's, it should be recognized that for both of them the forest and the attendant isolation it imposes serve as a setting for the encounters, testing and self-definition that each story involves. For both, the wilderness retains its traditional American nature as a locus for individual striving: in 1835, Americans, most characteristically, strove against Nature; by 1885, it was becoming increasingly evident that Americans had to strive to preserve the natural world, as Sylvy does.

More significant differences emerge as we move from the settings to the characters. Brown and Sylvy, though both the subjects of temptation, are in almost every other respect distinct from each other.

Unlike Sylvy, Young Goodman Brown is permitted by his role and circumstance to act out of choice rather than necessity. We see him brush aside Faith's objections to his trip into the woods, as he hastens to keep his appointment with the Devil. Even in the debate with Satan, Brown determines the agenda, holding up each of his idols—grandfather and father, the good people of New England, his own saintly minister—to be ritualistically knocked down by Satan's predictable responses. These are clearly straw men: at no point does Brown question, let alone reject, Satan's contentions that they are all of his party, beyond asking the Father of Lies, "Can this be so?" It is only the introduction of Faith into the debate that momentarily halts Brown's systematic destruction of his idols, and that last obstruction is overcome with his unquestioning acceptance of the flimsy and ambiguous pink ribbon as evidence of his wife's corruption. With each of these icons broken, Brown has freed himself to pursue his evil purpose.

At the same time, Brown, a creature of Original Sin, is appropriately aware of the role of the past in shaping the present. When he proposes to act virtuously, he bases his virtue on that of his ancestors. When he permits himself to be convinced that grandfather, father, minister, and Faith are all of the Devil's party, he commits himself absolutely to evil: "There is no good on earth; and sin is but a name. Come, devil; for to thee is this world given" (83). At the very last moment, he chooses once more, electing to deny Satan, apparently as absolutely as he had affirmed him.

Sylvy, on the other hand, exists until the conclusion of Jewett's story in a position of powerlessness. As a small, dependent, timid, female child, she is dominated by both her grandmother and the hunter. Her act of courage in discovering the heron's nest is performed as an act of propitiation to another. Her domination is most clearly signified by her silence; after reluctantly revealing her name at the hunter's insistence when they first encounter each other, Sylvy maintains an "awed silence" throughout the story: "the sound of her own unquestioned voice would have terrified her" (150). Her silence, however, which traditionally is a sign of subservience, becomes in the last scene of the story an instrument of power.[4] After a year in the woods and her adventure of the night before, the timid little town girl has found the courage to defy her elders. Sylvy's submissive silence is transformed into the silence of defiance, as she denies her grandmother and the hunter the knowledge she possesses. In a radical inversion of conventional order, Sylvy's denial turns the world upside down, silently declaring her independence.

Her act of denial is significantly different from Brown's and provides perspective on his rejection of Satan. About Brown's stranger there is no doubt in Brown's mind. He has announced his supernatural nature with his first words, and his snake-staff immediately establishes his identity. Though the careful reader may recognize ambiguities in his presentation, Brown believes he knows precisely with whom he is dealing. A sometime communicant of his saintly minister's church, Brown knows a whole body of appropriate, conditioned responses to the Evil One, to the Enemy, all of which support his ultimate denial. Rejecting Satan in the woods and then accepting his valuation of the world in the town, he in both instances acts consistently with the received knowledge and values of his community. Told by Satan in the woods that the nature of man is evil, Brown can well believe him because his venerable minister has preached exactly that tenet of faith in the town. Brown's brief involvement with Satanism is, as Gatsby might have said, only personal. In the absence of significant motivation, his denial of the Devil emerges as reflexive and communally conditioned by fear, not faith.

On the other hand, for Sylvy's young man there is no equivalent mechanism for rejection. Just the opposite: he is attractive, kindly, friendly; he has been welcomed as a guest by her grandmother. As a sportsman, as a scientist, he embodies some of the highest masculine values of his country and time. When Sylvy mysteriously changes her mind and decides not to reveal the heron's secret, she acts precisely against the received values of her community as they are represented by her grandmother and by the young man. She too acts personally, denying both the masculine "great world" apparently offered to her by the hunter and, at least as significantly, the matriarchal world of the grandmother who has cared for and protected her.

It is an act demanding much greater courage and sacrifice than Brown's last moment, trimmer's reversion to the safe and familiar. He, after all, saves only himself, leaving Faith behind at the alter, as he earlier left her behind in the village. "Sauve qui peut!" Sylvy, instead, sacrifices her grandmother's approval and the hunter's gratitude, reward, and friendship for the heron's sake and for the vision of Nature she has experienced at daybreak from the top of the tree.

This response to experience is significantly different from Brown's, who throughout his story denies his own personal experience when confronted by authority. Accepting the Devil's contentions and illusions, he disregards his own living knowledge of his grandfather and father whom he had believed to be "honest men and Christians," of his minister, "a good old man," and of his wife Faith, "a blessed angel on earth." Nine-year-old Sylvy, however, awed as she is by the young man and indebted as she is to her grandmother, rejects both adults' authority to affirm her own private experience.

The double nature of this rejection is often neglected by critics who focus exclusively on Sylvy's denial of the hunter. Those interpretations of "A White Heron" which limit it to a conflict between an aggressive patriarchal system represented by the young man and a supportive matriarchal community represented by Sylvy (cf. Donovan) do so only by eliding any consideration of the third character in the story, the grandmother. It is she who is the actual center of the matriarchal community, and it is she who gives in to temptation and allies herself with the hunter against Sylvy. The ideological reductivism that ignores the grandmother's role does violence to the story and undervalues the artistic complexity of Jewett's achievement.

The scene Jewett has created for the climax of her story confronts Sylvy with two possible futures. The hunter represents a combination of masculine aggressiveness and scientific detachment linked to "a wave of human interest," an entry into "the great world," and a hazy promise of love. The grandmother offers very real love, but represents the alternative to the hunter's promise: a world of actual experience, of loss, penury, and pain. To the elderly widow, left behind by her children and living in poverty on her isolated hardscrabble farm, the ten dollar reward promised by the hunter represents, not the child's fantasy of wealth, but the harsh difference between buying new shoes for Sylvy or buying another cow, or none. It is the presence of the grandmother that prevents "A White Heron" from sliding into formulaic allegory and roots it in the actual world of 19th century, decaying New England. This old farm woman who has buried four children, whose daughter has moved away to the city, and whose last son has disappeared into the West, possesses a solidity and credibility that the nameless young man never achieves. If he vaguely implies some golden future, she, more realistically, suggests another not nearly so bright. If the young man suggests power and wonder, the old woman represents the restrictiveness of experience, Nature, and circumstance.

Confronted with grandmother and hunter, the Emersonian polarities of Fate and Will, Sylvy—perhaps childishly, perhaps because she is a child—refuses allegiance to either, committing herself instead to a transcendent unity with Nature, achieved by a denial of self. Her distance from Young Goodman Brown could hardly be greater.

On the strength of the correspondences between these stories, the differences that distinguish them acquire special significance. The contrasting perceptions of wilderness and town and the contrasting conceptions of allegiance and community suggest some of the intellectual and cultural developments that had changed American literature and American society in the fifty years that separated the stories.

Other differences provide insights, perhaps more personal, into the writers themselves. Hawthorne's "good" young man is presented to us in terms which, while characteristically ambivalent, finally ask us to judge him and to deny his solitary claim to godliness. Writing in a period much less certain of the verities, Jewett is more tentative: Sylvy's act of refusal appears to us to be unquestionably right, yet it too amounts to an act of withdrawal from the human community and the conditions that circumscribe it; its consequences remain uncertain to Sylvy and to the narrator. Hawthorne can follow Brown for us to the hour of his gloomy death. We must leave Sylvy at the age of nine, all of the problematical consequences of her choice still before her. Jewett, who at forty-eight wrote, "This is my birthday and I am always nine years old," apparently was to remain uncertain of the correctness of Sylvy's choice into her own maturity (*Letters* 125).

Taken together, these stories can rewardingly be read as foils for each other, each putting the other into sharper outline. If Brown seems a little darker and Sylvy a little brighter for this procedure, they both come together in realizing for us worlds in which moral choices have profound consequences and must be made, however uncertainly. Beyond that, the stories suggest that many of the conventional distinctions we make separating our romantic and realistic writers can be profitably reexamined.

WORKS CITED

Brooks, Van Wyck. *New England: Indian Summer, 1865–1915.* New York: Dutton, 1940.

Fields, Annie, ed. *Letters of Sarah Orne Jewett.* Boston: n.p., 1911.

Garnett, Edward. "Books Too Little Known." *Academy and Literature* 11 July 1903: 40–41.

Hawthorne, Nathaniel. *Mosses from an Old Manse.* Columbus: Ohio State UP, 1974. 74–90

Huthe, Hans. *Nature and the American: Three Centuries of Changing Attitudes.* Los Angeles: U of California P, 1957.

Jewett, Sarah Orne. *Tales of New England.* Boston: Riverside, 1896. 138–58.

Kolodny, Annette. *The Lay of the Land.* Chapel Hill: U of North Carolina P, 1975.

Marx, Leo. *The Pilot and the Passenger.* New York: Oxford UP, 1988.

Person, Leland S., Jr. "Hester's Revenge: the Power of Silence in *The Scarlet Letter.*" *Nineteenth-Century Literature* 43 (1989): 465–83.

Renza, Louis A. *"A White Heron" and the Question of Minor Literature.* Madison: U of Wisconsin P, 1984.

Robertson, James 0. *American Myth, American Reality.* New York. Hill 1980.

Thompson, Charles M. "The Art of Miss Jewett." *Atlantic Monthly* October 1904: 485–97.

NOTES

1. Leo Marx points out in his description of the American pastoral that "the endings of these pastoral fables tend to be inconclusive if not deliberately equivocal" (301–02). Both "Young Goodman Brown" and "A White Heron" correspond to Marx's formulation to a very high degree.

2. The perception of nature as feminine and maternal and the corresponding perception of technology and destruction as masculine are discussed as dominating American metaphors by Kolodny.

3. For discussion of this shift in attitudes toward nature, see Huthe 87–104; Robertson 115–21.

4. Person discusses Hawthorne's use of silence as both a sign of submission and an instrument of revenge.

JOAN ELIZABETH EASTERLY

Lachrymal Imagery in Hawthorne's "Young Goodman Brown"

"Faith! Faith!" cried the husband. "Look up to Heaven, and resist the Wicked One!"

Whether Faith obeyed, he knew not. Hardly had he spoken, when he found himself amid calm night and solitude, listening to a roar of the wind, which died heavily away through the forest. He staggered against the rock and felt it chill and damp, while a hanging twig, that had been all on fire, besprinkled his cheek with the coldest dew. (Hawthorne 88)

Thus ends the crucial scene in Nathaniel Hawthorne's tale of "Young Goodman Brown," the story of a Puritan lad who leaves his bride of three months to secretly watch a witches' Sabbath in the deep forest outside Salem village. In so doing, he willfully betrays his commitment to his wife, the moral code of his society, and the teachings of his religion. The experience of this one night in the forest changes Goodman Brown for the rest of his life, for it poisons his relationship with his wife, isolates him from his neighbors, and destroys his ability to worship God. Whether dream or reality, one wild night is the turning point of Brown's existence; afterward he is "a stern, a sad, a darkly meditative, a distrustful, if not a desperate man" and, when he dies, "they carved no hopeful verse upon his tombstone" (90).

From *Studies in Short Fiction* 28, no. 3 (Summer 1991). ©1991 by *Studies in Short Fiction*, Inc.

Literary critics have interpreted the significance of Goodman Brown's experience in many fashions—allegorical, moral, philosophical, and psychological. However, there is an intriguing absence of any reference to the last line of the Sabbath scene to explain Hawthorne's characterization of the young Puritan, despite the fact that Hawthorne signals the importance of the cold drops of dew in a periodic sentence. In essence, Hawthorne here carefully delineates the image of a young man who has faced and failed a critical test of moral and spiritual maturity.

Young Goodman Brown, leaning against the cold rock after the witch-meeting vanishes, is reproached by his creator because he shows no compassion for the weaknesses he sees in others, no remorse for his own sin, and no sorrow for his loss of faith. The one action that would demonstrate such deep and redemptive human feelings does not take place. Goodman Brown does not weep. Therefore, Hawthorne quietly and gently sprinkles "the coldest dew" on his cheek to represent the absence of tears.

This lack of tears, the outward sign of an inward reality, posits the absence of the innate love and humility that would have made possible Brown's moral and spiritual progression. A meticulous artist and a master of symbolism, Hawthorne uses the twig and dewdrops deliberately. Drops of water on a man's cheek can only suggest tears.

The hanging twig that sprinkles the drops of water on Goodman Brown's face calls to mind a picture of the beadle perched on a high stool in the back of a Puritan meeting house, holding two long switches. According to legend, one switch had a feather attached to the end and the other a stone or burr. If a lady fell asleep during the long service, the beadle would awaken her by tickling her face with the feather, but any gentleman inclined to drowse or small boys inclined to mischief knew that the stone hung over their heads like the bait on a long fishing rod and that their recall to propriety would not be so gentle. Likewise, Goodman Brown is awakened to reality from his dream or vision by a "hanging twig" that had been burning during the witch meeting but now scatters cold dew on his cheek. Like the beadle's switch, a twig from on high is the vehicle for bringing to Brown's face the reminder of what would be correct behavior and attitude for a man in this situation. He should be weeping, but he is not.

The clear, cold drops of dew are a direct contrast to the flaming blood-like liquid with which the Satanic figure is about to baptize Faith and Goodman Brown when the young man's cry, "Look up to Heaven, and resist the Wicked One!" (88), interrupts the ceremony. The words—which trigger the disappearance of the witch-meeting—and the immediate sprinkling of dew on Goodman Brown's cheek suggest that the cold water is also a baptism, a sign of salvation, grace, and renewal. This interpretation would then imply that since Brown alone has resisted Satan, he would justly find his life intolerable in Salem, where all of those whom he has revered have betrayed his confidence in their faith. If the drops of water are a sign of blessing, then Goodman Brown's vision would seem to have been a true one, and he is consigned to live in the horror of being the one good man in a village of witches whose true maleficence is cloaked in piety. However, the placement and form of the water drops signify that they are not a reminder of Christian grace. In the story the devil's mark of baptism was to be laid on the communicants' foreheads as a mockery of the Christian sacrament. In contrast, the drops of dew that fall on Brown's cheek do not signify Christian baptism because this rite, by the oldest tradition, involves the forehead and flowing water rather than sprinkled water.

Instead, Hawthorne deliberately and ingenuously uses the image of dewdrops, suggestive of an uncomfortable, chilling dampness from the earth (rather than, for example, raindrops, which are associated with cleansing, warmth, and heaven), to reprove Goodman Brown. The Puritan has just seen the sinfulness of his neighbors and friends clearly exposed, and has become acutely aware of the evil in his own heart as the unholy celebration arouses in him a feeling of "loathful brotherhood" with the fiend worshipers. However, not only does Brown fail to display the pity indicative of a sense of moral maturity in regard to the weakness and depravity of others, he likewise shows no regret for his own wickedness, a response that would start him on the path to spiritual maturity. The spiritual implications of Brown's failure are emphasized by Hawthorne's presenting the young man's dilemma in the context of a witches' meeting, and Brown's assimilation of the Satanic figure's assertion that mankind is predominately wicked indicates his lack of faith in the power of God to overcome evil. On a moral level, Brown's acceptance of others as they are—imperfect and subject to temptation—would have made a mature adulthood and productive and healthy relationships with others possible. But his lack of remorse and compassion, as symbolized by the absence of tears, condemns him to an anguished life that is spiritually and emotionally desiccated. The drops that Hawthorne places on Brown's cheek are of "the coldest dew," devastating in their connotation, for they represent the coldness of a soul that is dying, in contrast to the regenerative warmth of true tears and love.

Young Goodman Brown's inability to cry after the shock of the witches' meeting would be a strong argument for those who typecast the tale as an "initiation story" in which the protagonist fails to achieve adulthood. As psychologists Carol Gilligan and John Murphy state in "Development from Adolescence to Adulthood":

> While formal logic and principles of justice can release adolescent judgment from the binding constraints of a conventional mode of moral reasoning, the choices that arise in adulthood impose a new context for moral decision ... an expanded ethic that encompasses compassion, tolerance, and respect. (410)

Using these criteria, Goodman Brown demonstrates none of the characteristics of the adult "expanded ethic." He shows no compassion for the sinfulness he sees in others (and which he shares), no tolerance for others' imperfections, and no respect for their attempts at faithful lives. Compassion is the most important of these characteristics because it could engender the other two emotions, and it is Brown's lack of compassion that Hawthorne wishes to emphasize in the story. Whether one classifies the young man's experience at the witches' Sabbath as a failed initiation into adulthood or as simply the critical moment in his moral and spiritual growth, Hawthorne's portrayal of a young Puritan of immature faith and simplistic morality is rendered more complete by the realization that Brown is a man who does not weep.

Human tears are an emotional response, and Hawthorne's allusion to the lack of tears underscores Brown's emotional barrenness. Critical analyses have hitherto focused primarily on Brown's faulty or immature moral reasoning, arguing that the Puritan fails the test of the Sabbath because he fails to *reason* on a mature moral level, either because of the legalism of Puritan doctrine or because of his refusal to admit his own sinfulness (Frank 209, Folsom 32, Fogle 23, Stubbs 73). Yet Hawthorne clearly indicates that Brown also destroys his chance to progress morally and spiritually because of his inability to respond intuitively to the shock of the experience with mature, positive *emotions* that would have enabled him to deal with the vision of evil in his neighbors as well as with the knowledge of his own wickedness. Goodman Brown does not weep tears of deep sorrow for others because he cannot love or forgive them. He does not weep for his own sins because he lacks a deeply felt faith, which tears of contrition—arising from a broken spirit sensitive to the baseness of sin and to God's loving mercy and grace— would signify.

Hawthorne emphasizes Brown's lack of positive emotions and implies his regression into emotional sterility by the cold, damp forest, which is in dramatic contrast to the description of the witches' meeting, where the trembling Puritan's horror is evoked by the blasphemy of the unholy worship and the loathsome kinship he feels with the congregation. The emotional prose intensifies with the dreadful, confused sounds of the fiends' hymn and the images of blazing fire, blood, and smoke as Brown becomes aware of the power of evil and the sinful nature of everyone whom he respects. When the vision disappears at Brown's anguished cry to Faith, the suddenly changed scenery of the next paragraph deliberately corresponds to young Brown's emotional state. Words like "solitude," "rock," "chill," "damp," and "coldest" suggest the absence or denial of positive feelings, which Brown demonstrates immediately afterward. The townspeople he encounters on his return from the witches' meeting are involved in good works—preparing a sermon, praying, catechizing a child—yet he rejects them, and when his young wife greets him with joy and affection, he spurns her. This heartlessness is the pattern for the rest of Brown's life, and Hawthorne, who was aware of the complexity and mystery of human nature, completes his portrait of a young man whose life is blighted in a single night by revealing in the crucial paragraph through chilly rock and coldest dew that young Goodman Brown's moral and spiritual disaster is also due to an inappropriate emotional response at the critical moment.

In conclusion, Nathaniel Hawthorne, the master of symbolism and suggestion, softly sprinkles cold tears on the cheek of young Goodman Brown. This lachrymal image, so delicately wrought, is the key to interpreting the young Puritan's failure to achieve moral and spiritual maturity. Brown cannot reconcile the conflict caused by his legalistic evaluation of others, nor can he transcend this moral dilemma by showing compassion and remorse. In final irony, Hawthorne tells us that the man who sheds no tears lives the rest of his life a "sad" man, whose "dying hour was gloom" (90).

WORKS CITED

Fogle, Richard Harter. *Hawthorne's Fiction: The Light and the Dark*. Norman: U of Oklahoma P, 1964.

Folsom, James K. *Man's Accidents and God's Purpose: Multiplicity in Hawthorne's Fiction*. New Haven: College & UP, 1963.

Frank, Neal *Hawthorne's Early Tales: A Critical Study*. Durham: Duke UP, 1972.

Gilligan, Carol, and John Michael Murphy. "Development From Adolescence to Adulthood: The Philosopher and the Dilemma of the Fact." *Readings in Developmental Psychology*, 2nd ed. Ed. Judith Krieger Gardner. Boston: Little, 1982. 400–12.

Hawthorne, Nathaniel. "Young Goodman Brown." *Mosses from an Old Manse*. Ohio State UP, 1974. 74–90.

Stubbs, John Caldwell. *The Pursuit of Form: A Study of Hawthorne and the Romance*. Chicago: U of Illinois P, 1970.

WALTER SHEAR

Cultural Fate and Social Freedom
in Three American Short Stories

When one compares James's "The Jolly Corner" to Irving's "Rip Van Winkle" and Hawthorne's "Young Goodman Brown," striking formal similarities present themselves. Each story focuses on a male protagonist and develops his relationship to his society in a triptych arrangement of settings. At its beginning each story places the central character in a domestic cultural environment, but with a treatment that emphasizes his detachment from that setting. The second section of the narrative transports the character to an outré environment where he encounters fabulous characters whose bizarre features are, nevertheless, haunted by what is familiar to the protagonist. Finally, the story returns the main character, in a rather dazed condition, to his society, in a manner that calls attention to his altered relationship to the others in his society, endowing him with such a perspective that he seems to transcend their social concerns.

The stories' formal divisions create two interrelated effects. On the one hand, each narrative is a story of change that calls attention to the way an accelerated flow of past into the present accents the difference between social identity and personal, psychological identity, creating a widening gap between public and private histories. On the other hand, through the social detachment such a division provides, the structure suggests that social access in America is multifaceted, not something restricted by an historic class

From *Studies in Short Fiction* 29, no. 4 (Fall 1992). ©1992 by *Studies in Short Fiction*, Inc.

structure and that, in this sense, history is the possibility of a beginning for the individual who will seize it. Since the individual is relatively secure in what is formally a kind of cultural sandwich, the rents in society that history generates can be regarded as the occasions for the disappearance and emergence of the private self.

However firmly Rip, Goodman Brown, and Spencer Brydon are placed in their environments, they are from the beginning separate from them, seen as individuals gradually imbibing premonitions of their precarious relationship to time and place. Brydon's is an obvious alienation. Returning to an America so charged with a dynamic materialism that he at first has difficulty recognizing it, he decides to respond as positively as he can to the new scene. His is initially an impetus to conformity and such a source of amusement and surprise that, as he informs Alice Staverton, "he scarce knew what to make of this lively stir, in a compartment of his mind never yet penetrated, of a capacity for business and a sense for construction" (James 438). At the root of his response is the idea of the environment as home (a place to be, which engenders, as the story develops, a literal being for place); yet it becomes also the source of conflict as Brydon's sentimental attachment for his old boyhood home, the house on the jolly corner, is threatened by the forces of progress that want this image of his and the country's past torn down to make way for the future. Brydon's eagerness to confront his alter ego indicates his anxiety about the cost of resolving that conflict, and he comes to believe that the image of what he would have become had he remained in America will yield him a sense of the historical reality in which the image might have lived. While Brydon is much more sophisticated than Rip or Goodman Brown, he finds that even his imaginative anticipations, his suspicions regarding the image's "monstrous" nature, are insufficient for the shocking force of historical cumulation and the accrued, apparently total, social commitment represented in the figure. Brydon's confrontation with this alien social being turns literally violent, becoming in one sense the measure of his shock at the persistence of his naiveté about social forces.

On a more casual level, Rip Van Winkle's naiveté has as well curious connections with a kind of alienation that leads to his separation from society. In Irving's wonderful deployment of eighteenth-century sentimentality, Rip as hen-pecked husband takes his aesthetic place comfortably in a caricatured society whose figures all come finally to manifest the smoothly carved outlines of provincial life. The pace of life seems appropriately suggested by Rip's laziness and the cultural stasis it implies. It is thus fitting that his social separation should proceed from a rather casual decision and seem a departure that has mainly an accidental meaning, resulting from the simple fact that he is an individual and therefore capable of being separated. Basically the coherence of this society, which Irving will reprise at the end in its transformed recurrent elements, makes it possible for small variants in individual qualities to take on rather significant status. Rip's quotidian decision is comically horrifying in its short-term effects, but amusingly reassuring as society finally opens again.

In this framework, history in the form of time is only gradually revealed. Temporal measurements in the village are familiar—and anticipated with comic certitude. We note,

> Nicholaus Vedder, a patriarch of the village, and landlord of the inn, at the door of which he took his seat from morning till night, just moving sufficiently to avoid the sun and keep in the shade of a large tree; so that the neighbours could tell the hour by his movements as accurately as by a sun dial. (Irving 32)

In most respects the scene is the opposite of the busyness of James's story, but the growing force of Dame Van Winkle serves to ignite the narrative and to render the dominant, strident note of a repressed time. Though they are held firmly but gently within the communal frame and its humorous aesthetic, the domestic relationships of the Van Winkles dramatize this sharper, more irritant quality of time as it works itself out in marriage, a representative social institution: "a tart temper never mellows with age, and a sharp tongue is the only edged tool that grows keener with constant use" (Irving 31).

While Irving's treatment of the social dimension of his character is as leisurely ample as James's is introspectively dramatic, Hawthorne seems, at the beginning, merely to acknowledge social ties as Goodman Brown says goodbye to his wife Faith and sets out for a night in the forest. From the first scene the emphasis is psychological, centered on the ironic relationship between innocent naiveté and the vague, free-floating quality of Goodman's intention:

> "after this one night I'll cling to her skirts and follow her to Heaven."
>
> With this excellent resolve for the future, Goodman Brown felt himself justified in making more haste on his present evil purpose. (Hawthorne 75)

In underestimating what one night's separation can mean, he underestimates the power of time, failing to see the degree to which he has in this domestic parting made himself a particular kind of individual, ultimately the prisoner of his own psychology. For while the story has within it a formal allegory of the loss of faith, the fact of the initial separation, representing as it does the departure from conventional belief, unleashes a social suspension that for him causes all communal relationships henceforth to be determined from within rather than from without.

The middle sections in each story involve social fantasies. Goodman Brown's experience in the woods involves projection, and because his basic means of order, his religious system, is absent, the society he was familiar with becomes nightmarish, inducing paranoia. As a third generation Puritan, Brown is historically the victim of an altered relationship to both God and nature, yet what the reader witnesses is the revenge of the id upon the ego, seemingly for the latter's social acquiescence. The people Brown apparently observes in the forest are most real in their absolute reverence for evil and in their complete contempt for naive social beliefs such as his. Under these terms Brown as individual must struggle against society for the very ground of personal value, ever alert for external threats (and everyone is a potential threat), continually betrayed by the double-edged nature (sign and significance) of all social meaning, and periodically forced to declare to himself that his beliefs can only be transcendent: "Look up to Heaven, and resist the Wicked One!" (Hawthorne 88).

In all the stories the fantasy dimension in the middle section tends to take the form of culture comporting itself on the dynamics of an individual psychology. Rip first senses himself in alien territory as he hears the strange voice that names him, "Rip Van Winkle," but then he sees characters dressed in antique Dutch fashion reminding him of the figures in an old Flemish painting. Despite the remnants of a recognizable social reality, the figures' peculiar silence on meeting him strengthens his sense of barrier: "There was something strange and incomprehensible about the unknown, that inspired awe and checked familiarity" (Irving 34). As he "discovers" later, what is happening here is time manifesting itself as history—not the past filtered through the rationale of memory, but an attribute of time, its linear flow, somehow dammed up and then suddenly inundating him as immediacy. More surprising than painful, it turns out to be a kind of game, a riddle and an amazement for the individual who thought he existed only in a socially-defined present.

History—in the form of competing personal histories—orchestrates as well the drama in the house on the jolly corner. Like Rip, Brydon fancies himself a hunter, but he discovers that it is he who is the game in the drama of time. Will and intention—the offensive powers of individuality—are undermined by Brydon's increasing awareness of his own vulnerability. Not simply the sophisticated, perceptive sensibility, he finds that he is as well the end of a point in time, someone who will seem horrifyingly strange once he is revealed to himself, and who may be for the detached perceiver simply what is seen and nothing more. His encounter with his alter ego results not in his individuality's strengthening by an alliance with the riches in his personal potential, but in the shock of the social image's alarming strangeness: "the presence before him was a presence, the horror within him a horror.... Such an identity fitted his at *no* point, made its alternative monstrous" (James 476). The alternate social history of himself, since it is simply so different as fact and experience, can only be for him the totally other.

Brydon is on his way to realizing that one's experience in time is, if not deterministic, at least unforgiving. What has been lived has been lived; experience cannot be canceled. As the violence of his encounter with the alter ego demonstrates, the power of otherness lies in its mirror reflection of the terrible social force confronting him as a result of his having become who he is.

After these implosions of history upon the protagonists, the assured resolutions of the final sections are, as closures, surprising returns to social order. Although their final social roles vary considerably, all three return to their respective societies culturally enhanced, both more acutely aware of themselves and the way they differ personally from their fellow citizens. And in each case a woman plays an Ariadne role, welcoming the male back to society with a recognition that seems to signal, at least for Rip and Brydon, a nurturing acceptance of love and affection. Because of the way the affectionate recognition builds to a communal dimension, Rip seems to take his place as one of the first American celebrities. And what the community chooses to have Rip represent has a happy coincidence with the passive existence he resumes. In his case context—chiefly the absence of critical viewpoints such as those of Dame Van Winkle—and the power of a past for a present that can perceive its relevance create the conditions for social happiness.

Much as Rip is embraced by his community, Spencer Brydon ends up in the lap of Alice Staverton. It is she who soothes away his anxieties about social identity, helping to erase the image of what he could have been with what he is. As a member of American society, she is able to imagine from the outside what Brydon conjures up from the inside. While from his subjective perspective, Brydon sees an alien alter ego, Alice sees and feels through the social channels for affection, surprising him by stating that this home-grown version of himself was someone she had accepted and "I *could* have liked him" (James 484). She could feel sympathy for the American's social existence and "it may have pleased him that I pitied him," she says as she imagines him "grim," "worn," and one to whom "things have happened" (485). Brydon, who suffers from that Jamesian social alienation in which "things" don't seem to happen to one, is puzzled and dismayed. Yet at the end he perceives, however dimly, that, despite lacking the million a year, he has the capacity for a subjective intensity that will see and feel Alice as one like him, someone who both recognizes and sees through social absolutes. Their exchange of insight that concludes the story—"he has n't you"; "he is n't—*you!*" (485)— suggests that the affectionate delight of shared cultural understanding is more than compensation for the rewards of social achievement, and that, in that sense, alienation is freedom for the self.

Goodman Brown's return is the most tragic, but perhaps, for that reason, the most illuminating in regard to social space. More clearly than the other figures, Brown is a cultural representative and in this context evokes that stage of Puritanism when a diminished conviction was beginning to be replaced by a somewhat hypocritical moral will. Whether the forest experience is seen as a loss of faith or not, Brown's return is marked by his deliberately ignoring his wife's proffered greeting. His calculated revulsion for his fellow citizens, presumably because they were in the evil forest, seems a part of a psychological strategy to repress his own wandering. However painful, the remainder of his life involves a deliberately chosen existence, one based on a cultural absolute that not only rejects social realities as mere appearances, but that also refuses to acknowledge any human quality outside his personal experience of that culture.

As the triptych structure creates sharp juxtapositions of past and present, society as one's basic reality is distanced. History thus engenders a power within the individual, but at a price. The individual is both temporal being and part of a cultural impulse that claims to know realities that are beyond time and thus to have a grasp upon the unknown future. But the full meaning of existence for the individual is either scattered in a future in the form of anticipation and desires, or is in the past in which experiences have preceded full knowledge and only exist in memory as history, individual and cultural. In these narratives the individual swings out of time, paradoxically and almost deliriously senses his power, and then moves abruptly back to contemplate his cultural fate—either with a resigned contentment at his place in the world or with an irreconcilable bitterness at his powerlessness.

Though all the stories tend to examine the protagonists in cultural constructs, each in its own way deconstructs the American person, unfolding what is viewed as a particular space and time to discover an asocial self within the social self. While the spatially structured form of each story insists on a definite cultural framework surrounding the subjective and seemingly free adventures of the protagonist, the narratives, simply as reading sequences, delight in unveiling, through the quickening and lessening of the pressures of time, the contingency of all social norms within the context of a cultural history.

I am not arguing that any direct influence exists between or among these stories, though Hawthorne obviously knew "Rip Van Winkle" (he praises the story in the introduction to "The Chimaera" *A Wonder Book*), and James would have known "Rip" and, as his book on Hawthorne indicates, was familiar with "Young Goodman Brown." What I would suggest is that in each case the demand for concentration and drama that the short story form invokes interacts with the scope history provides to produce peculiarly American treatments of the self, specifically stressing its resources for positive and negative possibilities beyond its social definitions. All three stories have their foundation in a sense of an American historical moment. Each story assumes that the self's cultural experience in America will be characterized by social and temporal disjunctures, but that the dynamics of history can provide, if not continuity, a form of cultural coherence for the individual who can find the right personal context for his experience.

How American is this version of the self? Readers of British literature have undoubtedly recognized that the triptych structure outline here fits almost exactly that of one of the most popular nineteenth-century English stories, *A Christmas Carol*. Scrooge's return from the fantastic visitations of Christmas spirits involves, as do the American stories, an altered relation to society. The difference, I would argue, is that Dickens's emphasis in his triptych-within-a-triptych is not merely on the security of linear time, but on cause-and-effect arguments made to Scrooge about his social obligations, and these become, presumably, in concert with his growing emotional attachments, the motive for his change. As a cultural occasion, Christmas signals Scrooge's spiritual connection to his culture. But there is no sense here of a re-connection to his society, from which he was never separated. By contrast, American fictions, here and elsewhere, seem almost fond of imagining the American individual apart from—and often in opposition to—his society.

WORKS CITED

Hawthorne, Nathaniel. "Young Goodman Brown." *Mosses from an Old Manse*. Ed. William Charvat et al. Columbus: Ohio State UP, 1974. 74–90. Vol. 10 of *The Centenary Edition of the Works of Nathaniel Hawthorne*. 20 vols. 1968–85.

Irving, Washington. "Rip Van Winkle." *The Sketch Book of Geoffrey Crayon, Gent*. Ed. Haskell Springer. Boston: Twayne, 1978. Vol. 8 of *The Complete Works of Washington Irving*. 30 vols. 1969–89.

James, Henry. "The Jolly Corner." *The Altar of the Dead, The Beast of the Jungle, The Birthplace, and Other Tales*. New York: Scribner's, 1909. 435–85. Vol. 17 of *The Novels and Tales of Henry James: The New York Edition*. 26 vols. 1907–17.

BENJAMIN FRANKLIN V

Goodman Brown and the Puritan Catechism

If the importance of an artistic creation may be gauged by the amount of critical attention it receives, then Hawthorne's "Young Goodman Brown" is surely one of the most significant stories ever written. From Melville's comments in 1850 to the present, this dark tale has engaged many of Hawthorne's best readers and is likely to continue attracting them. I would suggest, however, that while such scholars as Hyatt H. Waggoner, Richard Harter Fogle, Frederick Crews, and other, more recent critics have helped us understand Hawthorne in general and "Young Goodman Brown" in particular, they have overlooked a statement by Brown which, when analyzed, helps explain his inability to function satisfactorily in Puritan society.[1]

Soon after permitting his guide, the devil figure, to persuade him to go deeper into the woods than originally agreed, and after first seeing Goody Cloyse, Brown responds to her unexpected presence by saying, "A marvel, truly, that Goody Cloyse should be so far in the wilderness, at night-fall!"[2] But then, after observing and hearing most of what transpires between his guide and her and after she seems magically to leave for a meeting deep in the woods, he exclaims, "That old woman taught me my catechism!" In asserting that "there [is] a world of meaning in this simple comment" (80), the narrator insists that Brown's seemingly innocuous statement reveals something significant about the young man.

In an exhaustive historical examination of Hawthorne's art that

From *ESQ: A Journal of the American Renaissance* 40, no. 1 (1994). ©1994 ESQ.

encompasses this tale, Michael J. Colacurcio takes Brown's statement at face value, commenting that Brown "has been duly catechized, in his youth, by the dutiful Goody Cloyse." Neal Frank Doubleday, in a study of Hawthorne's early tales, mentions Brown's sentence but does not interpret it. Although Sheldon W. Liebman argues that the reader of the tale must "distinguish between appearance and reality by way of determining what happens in the story and why," he does not subject the sentence or its implications to such a test. Most surprisingly, critics like Melinda M. Ponder who examine the narrator of this story also ignore the sentence, despite the extraordinary claim, implicit in the narrator's remark, that any reader wishing to understand Brown must take it into account.[3]

As best as I can determine, only two critics analyze the sentence: Thomas E. Connolly in 1956 and Robert C. Grayson in 1990. Arguing that during his night in the woods Brown discovers the "full and terrible significance" of his faith and that the story "is Hawthorne's criticism of the teachings of Puritanic-Calvinism," Connolly posits that the "'world of meaning' in Brown's statement is that [Goody Cloyse's] catechism teaches the way to the devil and not the way to heaven."[4] Regrettably, Connolly seems merely to assume the nature of a Puritan catechism without having consulted one.

Grayson focuses much more sharply than Connolly on the importance of a catechism in "Young Goodman Brown." He argues that Hawthorne alludes to a specific catechism and that the four references to it in the tale collectively suggest the meaning of Brown's statement. Grayson identifies the catechism as John Cotton's and quotes from two of the answers (the sixth and the eighth) that catechumens, including Brown, would have given to questions asked by a catechist. Apparently on the basis of these answers, he concludes that "by its emphasis on total depravity, [the catechism] soured the milk of human kindness" in Puritans generally and in Brown specifically, so that it "actually undermined trust in mankind and thus did the work of the devil." As a result of studying with Goody Cloyse, Grayson asserts, Brown's "heart has been withered, at least in part, by the catechism."[5] However, only four sets of questions and answers (the fifth through the eighth) in the catechism of sixty-four such sets address the issue of innate depravity. In the remaining sixty sets, the author offers rules for living and addresses in considerable detail requirements for attaining salvation, the possibility of which children would have acknowledged in their first answer during catechism instruction. Failure to consider the entire text thus causes Grayson to assign greater importance to innate depravity than the catechism calls for, thus distorting the meaning of the catechism and misinterpreting its probable effect on Brown.

In this essay, I confirm Grayson's identification of the catechism to which Hawthorne alludes in his tale. I then examine the entire catechism and apply it to Brown, demonstrating that he never masters its meaning. I also show that the narrator speaks truthfully in his pregnant but elliptical comment about Brown's words.

By the year 1700, the Massachusetts Puritans had used a number of catechisms, including the Westminster Assembly's shorter version. As Grayson shows, Hawthorne consulted books that identify the specific catechism used in Salem Village in the late seventeenth century. Moreover, Marion L. Kesselring's catalogue of books that Hawthorne borrowed from the Salem Athenaeum reveals that before publishing "Young Goodman Brown" in the *New-England Magazine* in April 1835, he once withdrew (and his Aunt Mary Manning earlier twice withdrew, apparently for him) the sixth volume of *Collections of the Massachusetts Historical Society*. This volume contains "A Description and History of Salem," in which William Bentley specifies that the Salem Village Puritans of Brown's time used John Cotton's catechism, *Milk for Babes*.[6] Then, on 21 September 1833 and 30 December 1834, Hawthorne withdrew from the Athenaeum Joseph B. Felt's *Annals of Salem*, which records that on 10 September 1660 *Milk for Babes* was selected as the catechism for Salem children.[7] In referring to a catechism in "Young Goodman Brown," therefore, Hawthorne clearly has Cotton's in mind.[8]

Did Hawthorne then read the catechism in order to learn what it says? No evidence exists to indicate that he did. However, Hawthorne's close familiarity with the details of early American history is well known. In some of his tales he even alludes to or cites texts that illuminate the historical material he is presenting, as in "My Kinsman, Major Molineux" (Thomas Hutchinson's *History of Masachusetts*), "The Gentle Boy" (William Sewel's *History of the Rise, Increase, and Progress of the Christian People Called Quakers*), and "The May-Pole of Merry Mount" (Joseph Strutt's *Sports and Pastimes of the People of England*). Further, it seems unlikely that Hawthorne would have his narrator comment so boldly about Brown's allusion to a text if he, Hawthorne, were unaware of what the text says, especially when he knew its author's name and its title. In all probability, he sought out and read Cotton's text before completing "Young Goodman Brown."[9]

In his research, Hawthorne would have discovered that *Milk for Babes* addresses innate depravity only after a positive beginning, which raises the possibility of salvation and details the nature of God and humanity's relationship to him:

Q.   *What hath* GOD *done for you?*
A.   God hath made me, He keepeth me, and he can save me.

Q.   *Who is God?*
A.   God is a Spirit of himself, and for himself.

Q.   *How many Gods be there?*
A.   There is but one God in three Persons, the Father,
        the Son, and the Holy Ghost.

Q.   *How did God make you?*
A.   In my first Parents holy and righteous.

Q.   *Are you then born holy and righteous?*
A.   No, my first Father sinned, and I in him.

Q.   *Are you then born a Sinner[?]*
A.   I was conceived in sin, and born in iniquity.

Q.   *What is your Birth-sin?*
Answ.   *Adams* sin imputed to me, and a corrupt nature
        dwelling in me.

Q.   *What is your corrupt nature?*
Answ.   My corrupt nature is empty of Grace, bent unto sin,
        and onely unto sin, and that continually.

Q.   *What is sin?*
A.   Sin is the transgession of the Law [the Ten Commandments].[10]

At the beginning of each catechism lesson, then, catechumens like Brown would have acknowledged two of the primary tenets of Puritan faith: first, the possibility of salvation; then, humanity's certain sinful nature.

Although the treatment of innate depravity in the catechism is relatively brief, this was only one source of information about human corruption and its implications available to Puritan youth. As part of the Puritan upbringing that implicitly precedes Hawthorne's tale, Brown doubtless would have sat through many sermons that emphasized innate depravity, which his family of churchgoers presumably reinforced, if only by reading and discussing the book of Genesis. Even if he been inattentive during the sermons or if for some reason his family had been derelict in fulfilling their religious obligation to him, the Puritans of Salem Village would have taught him this belief, either directly or indirectly. Theirs was a religious society, after all; people talked about their faith. Young Brown might have encountered reading material conveying the same message about depravity, such as *The New-England Primer*, the reader that offers the verse "In *Adam's* Fall / We Sinned all" to help abecedarians master the letter *A*. And the same verse, or one expressing a similar sentiment, might have appeared on the hornbook Brown would have used to learn the alphabet, or elsewhere.[11] Because he has been reared and lives in Salem Village in the seventeenth century, Brown cannot have avoided regular exposure to the Puritan belief in innate depravity.

But before leaving the home he shares with his wife, Faith, does he believe—really believe—the gloomy philosophy presented in four sets of questions and answers at the beginning of Cotton's text? Clearly not. He thinks mortals good. How else explain the vow he makes, immediately after leaving home and while still observing his wife, that following his one night away from Faith, "a blessed angel on earth" he will "cling to her skirts and follow her to Heaven" (75)?[12] If he believed in the certainty of depravity and only the possibility of salvation, as the catechism teaches, he would know that even so righteous a person as Faith is corrupt and not necessarily of the elect, appearances notwithstanding. And how else explain his disappointment in Goody Cloyse, the minister, Deacon Gookin, and Faith when he apparently encounters them in the woods? Disappointed—and shocked—he surely is. After seeing his catechist, he says, "What if a wretched old woman do choose to go to the devil, when I thought she was going to Heaven!" (80); after hearing the minister and Deacon Gookin, "With Heaven above, and Faith below, I will yet stand firm against the devil!" (82); and after hearing Faith's voice and seeing her pink ribbon, "My Faith is gone! … There is no good on earth; and sin is but a name" (83). He now thinks that he was mistaken about these people he has "reverenced from youth" (87) and, by extension, about all people, especially those of his society. Only at this point does Brown finally comprehend the innate corruption of humanity. (The guilt he apparently feels at leaving Faith for the appointment with his guide seems to stem more from his violating her trust than from any belief in depravity.) As if to prove that he is one with the multitude he now views darkly—and possibly to demonstrate that he at last understands the full, somber reality of one part, if only one small part, of the catechism—Brown goes forward to participate in a fiendish version of the baptismal rite, which he finds the "Shape of Evil" conducting in the woods (88).[13]

Without addressing the catechism directly, Colacurcio, in calling Brown "theologically ill-prepared,"[14] offers one reason why Brown, before leaving home, has such an un-Puritan view of human nature: perhaps he does not comprehend the tenets of his faith, one important source of which is the catechism. Goody Cloyse might share this view. In terming her former student a "silly fellow" (79), she may intend to suggest that although he memorized the catechism answers, his latitudinarian attitude toward her, Faith, and others before he enters the woods signals his inability truly to understand and psychologically assimilate the full significance of *Milk for Babes*. Even if this is not what she means, the historical record indicates that many young people before, during, and after Brown's time have had difficulty mastering the meaning of a catechism.

This problem attracted the attention of several important seventeenth- and early eighteenth-century divines, both American and English. No less a figure than Richard Mather implies that too many people fail to master the meaning of a catechism. In his 1657 farewell sermon, he observes, "[C]omonly they that fall to erro [ur,] [ar]e defective in the knowledg of Catechistical points."[15] At almost precisely the same time that Brown would have been studying the catechism with Goody Cloyse, however, the English cleric Richard Baxter was suggesting that it is more important for children to memorize the words of a catechism than to understand what the words mean, at least initially. He writes: *"Cause your younger Children to learn the words, though they be not yet capable of understanding the matter....* A child of five or six years old can learn the words of a Catechism or Scripture, before they are capable of understanding them."[16] If this attitude prevailed in Salem Village during the time when Goody Cloyse would have been teaching *Milk for Babes*, it might help explain Brown's early inability to embrace the full significance of Cotton's text: there would have been no compelling reason for him to master it; he would have been required only to memorize the words. Yet he would have been expected to understand the catechism as he matured and to begin conducting his life according to its principles. He does neither.

Others also expressed opinions about the common deficiency in understanding a catechism. Cotton Mather, for example, addressed this problem in 1699, only seven years after the probable date of the events in "Young Goodman Brown." Clearly, he is less inclined than Baxter to make allowances for children's lack of comprehension:

> Be sure, that they [catechumens] Learn their *Catechism* very perfectly; But then content not your selves with hearing them say by Rote, the *Answers* in their *Catechism*; *Question* them very distinctly over again about every clause in the *Answers*; and bring all to ly so plain before them, that by their saying only, *Yes*, or, *No*, you may perceive that the sense of the Truth is Entred into their Souls.[17]

Three years later, Mather's concern had not abated. He includes the text of Cotton's catechism in one of his own publications and adds to it questions that can be answered affirmatively or negatively, precisely as he prescribed in 1699. He admonishes: "To *Remember*, and not *Understand*, is as *Tedious* as *Useless* a Thing. It is a thing of the first Importance, that our Children do *Understand*, what they *Remember*, of their *Catechism*, and not recite it, like meer *Parrots*, by rote."[18] In 1730, the English hymnographer and catechism writer Isaac Watts argued even more directly:

> [I]f by virtue of a faithful memory persons should retain the words which they have learned in childhood, they will vainly imagine themselves furnished with a set of principles of religion, though they feel no power of them upon conscience in the conduct of life; and all this because these articles do not lie in the heart, or even in the understanding, as a set of principles for practice, but rather in the head or memory as a set of phrases.[19]

In stating that children should not memorize what they cannot comprehend, the Mathers and Watts disagree with Baxter; to them, catechumens must understand a catechism from the outset. If they do not, they will be deluded into thinking themselves morally prepared for life and will therefore think as they should not and comport themselves poorly, as Watts avers. Such is the case with Brown. Clearly, his attitude before leaving for the woods is contrary to the Puritan way of thinking conveyed in *Milk for Babes*, a text he should have mastered. His decidedly non-Puritan faith in the goodness of humanity permits awareness of human corruption, once it comes, to destroy the young man's heart. David Levin, although he does not discuss the catechism, implies something similar in asserting that "Young Goodman Brown" is "about Brown's ... discovery of the *possibility* of universal evil."[20] I would amend Levin's statement by changing the word *possibility* to *certainty*. As a Puritan reared in Salem Village, Brown should not have to make such a discovery as a young adult, years after Goody Cloyse taught him the doctrine of innate depravity during their catechism lessons.

Even had Brown not understood human imperfection from the catechism or other sources as he progressed into adulthood, he should have suspected it because of his own moral shortcomings, his latent desires to violate religious precepts set forth in the catechism and especially the Ten Commandments. To the Puritans, the Commandments were extremely important: they served as a summary of scriptural instruction on proper behavior in every circumstance. In fact, Cotton stresses their significance by devoting twenty-seven sets of questions and answers to them in his catechism.[21] How successfully does Brown obey the Commandments? Either in his dream or in reality, in the woods or after returning to Salem Village, he disobeys all of them to one degree or another.

When Goody Cloyse, in the course of catechistical training, presumably asked young Brown to explain the meaning of the First Commandment, "Thou shalt have no other Gods but me," the proper response would have been, "That we should worship the onely true God, and no other beside him" (*MB*, 2). Similarly, when she asked for Brown's understanding of the Second Commandment, "Thou shalt not make to thy self any graven image, &c.," he would have said, "That we should worship the true God with true worship such as God hath ordained, not such as man hath invented" (*MB*, 2–3). But Brown violates both commandments. He might not worship his guide, the devil figure, but he permits his companion to manipulate him in an almost godlike manner. He obeys his cicerone. And as Brown moves toward the forest altar, he prepares to worship the "dark figure," the "Shape of Evil," who is about to initiate the converts into "the communion of [their] race" (86), which is to say into evil. Only awakening from his dream, if such it is, keeps Brown from worshiping under the direction of this minister, who is hardly the equivalent of a Puritan divine. Brown accepts and embraces for the remainder of his life the man's dark message that converts "shall exult to behold the whole earth one stain of guilt, one mighty blood-spot"—a message that differs from Cotton's at the beginning of the catechism by emphasizing only the negative and by urging mortals "to penetrate, in every bosom, the deep mystery of sin" (87).

In explaining his understanding of the Third Commandment, "Thou shalt not take the name of the Lord thy God in vain, &c.," Brown would have said, "To make use of God, and the good things of God, to his Glory, and our good; not vainly, not unreverently, nor unprofitably" (*MB*, 3). After observing (or dreaming about) people in the woods and then returning home, Brown cannot acknowledge that there are "good things of God" and that he lives among them, flawed as he believes Faith and the others are. Not only does he fail to use the townspeople to glorify God, he also distances himself from them emotionally, revealing his vanity and arrogance, his irreverence and ignorance. Instead of glorifying his creator, Brown cares only about preserving himself from the threat of spiritual contamination. As he finds others "unprofitable" to him, so too does he become to them, although Faith apparently continues loving him for the remainder of his life. In separating himself from his fellow mortals, he violates the Third Commandment.

Following his return to Salem Village, Brown might or might not rest on the Sabbath; certainly, though this morose young man never frolics then, or at any time. However, disillusioned with humanity and most especially with the church officials, he does not perform the Lord's work or feel close to God, even on Sunday. Therefore, he disobeys the Fourth Commandment, "Remember that thou keep holy the Sabbath day, &c.," which means that "we should rest from labor and much more from play on the Lord's day; that we may draw nigh to God in holy Duties" (*MB*, 3–4).

Brown also violates the Fifth Commandment, "Honour thy Father and thy Mother, that thy dayes may be long in the Land which the Lord thy God giveth thee." When Goody Cloyse asked Brown to define father and mother, he would have replied, "All our Superiors, whether in Family, School, Church, and Common-wealth"; and in detailing what honor he owes these people, he would have said, "Reverence, obedience, and (when I am able) Recompense" (*MB*, 4). Goody Cloyse, the minister, and Deacon Gookin are clearly Brown's religious superiors. Before his night in the woods, Brown had revered these people, but he did not truly obey them in the sense that he did not honor their teachings about human depravity. And after this night, he reveres them no more. To him they are now hypocrites whose apparent goodness veils corruption. In the woods, Brown does honor his father, or what he believes is "the shape of his own dead father" (86). The image of the elder Brown beckons him to the ceremony and Brown obeys. But a woman (the narrator suggests that she might be Brown's mother) warns him not to come forward. He disobeys her. And at the end of the tale, if not at the beginning, Faith is clearly Brown's superior. She obviously loves her husband, presumably functions more or less normally in her society, and exhibits an enthusiasm for life, whereas Brown, following his night in the woods, loves nobody (except possibly himself), quits functioning as a social being, and necessarily withdraws from life. In rejecting Faith upon returning to Salem Village, Brown humiliates and dishonors her. In fact, of the characters in the tale, Brown honors only the image of his father, the man who apparently conducts the ceremony in the woods, and his guide.

Just as surely as Brown fails to obey the Fifth Commandment, he also violates the Sixth, "Thou shalt do no murther." Religious novitiates indicated their understanding of this commandment by saying it means "[t]hat we should not shorten the life, or health of our selves or others, but preserve both" (*MB*, 4). Brown lives a long life, long enough to see Faith "an aged woman" (90) and to have grandchildren follow his corpse to its grave. But his emotional health, his psychological health, dies during his night in the woods; his long life is essentially a long nonlife. The murder Brown commits is spiritual suicide.

If Brown does not violate the Seventh Commandment, it is not for lack of trying. Even Puritan prepubescents must have known what "Thou shalt not commit Adultery" really means; but when asked to define it, they said, "To defile our selves, or others with unclean Lusts." And to indicate that they understood their responsibilities, they stated that their duty was to "[c]hastity, to possess [their] vessels in holiness and honour" (*MB*, 5). Definitions usually clarify, not obfuscate; but even today, adults might use euphemisms as vague and locutions as evasive as these in a similar context. At this late date, though, few would doubt that Brown goes to the woods primarily for sexual reasons.[22] Support for this interpretation emerges in sexual imagery, as when Goody Cloyse says that "there is a nice young man to be taken into communion to-night," or when Deacon Gookin says that "there is a goodly young woman to be taken into communion" (79, 81). Other evidence includes the apparent presence in the woods of the governor's wife and other women, many of them exalted, but all without their husbands. Their companions are "men of dissolute lives and women of spotted fame, wretches given over to all mean and filthy vice, and suspected even of horrid crimes" (85). I would suggest that Brown goes to the woods to participate in an orgy, in clear violation of the Seventh Commandment.

Puritan youth were taught that "Thou shalt not steal'" the Eighth Commandment, forbade them "to take away another mans goods, without his leave, or to spend [their] own without benefit to [them]selves or others" (*MB*, 5). In separating himself emotionally from Faith and their children for the remainder of his life, Brown steals from himself and from them the life of normal familial interaction that they might reasonably have anticipated.[23] In similarly subtle ways, he disobeys the Ninth Commandment: "Thou shalt not bear false witness against thy Neighbour." Brown would have explained to Goody Cloyse that bearing false witness means "to lye falsly, to think or speak untruly of our selves or others" (*MB*, 6). He certainly thinks "untruly." Not only does he perceive Faith, Goody Cloyse, the minister, and Deacon Gookin incorrectly, both before and after his night away from home, but in thinking himself superior to them upon returning to Salem Village, he thinks untruly about himself.

Finally, Brown violates the Tenth Commandment, "Thou shalt not covet, &c." This commandment forbids "[l]ust after the things of other men, and want of contentment with our own" (*MB*, 6). Brown is not content. Either he is unhappy with Faith, or he is not yet able to be faithful to her sexually, or both. Surely, when he goes to the woods, he knows what is happening there "this night ... of all nights in the year" (74), and he wants to participate. Even though he does not frolic with the women he desires, he consummates a physical relationship with more than one of them in his heart. This newlywed defiles himself with what he once would have identified, in explaining the Seventh Commandment to Goody Cloyse, as "unclean Lusts" (*MB*, 5).

The fact that Brown violates, or dreams of violating, the Commandments either in the woods or later in Salem Village suggests that he had urges to disobey them before leaving home. [24] And if so, he should have surmised from observing himself, if not from having studied the catechism with Goody Cloyse or from living in a Puritan society, that people are fundamentally corrupt, precisely as Cotton states in *Milk for Babes*. That Brown fails to honor the Commandments does not make him unique among mortals, however; nor does it mean that he is necessarily destined for eternal damnation. Rather, Cotton relates in the catechism that because of Adam's sin, no human is capable of keeping the Commandments:

> Q.   *Have you kept all these Commandments?*
> Ans.   No, I and all men are sinners.
>
> (*MB*, 6)

Had Brown understood from childhood that humans, all of whom are depraved, cannot obey the Commandments, that fidelity to God's law is impossible, he would not be so surprised to see, or to think he sees, the several worthies preparing to act in a decidedly non-Christian manner in the woods. But because he did not learn this lesson well, he is surprised; and as a result, he thinks that, in the words of Emily Miller Budick, "evil is our only reality and the devil our only God." [25] For the remainder of his life he retains this view, which destroys him.

After presenting the Ten Commandments, Cotton concludes the catechism by addressing salvation once again. Doing so is structurally appropriate because it reintroduces the hope expressed in the first catechism answer that God "can save me" (*MB*, 1). It is also theologically appropriate, the natural Christian conclusion to a traditional presentation of the gospel, as interpreted by St. Paul in Romans 8.[26] Cotton devotes twenty-eight sets of questions and answers to the possibility of salvation, illustrating its importance. Also, in this section, he requires catechism students to give their longest, most detailed answers, forcing them to address some of the fine points concerning salvation.

In helping Brown with the conclusion to the catechism, Goody Cloyse would have taught him that because all mortals are sinners, only Jesus can save them. But in order to gain salvation, they must look to the Bible, which teaches their need for a savior. Although unworthy of Christ's grace, they may attain it by denying themselves and demonstrating faith in him, by praying to God, by repenting (detesting their sins and asking forgiveness), and by attaining a new life (rejecting their corrupt state and walking before Christ as church members). The faithful of the church have a covenant wherein they give themselves to God, whom they worship, and to the church officials. Baptism and communion, the seals of the covenant, provide for resurrection from the dead on Judgment Day, a time when God will determine the fate of all souls on the basis of works performed in conjunction with the faith that gives them merit in God's sight.[27] Some souls will reside in heaven, some in hell.

Brown fulfills only one of the requirements for attaining salvation, and it is one in which he was necessarily passive. Assuming he was born in the late 1660s to church members, he would have been baptized as an infant. Even had his parents not demonstrated evidence of saving faith and therefore not been recognized as full church members, the Half-way Covenant of 1662 permitted the newborn Brown to be baptized.[28] But following his night in the woods, Brown apparently does not subject himself to the Bible, or at least not the New Testament, if his rejection of the imperfect but admirable members of his society and his long, somber life are any indications. In refusing to deny himself, Brown demonstrates a lack of faith in Christ, which makes praying for deliverance irrelevant. He does not repent his sins. While he attains a new life, it is, in its gloominess, the antithesis of the positive new life Cotton requires in the catechism. Since Brown probably no longer remains a member of the church, he cannot properly subject himself to God or the clergy, thus rendering himself ineligible to receive holy communion, one of the seals of the covenant.[29] According to Cotton's teachings, then, Brown's soul will not find eternal residence with God in heaven but will reside forever in hell.

Indeed, Connolly and Grayson state correctly that the Puritan catechism treats the issue of innate depravity, as any text detailing the tenets of Puritanism must. But *Milk for Babes* does so only briefly, at the beginning of the text. As the Bible progress from the talionic Old Testament to the caritative New Testament, so does Cotton's catechism progress, beginning with the fifth answer, from judgment to hope. Because it is essentially a *vade mecum* for living morally and attaining salvation, it is a hopeful, not a pessimistic, document. Clearly, then, Connolly misstates in claiming that the "catechism teaches the way to the devil and not the way to heaven"; and Grayson errs in proclaiming that "Connolly is right about the deleterious effects of the catechism."[30]

Aware that the Salem Village of Brown's time used *Milk for Babes*, Hawthorne astutely has his narrator state that "there was a world of meaning" in Brown's comment, "That old woman taught me my catechism" (80). Indeed, there is considerable meaning; the narrator does not speak idly—or ironically. Brown incriminates himself as one who has been unable to assimilate into his view of humanity the fundamental beliefs of his faith and of his society, as Cotton expresses them. Before leaving home, Brown thinks mortals close to perfection; an understanding of the catechism would have disabused him of this assumption. But after returning home from his night in the woods, he considers irredeemable these people he has revered. This judgment, too, is flawed. Since Brown never masters the lessons Goody Cloyse tried to teach him, he cannot fit spiritually, emotionally, or psychologically into his own society. As a result, he becomes, like Hawthorne's Wakefield, an "Outcast of the Universe"[31] on whose tombstone "they carved no hopeful verse ... ; for his dying hour was gloom" (90).

NOTES

1. See Herman Melville, "Hawthorne and His Mosses," in *The Piazza Tales and Other Prose Pieces, 1839–1860*, ed. Harrison Hayford et al., vol. 9 of *The Writings of Herman Melville* (Evanston and Chicago: Northwestern Univ. Press and The Newberry Library, 1987), 251–52; Hyatt H. Waggoner, *Hawthorne: A Critical Study*, rev. ed. (Cambridge: Harvard Univ. Press, 1963), 14, 59, 60–61, 119, 209–10, 253; Richard Harter Fogle, *Hawthorne's Fiction: The Light and the Dark*, rev. ed. (Norman: Univ. of Oklahoma Press, 1964), 15–32; and Frederick Crews, *The Sins of the Fathers: Hawthorne's Psychological Themes* (New York: Oxford Univ. Press, 1966; Berkeley and Los Angeles: Univ. of California Press, 1989), 98–106. Crews disavows the psychological underpinnings of his study in the afterword to the reprint edition; see especially 278–79.

2. Nathaniel Hawthorne, "Young Goodman Brown," in *Mosses from an Old Manse*, ed. William Charvat et al., vol. 10 of the Centenary Edition of *The Works of Nathaniel Hawthorne* (Columbus: Ohio State Univ. Press, 1974), 78; hereafter cited parenthetically by page number.

3. Michael J. Colacurcio, *The Province of Piety: Moral History in Hawthorne's Early Tales* (Cambridge: Harvard Univ. Press, 1984), 288; Neal Frank Doubleday, *Hawthorne's Early Tales: A Critically Study* (Durham: Duke Univ. Press, 1972), 205; Sheldon W. Liebman, "'The Reader in 'Young Goodman Brown,'" in *The Nathaniel Hawthorne Journal 1975*, ed. C.E Frazer Clark Jr. (Englewood, CO: Microcard Editions Books, 1975) 157; Melinda M. Ponder, *Hawthorne's Early Narrative Art* vol. 9 of *Studies in American Literature* (Lewiston, NY: Edwin Mellen, 1990), 52–62, 138–39.

4. Thomas E. Connolly, "Hawthorne's 'Young Goodman Brown': An Attack on Puritanic Calvinism," *American Literature* 28 (1956): 375, 373.

5. Robert C. Grayson, "Curdled Milk for Babes: The Role of the Catechism in 'Young Goodman Brown,'" *Nathaniel Hawthorne Review* 16 (Spring 1990): 1, 5, 3.

6. Marion L. Kesselring, *Hawthorne's Reading, 1828–1850: A Transcription and Identification of Titles Recorded in the Charge-Books of the Salem Athenaeum* (New York: New York Public Library, 1949), 56. Grayson mistakenly states that Hawthorne himself withdrew the volume three times ("Curdled Milk for Babes," 3). Also see William Bentley, "A Description and History of Salem," *Collections of the Massachusetts Historical Society* 6 (1799): 260.

7. See Kesselring, *Hawthorne's Reading*, 50, and Joseph B. Felt, *The Annals of Salem*,

From Its First Settlement (Salem: W[illiam] and S[tephen] B[radshaw] Ives, 1827), 207. The Salem church had jurisdiction over the Salem Village church until their separation in 1689 (Bentley, "A Description and History of Salem," 266). Therefore, until at least that date the catechism used in Salem, *Milk for Babes*, would have been used in Salem Village.

8. There are seven extant seventeenth-century editions of John Cotton's *Milk for Babes* in English, as well as a translation into Massachusett by Grindal Rawson:

> *Milk for Babes* (London: J[ane] Coe for Henry Overton, 1646).Wing 6443.
>
> *Spiritual Milk for Boston Babes in Either England* (Cambridg[e], MA: S[amuel] G[reen] for Hezekiah Usher, 1656). Evans 42.
>
> *Spiritual Milk for Boston Babes in Either England* (London: Henry Cripps, 1657). Wing 6462A.
>
> *Spiritual Milk for Babes* (London: Henry Cripps, 1662). Wing 6459A.
>
> *Spiritual Milk for Babes* (London: Peter Parker, 1668). Wing 6460.
>
> *Spiritual Milk for Babes* (London: Peter Parker, 1672). "Corrected in Quotations by *L.H.* 1665." Wing 6461.
>
> *Spiritual Milk for Boston Babes, in Either England* (Boston, 1684). Evans 39225.
>
> *Nashauanittue Meninnunk wutch Mukkiesog*, trans. Grindal Rawson (Cambridge, MA: Samuel Green for Bartholomew Green, 1691). Evans 550.

Although substantive textual differences exist among the editions in English, they do not affect meaning. Other editions reportedly were published in London in 1648, Cambridge in 1668, and Boston in 1690; and there might have been other seventeenth-century editions. See Wilberforce Eames, *Early New England Catechisms: A Bibliographical Account of Some Catechisms Published before the Year 1800, For Use in New England* (1898; reprint, New York: Burt Franklin, n.d.), 24–25. In this essay, I follow the established practice of referring to Cotton's catechism as *Milk for Babes*.

9. If *Milk for Babes* were unavailable to Hawthorne under its own title, he would nevertheless have had access to it in numerous eighteenth-century editions of *The New-England Primer*. See Charles F. Heartman, *The New-England Primer Issued Prior to 1830* (New York: Bowker, 1934).

10. John Cotton, *Spiritual Milk for Babes* (London: Peter Parker, 1672), 1–2; hereafter cited parenthetically as *MB*, with page number. In quoting from Cotton's text, I make no effort to reproduce the long *s*; I also do not include the marginal glosses to biblical verses. I base my use of this particular edition on the following reasoning: First, I assume that the tale in set in 1692 (due to the suggestions of witchcraft) and, further, that the protagonist is in his mid-twenties. In a demographic study of Andover, Massachusetts (fewer than fifteen miles from Salem Village), Philip J. Greven Jr. shows that from 1690 to 1694, Andover men married at the average age of 23.5 (see *Four Generations: Population, Land, and Family in Colonial Andover, Massachusetts* [Ithaca: Cornell Univ. Press, 1970], 117). Hawthorne had access to similar demographic data about Andover: in September 1834, only seven months before the publication of "Young Goodman Brown," he withdrew from the Salem Athenaeum Abiel Abbot's *History of Andover from Its Settlement to 1829* (Andover: Flagg and Gould, 1829), which includes, on 185–86, birth and death data from 1652

through 1700 (Kesselring, *Hawthorne's Reading*, 43). Assuming that Salem Village's data would be similar to Andover's, and that Brown married at the average age in 1692 (he and Faith have been married for only three months at the tale's opening), then were he a real person, he would have been born in 1668 or 1669. Because he would have begun catechism lessons around age five, it is likely that Goody Cloyse would have taught him using the 1672 edition of Cotton's text, the one I cite here. (Grayson cites the edition of 1646.)

11. *The New-England Primer Enlarged* (Boston: S[amuel] Kneeland and T[imothy] Green, 1727), 7. Evans 2927. This is the earliest extant text of the *Primer*, which was possibly first published before 1690. For further information, see Paul Leicester Ford, *The New-England Primer: A History of Its Origin and Development* (1897; reprint, n.p.: Columbia Univ., 1962); George Livermore, *The Origin, History and Character of the New England Primer* (1849; reprint, New York: Cha[rle]s Fred[erick] Heartman, 1915); Worthington Chauncey Ford, "The New England Primer," in *Bibliographical Essays: A Tribute to Wilberforce Eames* (1924; reprint, New York: Burt Franklin, 1968), 61–65; A.S.W. Rosenbach, *Early American Children's Books* (1933; reprint, New York: Kraus Reprint, 1966) Heartman, *New-England Primer Issued Prior to 1830;* William Sloane, *Children's Books in England and America in the Seventeenth Century* (New York: King's Crown Press/Columbia Univ., 1955), 191–93; Cornelia Meigs, ed., *A Critical History of Children's Literature: A Survey of Children's Books in English from Earliest Times to the Present*, rev. ed. (London: Collier-Macmillan, 1969), 110–19; Daniel A. Cohen, "The Origin and Development of the *New England Primer*," *Children's Literature* 5 (1976): 52–57; and David H. Watters, "'I Spake as a Child': Authority, Metaphor and *The New-England Primer*," *Early American Literature* 20 (1985–86): 193–213. No seventeenth-century hornbook is known to exist.

12. If Brown understood the catechism, he would know that a relationship with another person does not influence the ultimate disposition of one's soul. One does not gain salvation by proxy, as it were.

13. Cf. Nathaniel Hawthorne, "The Hollow of the Three Hills," in *Twice Told Tales*, ed. William Charvat et al., vol. 9 of the Centenary Edition of *The Works of Nathaniel Hawthorne* (Columbus: Ohio State Univ. Press, 1974), 200. Here, in what is possibly Hawthorne's earliest published tale, a "Power of Evil" performs the "impious baptismal rite."

14. Colacurcio, *Province of Piety*, 301.

15. Richard Mather, *A Farewel Exhortation to the Church and People of Dorchester in New-England* (Cambridg[e], MA: Samuel Green, (1657), 6.

16. Richard Baxter, *A Christian Directory; or, A Summ of Practical Theologie, and Cases of Conscience* (London: Robert White for Nevill Simmons, 1673), pt. 2, 582. Baxter argues that learning the words of a catechism without mastering their meaning will make understanding easier when children are capable of comprehending theological concepts. Then, instead of struggling to learn both words and meaning, they can focus on the latter. Also see David D. Hall, *Worlds of Wonder, Days of Judgment: Popular Religious Belief in Early New England* (New York: Alfred A. Knopf, 1989), 37.

17. Cotton Mather, *A Family Well-Ordered; or, An Essay to Render Parents and Children Happy in One Another* (Boston: B[artholomew] Green and J[ohn] Allen for Michael Perry and Benjamin Eliot, 1699),19–20.

18. Cotton Mather, *Maschil; or, The Faithful Instructor. Offering, Memorials of Christianity in Twenty Six Exercises upon the New-English Catechism* (Boston: B[artholomew] Green and J[ohn] Allen for Samuel Phillips, 1702), 11.

19. Isaac Watts, "A Discourse on the Way of Instruction by Catechisms, and of the

Best Method of Composing Them," in *The Works of the Reverend and Learned Isaac Watts, D.D. Containing, besides His Sermons, and Essays on Miscellaneous Subjects, Several Additional Pieces, Selected from His Manuscripts* (London: J[ohn] Barfield, 1810), 3:214.

20. David Levin, "Shadows of Doubt: Specter Evidence in Hawthorne's 'Young Goodman Brown,'" *American Literature* 34 (1962): 351.

21. Cotton also writes elsewhere about the importance of the Ten Commandments to the Puritans: "[A]ll the sins and good things found in the wlhoe [sic] Bible, are to be ranked within the compasse of the ten Commandments." See *A Practical Commentary; or, An Exposition with Observations, Reasons, and Uses upon the First Epistle Generall of John* (London: R[obert] I[bbitson] and E[dward] C[rouch] for Thomas Parkhurst, 1656), 235.

22. For a discussion of sexuality in "Young Goodman Brown," see Crews, *Sins of the Fathers*, 98–106.

23. Unless Faith is pregnant with more than one child before Brown leaves her for the woods, they have sexual intercourse after he returns, and probably more than once. Their "children" follow his body to the grave (90).

24. If Brown actually violates the Commandments, as opposed to merely dreaming about disobeying them, he might be violating civil as well as ecclesiastical law. In 1690 the General Court encouraged ministers to suppress such sins as "*Unbelief, Worldliness, Heresy, Pride, Wrath, Strife, Envy,* and the *Neglect* of communion with God, in both Natural and Instituted *Worship,* and the *Contempt* of the *everlasting Gospel,* with a shameful want of due *Family-Instruction,* which are the *Roots of Bitterness* in the midst of us" (*By the Governour and General Court of the Colony of the Massachusetts Bay* [Cambridge,1690], [2]).

25. Emily Miller Budick, *Fiction and Historical Consciousness: The American Romance Tradition* (New Haven: Yale Univ. Press, 1989), 91.

26. See, for example, Romans 8:38–39, quoted from the Authorized (King James) Version:

> For I am persuaded, that neither death, nor life, nor angels, nor principles
> nor powers, nor things present, nor things to come,
> Nor height, nor depth, nor any other creature, shall be able to separate us
> from the love of God, which is in Christ Jesus our Lord.

27. Cotton states elsewhere that mortals cannot know, on the basis of their works, if their souls are heaven bound: "Sanctification ... is no evidence, or witness of our union with Christ" (*A Treatise of the Covenant of Grace, As It Is Dispensed to the Elect Seed, Effectually unto Salvation,* 2nd ed. [London: William Miller, 1662], 43) This belief, of course, does not contradict Cotton's statement in the catechism that God judges souls according to mortals' works. For discussions of Cotton's attitude toward works, especially in the context of Anne Hutchinson and the Antinomian controversy, see Larzer Ziff, *The Career of John Cotton: Puritanism and the American Experience* (Princeton: Princeton Univ. Press, 1962), 110–12; William K. B. Stoever, "*A Faire and Easie Way to Heaven*": *Covenant Theology and Antinomianism in Early Massachusetts* (Middletown, CT: Wesleyan Univ. Press, 1978), 54–55; R. T. Kendall, *Calvin and English Calvinism to 1649* (Oxford: Oxford Univ. Press, 1979), 167–83; and Everett Emerson, *John Cotton,* rev. ed. (Boston: Twayne, 1990), 64–67, 85–96.

28. I refer to the fifth proposition in the Half-Way Covenant, which permits children of church members to be baptized:

> Church-members who were admitted in minority, understanding the
> Doctrine of Faith, and publickly professing their assent thereto; not

scandalous in life, and solemnly owning the Covenant before the Church, wherein they give up themselves and their children to the Lord, and subject themselves to the Government of Christ in the Church, their children are to be Baptized." (*Propositions Concerning the Subject of Baptism and Consociation of Churches* [Cambridge, MA: S(amuel) G(reen) for Hezekiah Usher, 1662], 19)

29. Colacurcio suggests otherwise. He says, "Goodman Brown evidently continued to be accepted at the communion table" (*Province of Piety*, 303). But following his return to Salem Village, Brown has no reason for wishing to remain in the church. Further, because he can no longer meet church membership requirements, as Cotton presents them, he could conceivably be excommunicated. Following the adoption of the Half-Way Covenant in 1662, Puritan churches continued to excommunicate members "for misconduct or for openly expressed heretical ideas" (Edmund S. Morgan, *Visible Saints: The History of a Puritan Idea* [New York: New York Univ. Press, 1963; Ithaca: Cornell Univ. Press, 1965], 127).

30. Connolly, "Hawthorne's 'Young Goodman Brown,'" 373; Grayson, "Curdled Milk for Babes," 5.

31. Nathaniel Hawthorne, "Wakefield," in *Twice-Told Tales*, 140.

JAMES C. KEIL

Hawthorne's "Young Goodman Brown": Early Nineteenth-Century and Puritan Constructions of Gender

N athaniel Hawthorn's "Young Goodman Brown" traditionally has been read as an examination of crises of faith, morality, and/or psychosexuality. Early readings focused on questions of theology and conduct,[1] but since the opening years of the 1950s, a second category of readings has emphasized the psychosexual elements. Roy Male, for example, argued that "the dark night in the forest is essentially a sexual experience, though it is also much more," while Frederick Crews observed that in his dream experience, the young, newly wed, and still oedipal Brown, fleeing from the sexuality of married love, removes himself to a place where he can voyeuristically and vicariously enjoy that which he directly shuns.[2] The third important category of readings attempts to ground the story in the late seventeenth- and early eighteenth-century documents about witchcraft to which Hawthorne had access. Most significant of these considerations are David Levin's contention that the most important topic of "Young Goodman Brown" is the theological and epistemological issue of "specter evidence" and Michael Colacurcio's thesis that the historical documents from which Hawthorne worked, especially those involving how you tell a saint from a witch or any other sinner, limit the scope of Hawthorne's investigation into Brown's (or his own) psyche to that made possible by the language and content of the Puritan documents.[3] In all three of these critical categories, the authors generally

From *The New England Quarterly* 69, no. 1 (March 1996). ©1996 by *The New England Quarterly*.

assume, if they address the matter at all, that Hawthorne is concerned with late seventeenth- and early eighteenth-century issues and events surrounding American Puritan life. We must recognize, however, that—contra the assumptions that some scholars make about Hawthorne as a Puritan historian—Hawthorne could not re-create Puritan history in his historical tales; he could only construct it, basing his construction upon his readings of Puritan documents and the experience that he, as a nineteenth-century, middle-class New Englander, brought to them.

At least one reader suggests that part of the experience Hawthorne brought to the Puritan documents was his familiarity with contemporary documents. Frank Shuffleton has pointed out convincingly that, in the climactic scene of the "witches' sabbath," Hawthorne appeared to have been working not only from Puritan archives but also from Frances Trollope's contemporary observations on the demonic aspects of evangelical tent meetings in *Domestic Manners of the Americans* (1832). Without denying the crises of faith, morality, and psychosexuality that earlier critics had discovered in "Young Goodman Brown," Shuffleton notes that Hawthorne was likely to find those issues in contemporary as well as Puritan documents and events. Moreover, in recognizing that "the story's meaning has an anchor in a specific social situation in Hawthorne's nineteenth-century present, we understand the balancing power of the specific richness of the story's historical knowledge as detailed by so many scholars."[4] If theology, morality, and psychosexuality were a devilish brew for Hawthorne's Puritan ancestors, they were no less so for Hawthorne and his contemporaries. Hawthorne places the story in the seventeenth century in order to explore the nexus of past and present in New Englanders' attitudes towards these central life experiences.

In addition to the Puritan problems of telling the saintly from the damned and the innocent from the corrupt, "Young Goodman Brown" takes as part of its context fundamental changes in gender and gender relations in the growing middle-class world of New England. One aspect of these changes in gender and sexuality with which the story surely is concerned is the nineteenth-century ideology of separate spheres. During the early decades of the nineteenth century, a discourse developed that sought to divide the world into public and private spheres based on gender.[5] Men and women had lived socially, economically, and politically distinct lives in the Puritan period, but what is significant about the new, nineteenth-century gender ideology is that it constructed a "male" world that was even more and decidedly self-consciously distinct from the "female." Men should be the "sole" economic providers of the household, working, increasingly, outside of it, in the public realm. Women should provide all the other needs of the family, laboring (although it was seldom seen as such) only within the house—a structure that during this period became known as the "home" and became identified primarily with women and their children.

Of particular relevance to Hawthorne's story, however, since its concerns are with transgression as much as catechism, is that in the last two decades historians have come to understand that the clear boundaries between male/female, public/private, and work/home were blurred–that these separate spheres, essential to constructions of the middle-class world and heretofore thought rigid barriers, more accurately should be seen as thresholds through which nineteenth-century Americans frequently passed.[6] Moreover, historians have also confirmed that the 1830s was a critical decade of change.[7] "Young Goodman Brown," probably written no earliest than the initial years of the decade and published anonymously in 1835, chronicles Hawthorne's observations about the anxieties caused by such discrepancies between ideology and behavior. Young Goodman Brown, who has come to believe with religious fervor what he has been taught prior to marriage about the separation of spheres, is disoriented by the behavioral expectations he confronts once he has entered that institution. The ideology of separate spheres was not transgressed, Hawthorne seems to suggest in "Young Goodman Brown," without some psychological and moral costs.

I

Michael Colacurcio has advised that readers look for the historical contexts of early Hawthorne stories in the opening paragraphs, and that is precisely where this reading will begin.[8] It is here in the opening paragraphs that we are introduced to both a Puritan setting and another of what Suffleton has called Hawthorne's contemporary "anchors." The story begins with an explicit presentation of issues of gender, sexuality, and intimacy, all of which take place in the doorway between public and private.

> Young Goodman Brown came forth, at sunset, into the street of Salem village, but put his head back, after crossing the threshold, to exchange a parting kiss with his young wife. And Faith, as the wife was aptly named, thrust her own pretty head into the street, letting the wind play with the pink ribbons of her caps, while she called to Goodman Brown.[9]

In this scene, we learn that the setting of the story is Salem village, the site of many mysterious activities in the minds of Hawthorne's contemporaries, and the time is sunset. The scene takes place in the doorway of the Browns' house, a threshold that both joins and separates not only private and public but, literally in this case, female and male. It is a threshold that both characters violate for reasons of intimacy, although she, as we see, is clearly the more intimate of the two. About the two characters we learn that the man is young, that he is embarking on a nighttime journey, and that, apparently, he is distracted or hurried, since he fails to kiss his wife before leaving the house. Of the woman, we learn that she is married to the young man, is named Faith, is pretty, and, although she modestly wears a cap over her hair, she has adorned it with pink ribbons.

The ambiguity in the description of Faith—is or is not her name a sign of her spirituality or faithfulness? is she modest or immodest?—will recur throughout the story, and this ambiguity is the cause of Brown's great sadness and the subject of much of the scholarship on the story. Here it is important to note that the ambiguity is repeated also in her not waiting for him to return to kiss her, in her thrusting her own head through the doorway and "letting" the breeze animate the ribbons with which she has dressed her cap. Not only is the "letting" ambiguous when combined with the thrusting, "letting" is an activity that itself raises questions about who is in control of the action. Having thrust her head through the doorway in order to give her husband his goodbye kiss, Faith whispers "softly and rather sadly, when her lips were close to his ear,"

> "Dearest heart, ... pr'y thee, put off your journey until sunrise, and sleep in your own bed to-night. A lone woman is troubled with such dreams and such thoughts, she's afeard of herself, sometimes. Pray, tarry with me this night, dear husband, of all nights in the year!" [P. 74]

Surely Hawthorne means for us to think of this story as taking place in Puritan Massachusetts.[10] Certain other factors, however—such as the threshold setting, the description of Faith, the couple's bad dreams, the implication that he has failed to sleep in his own bed on other occasions—suggest a more contemporary setting. John Demos indicates that the early decades of the nineteenth century produced scads of literature on domestic life, and the "shrill tone of the new advice betrayed deep anxieties about the evolving shape and future prospects of the family."[11] It is of course the Browns' prospects for the future about which they are most concerned. The family was changing in fundamental ways in Hawthorne's lifetime, and many New Englanders were writing and reading about the uncertainty they felt. That domestic literature was supplemented by sexual advice literature that portrayed men as sexually predatory and—a distinct difference from the

Puritan construction—women as virtually passionless. Unlike the Puritan ethos, this same nineteenth-century advice literature also threatened disaster if abstinence were not the rule in all aspects of non-procreative sexuality.[12] It is unlikely that Hawthorne was unaware of this new literature on domestic life and human sexuality, but at the very least his story betrays the same profound anxieties about contemporary family and sexual life.

Although much of Brown's anxiety later in the story involves traditional suspicions that women are especially sexual creatures, a failing of which men must beware, Faith herself may better fit an ideal of womanhood popular in the magazine literature of Hawthorne's time. According to Lois Banner, Hawthorne "gave [this ideal] epic representation in the dove-like Hilda of *The Marble Faun* and the manipulated Priscilla of *The Blithedale Romance*." Such a woman was known as the "steel-engraving lady" both for the "process by which she was created" and her own "moral rectitude": "When her pictorial representation is colored, her complexion is white, with a blush of pink in her cheeks."[13] Attending a gala New York City ball in 1822, James Fenimore Cooper encountered the real-life counterparts of this American ideal: "'There is something in the bloom, delicacy, and innocence of one of these young things, that reminds you of the conceptions which poets and painters have taken of the angels.'"[14] The ideal's delicacy and spirituality were important; later in the story, Brown will refer to Faith as a "'blessed angel on earth'" (p. 75). Another characteristic of the ideal is her youth, which "underscored her purity and reflected both the nineteenth-century romanticization of childhood and its tendency to infantilize women, to view them as creatures of childlike disposition."[15] Such characterizations of femininity contrast quite specifically with Puritan constructions of womanhood, which were based on Eve's seduction by the devil and her deception of Adam in the Garden of Eden.[16]

Perhaps as the last in a series of efforts to keep Brown home this night, Faith pleads with her husband not only to stay home but to sleep with her. The young wife's desire for intimacy with her husband could not be more explicit. Brown's reply is no less direct:

> "My love and my Faith, ... of all nights in the year, this one night must I tarry away from thee. My journey, as thou callest it, forth and back again, must needs be done 'twixt now and sunrise. What, my sweet, pretty wife, dost thou doubt me already, and we but three months married!" [P. 74]

In this passage Brown has deliberately conflated his wife's name with a belief system. Hawthorne's construction of Brown's speech in this manner, his association of religion with the role of wife, suggests both Puritan and contemporary possibilities. According to Edmund Morgan, for example, Puritans feared that love of spouse could rival and interfere with love of Christ. On the other hand, in Hawthorne's lifetime women, thought to be morally superior to men, were entrusted with preparing children for Christian salvation. Nancy Cott argues that the evangelicals of the early decades "linked moral agency to female character with a supporting link to passionlessness."[17] If Hawthorne's concerns are as much with contemporary as Puritan gender ideology, then having a wife named Faith seems an appropriate characteristic for his main character. However, except for Brown's distrust of Faith, it is at this point in Hawthorne's story that, although the setting seems Puritan and both periods sometimes confuse sex with "going to the devil," the gender relations begin to have more in common with nineteenth-century ideology and behavior than Puritan history.

In Brown's reply to Faith, there is an element of huffy self-importance, as if Brown were giving a prepared speech. Here we find an indication that the events of the forest are not entirely responsible for Brown's becoming a "darkly meditative, a distrustful" man (p. 89); for all his youth and inexperience, Brown is already very serious, and this hyper-seriousness is part of his foolishness. In insisting that he must leave Faith this night, Brown misreads her sexual desire and fear of being alone as anxiety about his marital fidelity. Note the irony of Brown's question: he doesn't realize that it is a sexual life with her that he is running away from when he portrays himself to his young wife ("dost thou doubt me already") as a licentious stud who would take other lovers after only three months of marriage, a self-portrait that suggests nineteenth-century manhood.

In the nineteenth century, with many men away from the home for long periods of time, middle-class Americans needed a gender ideology that sanctified woman's isolation among her children. Whereas men had played important roles in the moral upbringing, education, and socialization of children in former periods, in the early nineteenth century such responsibilities all but evaporated for many middle-class men. At the same time, women's important role in the economic production that sustained the household of the eighteenth century was, at least in the discourse, eliminated. "Having required the bourgeois woman to be both elegant and nonproductive," and leaving her on her own with the children all day, Carroll Smith-Rosenberg asks, "how could the bourgeois man ever trust her virtue or rest securely in the symbols of his class" (i.e., primarily, in his elegant woman and well-kept children)?[18] What was to keep this consumer, rather than producer, of resources from straying—economically, sexually, morally, religiously? The solution was a socially redeemed image of womanhood: woman as Angel of the Home. Middle-class woman's sole province became the production of "home" life, where the values of the culture could be instilled into the items she produced, her children.[19]

Yet Faith both conforms to and violates nineteenth-century ideology. Standing inside the doorway, she is pretty, modest, discreet, and her name suggests her spirituality and her devotion to her husband. At the same time, she is, within the terms of nineteenth-century ideology, aggressive in her sexuality. The reversal of the expected that we see Brown encounter on the threshold of his own home is probably not unprecedented. His language seems to suggest that marriage may have been a rude awakening for him. Brown's discovery of Faith's sexuality may have shattered his conception of the passivity and disinterest that women were supposed to demonstrate about sex, and this knowledge may have threatened the security of his home. The events that take place in the woods may be nothing more than his playing out of his anxious fantasies about Faith's sexuality and the ideology of separate spheres that he demonstrates in his speech and behavior at the entrance of his home.

The story's introduction, then, describes several threshold experiences, not just because it takes place in a doorway (although that too is important to our understanding of the action of the public/private discourse) but because it is this parting of Faith and Brown that defines their future intimacy. That is to say, from now on they will cross this threshold repeatedly. Intercourse is also physically and emotionally a threshold experience, and the act itself is suggested in the opening paragraphs where Faith and Brown repeatedly stick their heads in and out of a doorway graced by her pink ribbons.[20] There is much about the physical act of sex—the orgasms, the levels of intensity, the sleeping in one's own bed—that involves thresholds, but so too does the emotional aspect, particularly the intimacy that may proceed from as well as contribute to the physical experience. Whatever we may think today, coition and orgasm were not the *sine qua non* of human sexuality in the nineteenth century; a wide range of intimate activities constituted sexuality.[21] But notice also how those recurrent pink ribbons may have blurred Brown's whole notion of privacy, (woman's) purity, and the sanctity of the separate woman's sphere. Brown encounters these ribbons adorning the public world every-where he goes: each time he sees Faith sticking her head out of the doorway, he notices them, and later one floats down out of the forest sky to convince him that "'There is no good on earth'" and to the devil "'is this world given'" (p. 83).[22]

What happens in the woods, then, is also part of this public/private borderland, only here Brown realizes that the divisions are grotesquely blurred, and the sexual theme significantly expands to include the issues of manhood and fatherhood–much to Goodman Brown's chagrin.

II

As we follow our new husband into the woods, we notices that the image of the threshold recurs when Brown looks back at Faith before turning the corner of the meetinghouse and, presumably, going out of her sight. Upon entering the woods, he finds that the "dreary road" he has chosen is "darkened by all the gloomiest trees of the forest, which barely stood aside to let the narrow path creep through, and closed immediately behind." The trees seem to cut him off effectively from his life with Faith and from Salem village. He will soon pass a "crook" in the road, which will further isolate him. Or so it would seem. His only emotions at this point are his loneliness— the same emotion his wife is, presumably, experiencing—and his guilt. However, even this guilt and loneliness, we are told on two occasions, may be occurring in the midst of "an unseen multitude" (p. 75). Having left the private sphere for the public as the story begins, Brown now apparently enters another sphere in which the public and private have been completely blurred.

As for Brown's thoughts of his wife and his pangs, if any, about his mission, we read:

> "Poor Little Faith!" thought he, for his heart smote him. "What a wretch I am, to leave her on such an errand! ... Methought, as she spoke, there was trouble in her face, as if a dream had warned her what work is to be done to-night. But no, no! 'twould kill her to think it. Well; she's a blessed angel on earth; and after this one night. I'll cling to her skirts and follow her to Heaven." [P. 75]

Brown finds it impossible to believe that Faith could imagine her husband so immoral.[23] As we soon learn, however, Faith not only can imagine Brown on such a mission, she herself takes part in one. More interesting, perhaps, is his conviction that later he will "cling to her skirts and follow her to heaven." This vision suggests the strength of Brown's *au courant* identification of his wife as a morally superior "blessed angel." But modern too is Brown's figuring of his wife as a mother to whose skirts he can cling, an image that bears witness to the difficulty Brown has in differentiating love of mother from love of wife, a dilemma with which Hawthorne and his contemporaries were not unfamiliar.

Wife came to replace mother as the moral guardian and disciplinarian of a nineteenth-century, middle-class young man's family. The move from mother's home to wife's, from child's world to man's world should not, then, be all that difficult. Of course, in reality it is far from simple, particularly because the grown son must spend half his life away from mother-wife in the world of men for which his childhood in woman's sphere has not prepared him. Many young men must have found adult life frightening and confusing. T. Walter Herbert believes that Hawthorne did: "Nathaniel maintained a 'childlike' persona because his effort to become a 'man' was complicated by the difficulties of crossing the gap between the maternal/marital sphere and the world beyond."[24]

Faith has referred to what Brown is leaving home for as a "journey," but it is clear that he does not think of it as such. He first refers to what he is about to do as an "'errand'" and two sentences later as "'work.'" There is also no doubt that Brown is both fleeing Faith and setting out to "go to the devil," as he phrases his errand when talking about Goody Cloyse further on. What is it the devil can offer him that his Faith cannot? When Brown meets up with the devil, the gravely dressed man, mentioning the striking of the clock on Boston's Old South Church, reprimands Brown for being a "'full fifteen minutes'" late (p. 75). In this reference to the clock, the "devil's work" becomes associated with contemporary work—labor of a modern, rational, time-ordered sort—and thus "going to the devil" carries the connotation of "men's business." Here also in this encounter we notice that the devil has been expecting Brown and knows him by name and appearance, as if the two had met before (and we are reminded of Faith's implication that this is not the first night she has spent alone). When to the devil's reprimand Brown replies, "'Faith kept me back a while,'" we realize that he knows the devil well enough to use his wife's first name with him and, further, that he believes the devil will accept the explanation that a woman was interfering with his ability to set to the "errand" or "work" that is to be done (p. 76).

Brown's morality is Manichean, gendered, as is his religious sensibility, which is reminiscent of the Puritans and evangelicals. He has been catechized to believe in the ideology of separate spheres, and his faith brooks no blurring of them. Figuring the world of wife/mother/home as on the side of good, angels, and heaven, Brown constructs the world of men/father/non-home as siding with evil and the devil. Hence, we meet the devil in the shape of Brown's father and grandfather.

Brown's new traveling companion is described as being "about fifty years old, apparently in the same rank of life as Goodman Brown, and bearing a considerable resemblance to him, though perhaps more in expression than features." So similar are their appearances that "they might have been taken for father and son"; indeed, Goody Cloyse later recognizes the similarity immediately (p. 76). But Brown does not.[25] Within the context of our present concerns, that lack of recognition can be understood as reflecting middle-class father's absence from the home. Middle-class mothers and children were not to cross the threshold of the father's soiled workplace (the disaster that could result when masculine space was invaded by the feminine is the subject of Hawthorne's "The Birthmark"), and so increasingly sons' experiences of what fathers did and who they were were limited to a few hours a day. Advice literature even urged that the son's sexual education be supervised by the mother.[26]

Brown's failure to recognize his father and to see the world as anything other than devil's work might also be attributed to the devil-father's magical power: "the only thing about [the devil-father], that could be fixed upon as remarkable, was his staff, which bore the likeness of a great black snake, so curiously wrought, that it might almost be seen to twist and wriggle itself, like a living serpent" (p. 76). In Brown's immature sensibility, in his underdeveloped sense of fatherhood and manhood, the father has never escaped the expression of his mature sexuality, his erect and animated phallus. It is in Brown's mind the most significant feature about him, in fact the devil-father's only remarkable feature.

The devil-father wishes to speed the pace of their travels and taunts Brown, saying: "'this is a dull pace for the beginning of a journey. Take my staff, if you are so soon weary.'"[27] Instead of accepting the challenge, Brown gives his companion his reasons for refusing to take up the staff: "'having kept covenant by meeting thee here, it is my purpose now to return whence I came. I have scruples, touching the matter thou wot'st of'" (p. 76). That is to say, the son replies to the devil-father's taunt by challenging his moral authority by virtue of the "scruples" he learned in the woman's sphere to which he now would return.

In this passage we also learn why the appearance of the devil-father was not unexpected: the son had previously agreed to the rendezvous. It is nothing other than the sight and offering of that twisting, writhing, serpentine staff, then, that energizes the newlywed's scruples. As he has done more than once since he walked through the door of his home, young Goodman Brown hesitates, pauses, looks back. Even as he unconsciously walks on, urged forward by the devil-father, identified in all his "evil" sexuality as "he of the serpent," the son objects to proceeding any further; again he renounces his "friend's" paternal relationship to him, claiming that *his* "'father never went into the woods on such an errand, nor his father before him.'" The devil-father, smilingly reassuring young Brown that he need not fear being "'the first of the name of Brown, that ever took this path,'" confides that "'I have been as well acquainted with your family as

with ever a one among the Puritans.... They were my good friends, both....
I would fain be friends with you, for their sake'" (pp. 76–77). The devil-
father comforts Brown by promising him that he is following in his father's
and grandfather's footsteps (which of course he literally is in this scene); he
is fulfilling an honorable paternal tradition, and the devil-father would
befriend Brown so that the tradition of the fathers might be perpetuated. Of
course, the foremost and essential tradition of the fathers of any multi-
generational family is the continuity of past, present, and future achieved
through the production of a family, through intercourse and sexual intimacy,
through the literal blurring of many boundaries between the genders.

When the naive young man insists that none of the patriarchs of his
family engaged in '"such wickedness,'" all being men of prayer and good
works, the devil-father replies that, wicked or not, such behavior is common
among all the patriarchs of the colony (p. 77). In the midst of going about his
father's business, Brown next encounters, much to his surprise, a woman
intruding upon their forest space; she is not just any woman, this Goody
Cloyse, but Brown's religion teacher. Hiding out of her sight, Brown
overhears an exchange between his traveling companion and his teacher
which begins with the devil-father touching her neck with his staff and the
old hag recognizing him as the devil "'in the very image of old gossip,
Goodman Brown, the grandfather of the silly fellow that now is.'" Despite
the fact that someone has stolen her broomstick and the old woman must
travel on foot, she is determined to get to the meeting because, she says,
"'they tell me, there is a nice young man to be taken into communion to-
night'" (p. 79). As he had once extended it to Brown, the devil father now
offers his staff to Goody Cloyse to aid her on her journey to the evening's
assembly, and she disappears from sight.

Goody Cloyse's interest in things sexual is explicit in this encounter;
this and her appearance in the woods break down the supposed barrier
between male and female, public and private, work and home, husband and
wife.[28] Brown calls it a "'marvel'" to find Cloyse in the woods at night, and
the narrator points out that it was Cloyse "who had taught [Brown] his
catechism, in youth, and was still his moral and spiritual adviser, jointly with
the minister and Deacon Gookin" (p. 78). After witnessing her intimacy with
the devil-father, Brown reiterates that "'[t]hat old woman taught me my
catechism.'" Hawthorne's narrator emphasizes that "there was a world of
meaning in this simple comment" (p. 80). Hawthorne's association of women
and ministers with the religious education and spiritual welfare of the
community is another characteristic of this part of the story that is more
reminiscent of nineteenth-century gender relations than those of the Puritan
period.[29] Goody Cloyse's reference to Brown as that "silly fellow" indicates

some sense on her part, too, that much of his life Brown may have had trouble distinguishing belief from practice. Moreover, Goody Cloyse, in her references to "'that silly fellow'" and the "'nice young man to be taken into communion to-night,'" unwittingly has confused two aspects of Brown's identity: as child/innocent and as man/sexual creature.

As the devil-father and Brown proceed through the forest, the older man breaks off a branch of maple limb and fashions yet another walking staff. When Brown once again refuses to go any further, the devil-father suggests that he rest for a while and, before disappearing, throws the young man his staff. Brown then thinks he hears in the forest the voices of his spiritual patriarchs, his minister and Deacon Gookin, conversing about tonight's meeting. When one of them also stop to "pluck a switch," Brown overhears Deacon Gookin saying that he is looking forward to the impending ceremony, where they will find "'a goodly young woman to be taken into communion'" (p. 81). Shaken, Brown cannot decide whether or not what he is witnessing is real. His doubt is so great that, looking up into the night sky, he cannot make up his mind whether "there really was a Heaven above him" (p. 82).

Brown's belief system, his moral certainty, dependent as it seems to be on the nineteenth-century ideology of separate spheres with which he has been catechized, is quickly shattering in the heavily peopled forest. The voices of additional fellow townspeople fall on his ears, and it is obvious that all are hurrying to a late-night rendezvous. In the heart of this commotion, Brown hears "one voice, of a young woman, uttering lamentations, yet with an uncertain sorrow, and entreating for some favor, which, perhaps, it would grieve her to obtain" and for which the townspeople "both saints and sinners, seemed to encourage her onward" (p. 82). Brown immediately recognizes the woman's voice as Faith's. But how much more ambiguous could Faith's voice be? She both is and is not a sexual creature in this description of her cries. She both is and is not present. Faith's disembodied voice, as well as Goody Cloyse's ability to fly, to travel effortlessly, without labor, may speak to the nature of Brown's gender fantasy. One recent scholar has suggested about the ideology of separate spheres that as it "engenders and demarcates the spaces of work and personal (as opposed to working) life, both labor and women are divested of their corporeality, defined as different rather than extensive with the body."[30] Brown screams Faith's name out into the night, only to have the forest mockingly echo his "cry of grief, rage, and terror." Brown should indeed be terrorized by this experiences, for he has built his entire belief system on the moral rectitude of his mother and wife—and on their rightful place nowhere but in the home.

Surely, Goody Cloyse and his Faith have no business in this forest of moral uncertainties. Brown listens in silence for a response to his cries, only to hear "a scream, drowned immediately in a loud murmur of voices, fading into far-off laughter, as the dark cloud swept" by. Something substantial floats down out of the sky, filled as it is with insubstantial voices, and Brown snatches it off of a tree limb. It is one of Faith's pink ribbons. Just as the serpentine staff is Hawthorne's synecdoche for the sexual potential of the father, this pink ribbon is, as earlier implied, his synecdoche for the sexuality of Faith. Brown cries out, "'My Faith is gone!'" It is usually argued that with this outburst, Brown proclaims his lost religious belief, but much more has been lost: his wife Faith is also literally gone; if she is present in the forest, then she cannot, according to his belief system, be who he thought her to be.

Now Brown takes up the devil-father's staff and hurries to the communion. Along the way he encounters a forest "peopled with frightful sounds." And soon the scariest noisemaker in the forest is he: "all through the haunted forest, there could be nothing more frightful than the figure of Goodman Brown" (p. 83). Now deep in the heart of the forest, where no trail remains, Brown encounters "a numerous congregation ... peopling the heart of the solitary woods" (p. 84). In fact, much of the adult population of Salem village has crowded into this space, both the "grave, reputable, and pious people" and "men of dissolute lives and women of spotted fame, wretches given over to all mean and filthy vice, and suspected even of horrid crimes." Most telling is the narrator's comment that it "was strange to see, that the good shrank not from the wicked, nor were the sinners abashed by the saints" (p. 85). Here in the forest private and public spheres blur into one another; or, perhaps, the difference between public and private is nowhere as certain as Brown once thought it was.

As Goodman Brown feels himself called forth with the rest of the converts, he "could have well-nigh sworn, that the shape of his own dead father beckoned him to advance." Indeed, he meets his spiritual fathers when his village "minister and good old Deacon Gookin seized his arms, and led him to the blazing rock" to be initiated. But this "community of men, as we have seen, includes both men and women. Even his mother seems to appear, if only, in keeping with her role as angel of the home, to throw "out her hand to warn him back" (p. 86). The master of ceremonies, a kind of devil-preacher, then invites his "children" to turn around and see "'all whom ye have reverenced from youth'" for their "'righteousness, and prayerful aspirations.'" This night of their conversion, the children will learn of their spiritual leaders' "'secret deeds'":

> "how hoary-bearded elders of the church have whispered wanton
> words to the young maids of their households; how many a

woman, eager for widows' weeds, has given her husband a drink
at bedtime, and let him sleep his last sleep in her bosom; how
beardless youths have made haste to inherit their fathers' wealth;
and how fair damsels—blush not, sweet ones!—have dug little
graves in the garden, and bidden me, the sole guest, to an infant's
funeral." [p. 87]

These deeds are, broadly speaking, crimes of human sexuality. Clearly
Brown's devil-preacher associates sin with sexuality.

The promised knowledge of the secret deeds will give the converts the
ability to determine

"all the places—whether in church, bed-chamber, street, field, or
forest—where crime has been committed, and [they] shall exult
to behold the whole earth one stain of guilt, one mighty blood-
spot. Far more than this! It shall be [theirs] to penetrate, in every
bosom, the deep mystery of sin, the fountain of all wicked arts,
and which inexhaustibly supplies more evil impulses than human
power ... can make manifest in deeds." [p. 87]

The language of human sexuality is omnipresent: "one mighty blood-spot,"
"penetrate," "bosom," "fountain," and "deep mystery." Notice also the
language of unification, of the "communion of [the] race," and the way in
which the devil-preacher contradicts Brown's belief in separate spheres,
especially his belief that only certain wicked people, usually men, have "evil"
sexual longings (p. 86).

When Brown is finally face to face with his wife, just as the "Shape of
Evil" prepares "to lay the mark of baptism upon their foreheads, that they
might be partakers of the mystery of sin," he looks at his Faith and realizes
what "polluted wretches would the next glance" mutually reveal them to be.
He cries out to his wife to forego this baptism into adult sexuality and to
"'[l]ook up to heaven, and resist the Wicked One'" (p. 88). Brown actually
reverses roles here, now imagining himself leading Faith up to heaven. But
it is all too late. The entire forest scene, including his wife, vanishes. He is
alone because he has refused to acknowledge his wife's sexuality in this
threshold experience, just as he had refused it in the doorway of his home.
He has rejected the blurring of separate spheres that is the reality of adult
life. Once peopled with an invisible multitude, the forest around him now is
calm and quiet.

The reader is unsure what has happened to Brown, but Brown himself
is quite certain that in his last words to Faith in the forest, he has resisted the

devil; every inhabitant of Salem village he had formerly trusted, however, is in league with the devil or, at the very least, has secret sins of which each should be ashamed. Brown is quite right, of course, but his very lack of sin is a crime.[31] He returns to a community in which the blurring of the separate spheres is for the first time apparent to him, and he rejects it nonetheless. Deacon Gookin is inside his home now, but his words can be heard coming through his open window. Goody Cloyse, "that excellent old Christian," stands outside her house at the latticed gate "catechising a little girl." Brown's reaction—he snatches away the "child, as from the grasp of the fiend himself"—acknowledges his fears that the little girl could be deceived as he was—not by Goody Cloyse's catechizing, because Brown still believes in what he was taught, but by the old woman's failure to live what she preached. Approaching his home, he sees "the head of Faith, with the pink ribbons, gazing anxiously forth, and bursting into such joy at sight of him, that she skipt along the street, and almost kissed her husband before the whole village." But whatever attractions Brown had to human sexuality when he left the village—as, for example, when he turned back to kiss his wife in the doorway—are now banished by the events he witnessed in the forest. So convinced is he of her sinfulness that "Goodman Brown looked sternly and sadly into her face, and passed on without a greeting" (p. 89).

Goodman Brown becomes a "stern, a sad, a darkly meditative, a distrustful, if not a desperate man ... from the night of that fearful dream" (p. 89). Whatever huffiness and silliness Brown possessed before leaving home has been tragically transformed by his forest refusal to recognize the blurring of spheres. Brown has "a goodly procession" of children and grandchildren, but clearly there was little joy in those sexual experiences (p. 90). The initiative was seldom his it seems: "Often, waking suddenly at midnight, he shrank from the bosom of Faith" (p. 89). And when he dies, "they carved no hopeful verse upon his tombstone, for his dying hour was gloom" (p. 90).

III

When we penetrate the oedipal and sexual anxieties of Hawthorne's early fiction, we tend to divorce them from the historical, and when we unearth the stories' historical concerns, we tend to separate them from the psychosexual and from Hawthorne's immediate social environment. In "Young Goodman Brown," Hawthorne was not only asking his readers to imagine the synthesis of the historical and the psychosexual; he was investigating for them the relationship between Puritan anxieties about faith, morality, sexuality, and gender and his contemporaries' and his own anxieties about those subjects. A renewed interest during the 1830s in the Puritan experience and what it could offer the present probably led Hawthorne to believe that his ancestral line and his own research into Puritan history uniquely qualified him to contribute to the discourse that sought to construct a bridge between past and present New England.

In addition to recognizing Hawthorne's examination of the nexus of Puritan and contemporary experience in "Young Goodman Brown," we must also consider the importance of contemporary gender issues. Nina Baym has argued that a sophisticated feminist criticism of Hawthorne's work "would be based on the presumption that the question of women is *the* determining motive in Hawthorne's works, driving [his female characters] as it drives Hawthorne's male characters."[32] Recent works by T. Walter Herbert and Gillian Brown have, while throwing men into the equation, largely heeded this call.[33] But when scholars turn their attention to issues of gender as well as other nineteenth-century contexts in Hawthorne, they tend to focus on the later works. This virtual neglect of the early material is repeated by David Leverenz, Joel Pfister, Richard H. Millington, and the above critics in their recent books focusing on Hawthorne as an observer of contemporary middle-class culture.[34] It appears, then, that adequately to give Hawthorne his due, we must focus on the whole question of gender—both masculine and feminine—in *all* of his works—early and late. Such a masterful critic of human nature deserves no less than a fully comprehensive view.

NOTES

The research for this article was supported from the Faculty Research Program in the Social Sciences, Humanities, and Education at Howard University.

1. For a categorization of these readings, see D.M. McKeithan, "Hawthorne's 'Young Goodman Brown': An Interpretation," *Modern Language Notes* 67 (1952): 93.

2. Roy R. Male, *Hawthorne's Tragic Vision* (Austin: University of Texas Press, 1957), p. 77; Frederick C. Crews, *The Sins of the Fathers: Hawthorne's Psychological Themes* (New York: Oxford University Press, 1966). p. 102

3. David Levin, "Shadows of Doubt: Specter Evidence in Hawthorne's 'Young Goodman Brown'" *American Literature* 34 (November 1962): 344–52; Michael J. Colacurcio, "Visible Sanctity and Specter Evidence: The Moral World of Hawthorne's 'Young Goodman Brown,'" *Essex Institute Historical Collections* 110 (1974): 259–99.

4. Frank Shuffleton, "Nathaniel Hawthorne and the Revival Movement," *American Transcendental Quarterly* 44 (Fall 1979): 321.

5. I have tried wherever possible to pinpoint developments to the decade or decades in which they occurred, but many changes experienced by the middle class in the late eighteenth and early nineteenth centuries continued into and only rose to hegemony in the middle of the nineteenth century. Hence, what is true for Hawthorne's family in his youth and for seacoast New England towns like Salem—where the absence of fathers away on work for long periods of time, for example, was a common phenomenon—may not yet be true of America in general until mid century or later. Hawthorne is writing, in part,

about the world he knows and for a geographically limited, middle-class reading audience cognizant of these developments from other domestic literature.

6. Carl N. Degler, *At Odds: Women and the Family in America from the Revolution to the Present* (New York: Oxford University Press, 1980); Ellen Rothman, *Hands and Hearts: A History of Courtship in America* (New York: Basic Books, 1984); Karen Lystra, *Searching the Heart: Women, Men, and Romantic Love in Nineteenth-Century America* (New York: Oxford University Press, 1989). Nina Baym claims that woman's fiction "showed the home thoroughly penetrated at every point by the world, dominated by man" and that it held out the hope that perhaps "the direction of influence could be reversed so that home values dominated the world" (*Woman's Fiction: A Guide to Novels By and About Women in America, 1820–1870* [Ithaca: Cornell University Press, 1978], p. 48).

7. For example, Nancy F. Cott argues in *The Bonds of Womanhood: "Woman's Sphere" in New England, 1780–1835* (New Haven: Yale University Press, 1977), pp. 6 ff., that the 1830s "became a turning point in women's economic participation, public activities, and social visibility." Stephanie Coontz points out in *The Social Origins of Private Life: A History of American Families, 1600–1900* (London: Verso, 1988), p. 34, that "about the 1820s a new family system emerged"; and Joe L. Dubbert notes in *A Man's Place: Masculinity in Transition* (Englewood Cliffs, N.J.: Prentice Hall, 1979), p. 27, that "around 1830 the number of [guidebooks to male behavior] increased and their tone became more serious, especially in discussing sexual purity." See also Jack Larkin, *The Reshaping of Everyday Life, 1790–1840* (New York: Harper & Row, 1988), pp. 199–201; Lystra, *Searching the Heart*, pp. 28–32; Stephen Nissenbaum, *Sex, Diet and Debility in Jacksonian America: Sylvester Graham and Health Reform* (Westport Conn.: Greenwood Press, 1980), pp. 4, 25–29; and Rothman, *Hands and Hearts*, pp. 51, 91.

8. Michael J. Colacurcio, *The Province of Piety: Moral History in Hawthorne's Early Tales* (Cambridge: Harvard University Press, 1984).

9. Nathaniel Hawthorne, "Young Goodman Brown," in *Mosses from an Old Manse*, vol. 10 of *The Centenary Edition of the Works of Nathaniel Hawthorne*, ed. William Charvat et al. (Columbus: Ohio State University Press, 1974), p. 74. All further references are to this edition and are identified parenthetically.

10. Levin and Colacurico, in particular, have strengthened this sense by revealing the depth of Hawthorne's familiarity with Puritan sources. See also E. Arthur Robinson. "The Vision of Goodman Brown: A Source and Interpretation" *American Literature* 35 (May 1963): 218–25; B. Bernard Cohen, "Deodat Lawson's *Christ's Fidelity* and Hawthorne's 'Young Goodman Brown," *Essex Institute Historical Collections* 104 (1968): 349–70; James W. Clark, Jr., "Hawthorne's Use of Evidence in 'Young Goodman Brown," *Essex Institute Historical Collections* 111 (1975): 12–34 and Robert C. Grayson, "Young Goodman Hawthorne," *American Notes and Queries* 21 (March–April 1983): 103–6.

11. John Demos, *Past, Present and Personal: The Family and the Life Course in American History* (New York: Oxford University Press, 1986), p. 49

12. Nancy F.Cott, "Passionlessness: An Interpretation of Victorian Sexual Ideology, 1790–1850," in *A Heritage of Her Own*, ed. Nancy F. Cott and Elizabeth H. Pleck (New York: Simon & Schuster, 1979), pp. 162–81; Nissenbaum, *Sex, Diet and Debility in Jacksonian America*.

13. Lois Banner, *American Beauty* (New York; Knopf, 1983), pp. 45, 46.

14. Cooper, quoted by Banner, in *American Beauty*, p. 46.

15. Banner, *American Beauty*, p. 53.

16. John Demos, *A Little Commonwealth: Family Life in Plymouth Colony* (New York: Oxford University Press, 1970), pp. 82–83.

17. Edmund S. Morgan, *The Puritan Family: Region and Domestic Relations in Seventeenth-Century New England* (1944; revised ed., New York: Harper & Row, 1966), pp. 166–68; Cott, "Passionlessness," p. 167.

18. Carroll Smith-Rosenberg, "Domesticating 'Virtue': Coquettes and Revolutionaries in Young America," in *Literature and the Body: Essays on Populations and Persons*, ed. Elaine Scarry (Baltimore: Johns Hopkins University Press, 1988), p.166.

19. On woman's work as social reproduction, see Coontz, *The Social Origins of Private Life*.

20. For a psychoanalytic reading of this opening passage as explicitly sexual, see Edward Jayne, "Pray Tarry with Me Young Goodman Brown," *Literature and Psychology* 29 (1979); 103–4.

21. See Lystra, *Searching the Heart*, pp. 57–58.

22. Perhaps Brown's insistence that Faith and her ribbons remain inside the public/private threshold is related also to the taboo that menstruation has a chaotic effect on social behavior. One best-selling marriage manual of the 1830s declared that menstruating women were "'out of order'" and should be kept at home (see Charles Knowlton's *Fruits of Philosophy*, quoted in Joel Pfister's *The Production of Personal Life: Class, Gender, and the Psychological in Hawthorne's Fiction* [Stanford: Stanford University Press, 1991], p. 35). In addition, the repetition of "of all nights in the year" suggests that this particular night is important to both of them. Perhaps her ribbons are a sign that she is ovulating. It was generally held prior to the twentieth century that when a woman was menstruating she was also ovulating (see Thomas Laqueur, "Orgasm, Generation, and the Politics of Reproductive Biology," in *The Making of the Modern Body: Sexuality and Society in the Nineteenth Century*, ed. Catherine Gallagher and Thomas Laqueur [Berkeley: University of California Press, 1987], p. 3). Hence, Faith's omnipresent pink ribbons and sexual desire may be signs of her wish to pull her husband through yet another threshold into the joys of parenthood.

23. That many husbands, including Hawthorne, could, following the advice literature of the early decades of the nineteenth century, accept the moral superiority of their wives is clear from their letters and diaries. See Degler, *At Odds*, p. 30, and T. Walter Herbert, *Dearest Beloved: The Hawthornes and the Making of the Middle-Class Family* (Berkeley: University of California Press, 1993).

24. Herbert, *Dearest Beloved*, pp. 131–32; see also chaps. 8 and 10. In later decades, historian E. Anthony Rotundo proposes, a distinct "boy culture" grew up to counter the forces of "tender affection and moral suasion" each boy encountered when he crossed the threshold into his mother's home. This more "masculine" youth culture outside the home helped prepare boys for a manhood in which crossing the threshold between male and female worlds was more natural. In fact, some "of the most important lessons that a youngster learned from boy culture were those about living a life divided by a boundary between the two spheres." But in the early decades, such acculturation was quite limited. E. Anthony Rotundo, "Boy Culture: Middle-class Boyhood in Nineteenth-Century America," in *Meanings for Manhood: Constructions of Masculinity in Victorian America*, ed. Mark C. Carnes and Clyde Griffen (Chicago: University of Chicago Press, 1990), pp. 16, 29.

25. Levin and Colacurcio read this story as, in part, concerned with the theological and epistemological problems the Puritans had with the specter evidence, that Brown might mistake the specters in the forest for the people of the colony. Yet neither critic asks what specter evidence has to do with not recognizing that your companion is the "specter" of your father. Clearly the issue at this point in the story is not that Brown cannot tell a

specter from a person or a saint from a sinner but that he does not recognize that someone looks like his father.

26. Carroll Smith-Rosenberg, "Beauty, the Beast and the Militant Woman: A Case Study in Sex Roles and Social Stress in Jacksonian America," *American Quarterly* 23 (1971): 575.

27. We might see this taunt as well as the serpentine phallus as challenges to Brown's manhood. The devil-father offers the competition and possible humiliation that a nineteenth-century son might find outside the home. David Leverenz argues that "any intensified ideology of manhood is a compensatory response to fears of humiliation" and that throughout his career Hawthorne "dramatizes manhood as demonic possession, often explicitly." But Leverenz virtually ignores "Young Goodman Brown," preferring to focus for the most part on one or two late stories and the novels. *Manhood and the American Renaissance* (Ithaca: Cornell University Press, 1989), pp. 4, 239.

28. On the possible sexual implications of Goody Cloyse being Brown's grandfather's gossip, see Daniel Hoffman, *Form and Fable in American Fiction* (New York: Oxford University Press, 1961), p. 163. For additional discussion of these sexually-laden paragraphs and the sexual aspects of the story, see Robinson, "The Vision of Goodman Brown," pp. 221–24; Jayne, "Pray Tarry with Me Young Goodman Brown," pp. 100–113; Male, *Hawthorne's Tragic Vision*, pp. 77–78; Crews, *Sins of the Fathers*, pp. 96–106; and Elizabeth Wright, "The New Psychoanalysis and Literary Criticism: A Reading of Melville and Hawthorne," *Poetics Today* 3 (Spring 1982): 89–105.

29. Ann Douglas, *The Feminization of American Culture* (New York: Knopf, 1977).

30. Gillian Brown, *Domestic Individualism: Imagining Self in Nineteenth-Century America* (Berkeley: University of California Press, 1990), p. 63.

31. That Brown is so confident that he is sin free leads to the possibility that he is pure of sexual "sin," that he left his wife and came to the forest still a virgin. This idea has been suggested to me by Professor Elizabeth Jane Hinds. Such a possibility would make Faith's pleas at the beginning of the tale all the more poignant, Brown's focus on stains and bloodspots covering the earth that much more vivid and significant, and his return to the village and his future life as the father of "a goodly procession" of children all that more personally tragic.

32. Nina Baym, "Thwarted Nature: Nathaniel Hawthorne as Feminist," in *American Novelists Revisited: Essays in Feminist Criticism*, ed. Fritz Fleischmann (Boston: G.K. Hall, 1982), p. 62.

33. Herbert, *Dearest Beloved*, and Gillian Brown, "Hawthorne, Inheritance, and Women's Property," *Studies in the Novel* 23 (1991): 107–18.

34. Leverenz, *Manhood and the American Renaissance*; Pfister, *The Production of Personal Life*; and Richard H. Millington, *Practicing Romance: Narrative Form and Cultural Engagement in Hawthorne's Fiction* (Princeton: Princeton University Press, 1992). For some explanation of Pfister's preference for the later Hawthorne, see *Production of Personal Life*, p. 43.

DEBRA JOHANYAK

Romanticism's Fallen Edens: The Malignant Contribution of Hawthorne's Literary Landscapes

America's stern puritannical history provided nineteenth century writers with ideal plots and settings for the age-old conflict between good and evil. Edenic gardens and pastoral woodlands grace countless works of the Romantic era, wherein Adam- and Eve-like lovers succumb to temptation and find themselves not only cast out of their normative societies, but often torn from each other as well—whether spiritually, emotionally, or literally. Significantly, the forest settings of these tales contribute substantially and malignantly to the plot development of such stories.

None used the Edenic motif so pervasively as Nathaniel Hawthorne. His tales initially seem to draw our focus to a narrator who introduces characters and events. But Hawthorne's stories begin much earlier, in fact, commencing with landscape descriptions that set our goose bumps in motion. He accomplishes this in so artful a way that we are scarcely aware of it; hence we focus our mounting apprehension on a principal hero or heroine appearing signally in the narrative spotlight.

It is especially interesting that tales utilizing a contributory landscape are those emphasizing a Puritan backdrop against which a conflict-laced love story unfolds. Specifically, "The Maypole of Merry Mount," "Young Goodman Brown," and *The Scarlet Letter* are Hawthorne's strongest revivals of the Edenic legend featuring Puritan protagonists. And although the

From *CLA Journal* 42, no. 3 (March 1999). ©1999 by the College Language Assocation.

couples remain bonded, legally or emotionally, until death's separation tears them asunder, a shared moral flaw or spiritual weakness blocks their enjoyment of a true or joyous marriage.

"Young Goodman Brown" (1835) places the protagonist in a haunted forest representing the hero's troubled state of mind as he secretly hurries toward a midnight rendezvous. Leaving his wife secure, as he believes, in the heart of their Puritan community, Goodman Brown begins a journey at dusk toward a universal temptation which dooms his relationship to Faith—his literal wife and metaphorical spirituality—when he is forced to face the all-pervasive weak and sinful nature of humanity. The woodland path parallels his morally dangerous purpose and enhances the tone—and moral—of Hawthorne's plot:

> He had taken a dreary road, darkened by all the gloomiest trees of the forest, which barely stood aside to let the narrow path creep through, and closed immediately behind. It was all as lonely as could be; and there is this peculiarity in such a solitude, that the traveller knows not who may be concealed by the innumerable trunks and the thick boughs overhead; so that with lonely footsteps he may yet be passing through an unseen multitude.[1]

The separation at sundown of Brown from his wife suggests the divisive nature of his temptation. Brown wrongly assumes that his is an isolated, one-time distraction to be easily rectified by returning to the Puritan fold the next morning. As Brown commences traveling, Hawthorne likens his forest path to the spiritual journey of a man questioning his religious faith. Rather than adhering to the superficial community standards of his Puritan counterparts, Brown moves alone down the woodland route to consummate a deep, secret longing—one that he little expects is universally shared. Allegorically—like much of Hawthorne's writing—the road depicts Brown's journey to the depths of his own soul as he questions his personal human nature and, later, that of his wife and surrounding community. Hawthorne describes the woodland setting in terms corresponding to Goodman Brown's desperate self-search. The Puritan's eagerness to reach his midnight goal parallels a dwindling moral reserve as his hopes, like the gloomy woodland path, become increasingly narrow, twisted, and obscure.

The haunted forest frames young Brown's spiritual wanderings, suggesting that human sinfulness is inextricably bound to Nature.[2] As the hero moves—at first hesitantly, but then quite purposefully—toward a seductive tryst in the heart of this wild woodland, it becomes apparent that he has exchanged his Puritan identity for pagan revelry. As Michael Bell notes, "[F]or Hawthorne nature itself is more a part of the European character than of the American.... '[N]ature' and the Old World are both comprehended, for Hawthorne, in the notion of the pagan."[3] Prefiguring Hester Prynne's escape plan to flee America for the Old World with Dimmesdale, Goodman Brown attempts to renounce his Puritan community, his Puritan faith, and his Puritan wife, in order to pursue Old World temptations embodied in the dark, mysterious depths of Nature. The woodland path, growing "wilder and drearier and more faintly traced," is enlivened by "frightful sounds" (62) which animate the otherwise-dead terrain, giving it human likeness. Into this eerie setting comes literal temptation, personified in an older gentleman who accompanies Brown through the wood where it is "deep dusk ... and deepest in that part of it where these two were journeying" (55).

Thinking to escape his heritage, his marriage, and his humanity, Brown is instead lured along the forest path toward these restrictive elements in a shocking and irreparable recognition of all creation's spiritual degeneration. His bridegroom's love for wifely Faith is assaulted by her metaphorical adultery with the Satanic mass when she betrays both faith and husband by participating in the group's devil worship. As Brown plods along the dreary route, his darkening path finally disappears, symbolizing the youth's complete lapse into spiritual depravity.

The journey climaxes when Brown arrives at the ritual in progress deep in the "heathen wilderness" (61), grimly portrayed by Hawthorne's lurid descriptions of the forest clearing:

> At one extremity of an open space, hemmed in by the dark wall of the forest, arose a rock, bearing some rude, natural resemblance either to an altar or a pulpit, and surrounded by four blazing pines, their tops aflame, their stems untouched, like candles at an evening meeting. The mass of foliage that had overgrown the summit of the rock was all on fire, blazing high into the night and fitfully illuminating the whole field.... As the red light arose and fell, a numerous congregation alternately shone forth, then disappeared in shadow, and again grew, as it were, out of the darkness, peopling the heart of the solitary woods at once. (63)

This devilish scene is heightened by a worship hymn, "not of human voices, but of all the sounds of the benighted wilderness pealing in awful harmony together" (63). Although the anguished husband cries out in despair, his voice blends in "unison with the cry of the desert" (63), and his unique lament of dissent is swallowed up by the encompassing evil about him, embodied as much in the wilderness setting as in the human celebrants. Eden's pathetic fallacy is inverted, like other biblical images, to conform to the Satan-worship of this story in honoring the "Prince of this World" and rejecting the heavenly Christ.

The climactical welcome chant to the lord of darkness is epitomized by cacophonic screams of "the roaring wind, the rushing streams, the howling beasts, and every other voice of the unconcerted wilderness ... mingling and according with the voice of guilty man in homage to the prince of all" (65). Fallen Eden offers a grotesque parody of creation praise, as nature's wildest voices join and overtake the Puritans' lewd celebration.

Surrounded by humanity's and nature's evil, Goodman Brown is nearly powerless to resist Satan's draw. Somehow he finds strength to glance heavenward and urges his wife to do likewise. Ultimately he saves himself, unassisted by Faith, who remains an allegorical symbol of failed religious hope.

Unsure of whether his life is now a dream or reality, Brown abruptly faces a desolate future

> amid calm night and solitude, listening to a roar of the wind
> which died heavily away through the forest. He staggered against
> the rock, and felt it chill and damp; while a hanging twig, that had
> been all on fire, besprinkled his cheek with the coldest dew. (67)

Despite his harrowing escape, Brown's familiar world is scarcely more welcoming than the evil one of the previous night. Nature now appears dispassionate at best. The fire's midnight blaze is replaced by dawn's clammy cold; the warmth of his bed and comfort of his hope are as lost as his religious and wifely Faith.

Thus, it comes as no surprise that Young Goodman Brown's "dying hour was gloom" (68). The grave receives him devoid of "hopeful verse" (68), his happiness sacrificed in that one night's compromising journey. Although Hawthorne's young Puritan acknowledges his own and his wife's fleshly weaknesses, knowledge of the world's pervasive evil—represented in the personified forest—haunts him all his days. The woodland's midnight shades coupled with the town's gloomy daylight remind us that we are everywhere surrounded by evil; our only escape lies in this realization and in an attempt to find—and keep—a straight moral path. Hawthorne emphasizes in this tale, as in the others that follow, that the key to understanding and accepting humanity's natural depravity is a sense of balance between the values of head and heart;[4] thus Brown's lifelong gloom is as unhealthy as the Puritans' hypocritical double standards.

Another woodland scene witnesses a confrontation between Puritanism and paganism in "The Maypole of Merry Mount" (1836). Taking liberties with New England historicity, Hawthorne neglects to mention that the original location was more than a revel site; "located on the South shore from Boston in what is now Quincy, the Merry Mount Plantation was a fur-trading and merchandising venture, not a mere festival."[5] Overlooking the commercial aspects of this community, Hawthorne instead presents images of Bacchanalian revelry with a clear focus on surrounding Nature as the setting rather than making mention of the nearby settlement buildings. An important subplot to this tale, then, highlights the conflict between humanity and nature: "Hawthornian man ... enters 'the dreary and perilous wilderness'...., imposes on it his own will and design, and transforms it, little by little, until it finally gives way to a world made in his image and subject to his control."[6] Consequently, Nature settings in Hawthorne's Puritan tales often adapt characteristics of the invading or dominant class or group of settlers.

A tension-fraught landscape is introduced when Hawthorne writes in the first paragraph that "Jollity and gloom were contending for an empire."[7] As Puritans look on from their wooded hiding place and prepare to seize the revelers, Hawthorne likens them to their surroundings: "[S]ome of these black shadows have rushed forth in human shape" (48). Pine trees (50) are used to whip the Merry Mount natives as the pastoral scene fades to horrific images of judgment and castigation. Endicott, "the severest Puritan of all" (53), criticizes and condemns the frivolous joys of the nuptial couple celebrating their wedding and May Day festivities amid Nature's beauteous flowers and trees, and Hawthorne allows this stern justice to overshadow the lovely New England landscape: "As the moral gloom of the world overpowers all systematic gayety, even so was their home of wild mirth made desolate amid the sad forest" (53).

In this tale a pastoral bacchanal is turned into a doomridden nightmare of Puritan justice imposed on the youthful revelers. The authoritarian Puritans relate these revelers, however, to "those devils and ruined souls with whom their superstition peopled the black wilderness" (42) in the Old Country, presumably England. Depending on perspective, the setting adopts overtones of the dominant habitants. For the May celebrants, the natural wilderness boasted "[g]arden flowers, and blossoms [that] ... laughed gladly forth amid the verdure, so fresh and dewy that they must have grown by magic ... " (41). Such descriptions project the idea that Nature is "lush, fecund, frolicsome."[8] For the sober Puritans, however, the wilderness was to be "a land of clouded visages, of hard toil, of sermon and psalm forever" (48). Thus Nature's fertility reverts to an austere sterility paralleling that of the Puritans as the revelers' gay freedom comes under Puritan control. When Endicott assaults the Maypole—Nature's symbol of joy and fruition—the setting dims accordingly: "[T]he evening sky grew darker, and the woods threw forth a more sombre shadow" (48); the scene recalls Christ's torture and death on the pole of crucifixion.

Following the biblical Eden, the once lovely setting becomes a desolate cloud of labor for the young couple whose tender love and nuptial joy is dimmed by the harsh reality of Endicott's threatened punishment and overriding manipulation. Allegorically, the tale suggests that even nature's loveliness and freedom must submit to man's tyrannical government. Laughter and spontaneity are banished by the stern enforcement of reason's reign over joy's merriment as Hawthorne's pantheistic protagonists fall under the authority of the punishing deity, Endicott.

Hawthorne's largest work utilizing this theme, *The Scarlet Letter* (1850), is centered in a haunting setting distanced from reality in time and location. Hester, the fallen woman, finds no sympathy with her Puritan townspeople, and this tale emphasizes a woodland setting that provides an alternative and somewhat softened framework for her isolated character.

The surrounding forest beckons Hester's company, "having also the passes of the dark, inscrutable forest open to her, where the wilderness of her nature might assimilate itself with a people whose customs and life were alien from the law that had condemned her."[9] Pearl plays comfortably in the woodland sunshine and shadow, finding acceptance and joy in nature that are denied her by the ostracizing community.

Dimmesdale, too, travels frequently through the isolated forest on errands of pious mercy. Thus these three focal characters—separated by their community and divided by sin—draw together in the brooding landscape. This woodland setting provides a trysting place for the unique family's last private encounter. Darkly silent and uninhabited, the forest offers a neutral refuge where Hester can one last time reveal her femininity to the man she still loves. Here, too, she shares with him a plan to escape to the Old Country of their origins and future hope of a shared eternity.

On a "chill and sombre" (468) day, the forest stands "black and dense" (468) on either side of the footpath, and young Pearl races to catch a winsome sunbeam, which vanishes as Hester approaches and stretches forth her hand. Finding a seat on a rotted pine near a blackish stream, the surrounding area seems to parallel the dark mysteries of her past and present life, reminiscent in the bewilderment of tree-trunks and underbrush, and here and there a huge rock, covered over with gray lichens. All of these giant trees and boulders seemed intent on making a mystery of the course of this small brook; fearing, perhaps, that with its never-ceasing loquacity, it should whisper tales out of the heart of the old forest whence it flowed, or mirror its revelations on the smooth surface of a pool. (471–72)

Hester not only observes this setting; she becomes part of it, exposing her wild nature to its nonjudgmental, peaceful environment that accepts her as she truly is, a "natural" creature, more comfortable in the forest than in the rejecting Puritan community. Only in this wild, secluded microcosm can Hester dare become, once again, the woman she used to be, and Arthur dare reveal, for a moment, the man he has become. In Nature's timeless vacuum, Dimmesdale, like Hester, "has breathed the 'wild, true atmosphere of an unredeemed, unchristianizd [sic], lawless region' and now has a 'knowledge of hidden mysteries,' a suspicion that society may rest on no transcendent ground but may be merely the magical creation of man's will."[10] Within Nature's confines and Hester's embrace, Arthur, for a short time, breathes the air of a free man. Divorced from past and future, the pair relive their earlier meetings and revise their original relationship—even Pearl has scampered away, leaving them alone with each other. But the original sin, inherent in each of us, resurfaces to lead them down the fallen path once more. Lacking social structure and Puritan mores in their primitive bower, Hawthorne's Adam and Eve again succumb to the serpent's lure of a tempting paradise, by hoping to escape the consequences of their actions in leaving Boston.

Because each has become acclimated to a life without the other, their woodland joining is laced with ghostly surrealism. And yet it is within this private but temporary setting that plans are laid for a hopeful reunion, when the couple conspires to flee in a departing ship days hence. The forest provides not only respite for Hester—who has wandered in a "moral wilderness" (484) for the past seven years—but also invigoration and a framework for rededication of her love to Arthur. In Nature's darkly secure womb, Dimmesdale luxuriates in his only reprieve from seven years' guilt and fear when he relaxes in the shelter of the covering trees and Hester's maternal nurturing. The lonely wilderness around them provides secrecy and privacy which strengthens and protects—at least briefly—their love for, and commitment to, each other. Thus, Nature's solace elicits Hester's repressed rebellion, which "finds its equivalent in the joyous gaiety of nature"[11] and encourages their desperate plan:

> And, as if the gloom of the earth and sky had been but the
> effluence of these two mortal hearts, it vanished with their
> sorrow. All at once, as with a sudden smile of heaven, forth burst
> the sunshine, pouring a very flood into the obscure forest....The
> objects that had made a shadow hitherto, embodied the
> brightness now.... Such was the sympathy of Nature—that wild,
> heathen Nature of the forest, never subjugated by human law, nor
> illumined by higher truth—with the bliss of these two spirits!
> (202–03)

Despite surging emotions, the couple's rekindled love is doomed, rooted in idealism rather than conventionality. In leaving their forest sanctuary, their temporary respite is overshadowed by malignant foreshadowings. Approaching the town after leaving Hester in the woods, Dimmesdale experiences devilish impulses he can scarcely control. Just days later, Hester, observing his participation in the governor's inaugural celebration, struggles with loneliness and insecurity as she questions Arthur's love and commitment. Briefly strengthened by their forest reunion, Dimmesdale's life is shortly thereafter drained in his final public appearance to their Puritan society. Unable to resist death's pull any longer, he weakly proclaims his guilt on the public scaffold before dying a martyr in the townspeople's eyes.

In this romance, the forest provides a bower setting for refueling the lovers' ardor, which paradoxically seals their tragic doom. The sympathetic security of the dark woodland provides a tempting but futile mirage of daring rebellion and eleventh-hour hope. It is only outside the mainstream of Puritan life, in this shadowy retreat, that Hester and Arthur sustain a dying ember of shared love and mutual dependence which cannot be maintained in the Puritan community, later resulting in Arthur's death and the lovers' separation.

Hawthorne marries Puritan themes to forest settings in ways that are often ambivalent; sometimes Nature projects celebration and joy, while at other times it depicts the evil characteristics and threatening gestures of menacing invaders. But like no other romancer, Hawthorne uses the native American soil to tremendous advantage in enhancing scenes, moods, and characters in stories featuring Puritan-based plots and conflict-challenged romances.

NOTES

1. Nathaniel Hawthorne, "Young Goodman Brown," in *The Portable Hawthorne*, ed. Malcolm Crowley (New York: Penguin, 1948) 54. Hereafter cited parenthetically in the text.

2. Nancy Bunge, *Nathanial Hawthorne: A Study of the Short Fiction* (New York: Twayne, 1993) 13.

3. Michael Davitt Bell, *Hawthorn and the Historical Romance of New England* (Princeton: Princeton UP, 1971) 131.

4. J. Golden Taylor, *Hawthorne's Ambivalence Toward Puritanism* (Logan: Utah State UP, 1965) 28.

5. Taylor 30.

6. Edgar A. Dryden, *Nathaniel Hawthorne: The Poetics of Enchantment* (Ithaca: Cornell UP, 1977) 39-40.

7. Nathaniel Hawthorne, "The Maypole of Merry Mount," in *The Portable Hawthorne*. ed. Malcolm Crowley (New York: Penguin, 1948) 40. Hereafter cited parenthetically in the text.

8. John F. Birk, "New Roots for 'Merry Mount': Barking Up the Wrong Tree?" *SSF* Summer 1991: 349.

9. Nathaniel Hawthorne, *The Scarlet Letter*, in *The Portable Hawthorne*, ed. Malcolm Cowley (New York: Penguin, 1948) 368. Hereafter cited parenthetically in the text.

10. Dryden 42.

11. Michael Davitt Bell, "Another View of Hester," in *Hester Prynne*, ed. Harold Bloom (New York: Chelsea House, 1990) 93.

EDWARD JAYNE

Pray Tarry With Me Young Goodman Brown

Hawthorne's almost transparent use of paranoia as an organizing principle has been generally overlooked even in psychoanalytic studies of his fiction. There have been many critical approaches to Hawthorne, but most if not all of them have provided an essentially "normal" response to his paranoid manipulation of experience. It almost seems as if his uncompromising delusional intensity has provoked a variety of normal defenses among those who are sufficiently tantalized to want to deal with it without coming to terms with its fullest implications. By doing so they both accept and deny whatever resonance this manipulation of experience has produced in themselves, as would be demonstrated by their indignation when challenged on these grounds. Nevertheless, once noticed, unmistakable symptoms of paranoia are everywhere to be observed in Hawthorne's fiction, and these can and should be investigated as a pattern of behavior which is consistent enough to justify its independent clinical evaluation. It is Hawthorne's fiction which should be diagnosed, not Hawthorne, his sympathetic audience, nor even his tormented and guilt-ridden characters. Magnificent in its brooding solitude, his fiction literally organizes itself as an intact delusional system which may be tried out for size by its author and readers who are able to share in the nightmarish experience it imposes upon its characters.

From *Literature and Psychology* 29, no. 3 (1979). © 1979 *Literature and Psychology*.

One of the most obvious examples of paranoid consciousness in the canon of Hawthorne's works is "Young Goodman Brown," a short story which is fully as relevant to the central tradition of American fiction as it is to the personal circumstances of either Hawthorne or his readers. The story can be explained, I think, both as a remarkable case history of paranoid aberration and as a "negative" example of the wilderness consciousness which has persisted from Natty Bumppo's exploits to those of the detectives, cowboys and anti-heroes who crowd our media today. The principal difference would be that Young Goodman Brown briefly tests and rejects the adventures to which they dedicate their lifetime endeavors. But in doing so, he successfully exposes the inadequacies he shares with them despite the restraint which supplants material accomplishment with the suspicion and bitterness which he must endure for the greater part of his life. The temporary forest ritual he denies in himself expresses the syndrome he shares with them except to the extent that he is complicated enough to try to reject it.

Briefly recounted, Hawthorne's narrative tells how the sensitive and vulnerable Young Goodman Brown goes into the forest to carry out his overnight assignation with Satan. Faith, his equally vulnerable young bride, pleads with him to "tarry" with her at home, but he feels inexplicably compelled to leave and fulfill his mysterious obligation. Once in the forest he meets Satan, who leads him toward the site where an unexplained midnight ritual is to be conducted. The two of them soon overtake his old nurse, Goody Cloyse, who had taught him his catechism in his childhood. He is shocked to learn that she is on her way to the same ceremony and has been a long-standing friend of Satan on the most intimate of terms. When she accepts Satan's staff to fly like a witch to their destination, Young Goodman Brown decides to profit from Faith's example by refusing to cooperate any further. Abandoned by Satan, who has become impatient with his naiveté, Young Goodman Brown finds himself alone in the dark and listening to voices in the clouds overhead, evidently of other women flying to the same event. One of these sounds as if she is Faith, his young wife, and a red ribbon which descends from the sky seems to be hers. With this discovery he loses his composure and frantically rushes to join in the evil proceedings, spurred on by the voices of two respectable local clergymen riding on horseback to the same destination.

Young Goodman Brown finally stumbles into a clearing illuminated by four burning pines and full of local citizens, many of them from among the most pious and prosperous families he knows. He finds that everybody has gathered and been waiting to perform the ritual baptism of Faith and himself as two new converts into what Satan describes as "the communion of their race." Only one figure, probably his mother, motions him not to participate, but she seems to be lost in the crowd. Satan begins his invocation before a blood-filled basin when Young Goodman Brown suddenly changes his mind and cries to Faith, who stands next to him, to join in resisting "the wicked one." Exactly at this instant the entire gathering disappears, Faith included, and Young Goodman Brown once again finds himself alone in the dark forest. The next day he returns home again entirely disillusioned. He does stay on with Faith to raise a family of children and grandchildren, but he can never determine whether his extraordinary experiences had been a dream or not. As a result he remains suspicious and embittered until he finally dies of old age still unreconciled with those about him.

Before the origins of the paranoid syndrome are explored as suggested in the story, it would be useful to list some of the many overt paranoid symptoms which occur throughout its narrative. The cause-and-effect interaction between vulnerability and its projective defenses typical of paranoia is carried out in this story in almost textbook fashion, but a discussion of its more obvious paranoid traits seems necessary before launching into their etiology.[1] Listed, these traits stand as follows:

1. There is a complete and intact delusional system, an elaborate explanation of events which justifies Young Goodman Brown's final hostility against all others.

2. Young Goodman Brown is pitted against a conspiracy so pervasive that everybody, even his trusted bride, is probably involved. It is only his rigid commitment to virtue that prevents him from succumbing to it, and because of his refusal he becomes alienated from the entire town, a "pseudo-community" of potential enemies.[2]

3. Paranoid "centrality" is gained by Young Goodman Brown because his evil communion is supposed to be celebrated by all of society and because his salvation becomes the principle battlefield, however temporary, in the cosmic struggle between God and Satan.

4. There is supernatural interference by powers too enormous to be resisted except by soliciting one in the struggle against the other. Young Goodman Brown is nothing more than a pawn in the "cold war" between forces he cannot entirely understand.

5. Undue emphasis is put upon the exaggerated Manichaean choice between sin and virtue. Young Goodman Brown stakes his life and happiness upon a clear-cut ethical issue,

all-good versus all-bad, and he must remain steadfast in his commitment to "the good" despite evil temptations to which everybody else has very probably succumbed.

6. There is a pronounced tendency toward "premature closure" in the judgment of others. We are never certain whether Young Goodman Brown's experience is real, but following his single evening's ordeal he absolutely and humorlessly commits himself to the perpetual rejection of his family and neighbors.

7. The possibility of compromise is totally excluded. Once Young Goodman Brown has made his choice, his fate is determined and no accommodation can be made for the rest of his life with his relatives and neighbors.

8. There is an excessive emphasis upon the detection of clues to expose the truth to Young Goodman Brown about the conspiracy against him: his wife's hair ribbon, peculiar resemblances, snatches of familiar voices heard in the dark, etc. All of these must be sifted as evidence to be used to save Young Goodman Brown from the fate which would otherwise await him.

9. There is an overcompensatory reduction of sexual roles to simplified stereotypes. Women are divided into pure beings such as Young Goodman Brown's mother and threatening temptresses and/or witches such as Goody Cloyse. Unfortunately, Faith seems willing to join the devil's party, so the temptation she represents would bring about his destruction if he didn't have the will power to withstand it.

10. There is prolonged uncertainty whether events are real or imaginary. Particularly noteworthy are the voices heard in the dark of the clergymen and the women passing by on the cloud overhead. Hearing voices is of course one of the typical symptoms of advanced paranoia, even in a story such as "Young Goodman Brown" in which forest darkness provides a kind of secondary elaboration to justify its occurrence.

11. The story of Young Goodman Brown is told with a disarming candor which emphasizes the truth at one level of interpretation in order to obscure it at another. The narrator is always careful to differentiate uncertainty from the clear-cut truth, and of course a struggle must be understood to occur between satanic deception and the

ultimate truth. However, the central issue of the story, Young Goodman Brown's rejection of his role as husband, is kept almost entirely excluded from conscious recognition, as are the more fundamental reasons for his choice through his fear of sex.

12. Finally, there is even a good deal of paranoid imagery to the story. Young Goodman Brown makes his regressive journey along a dark and threatening trail in order to participate in a ghastly ritual dominated by burning pines and a rock basin full of blood. An enormous crowd has gathered to watch his humiliating baptism, but it suddenly disappears to leave him stranded in the darkness. This kind of oneiric intensity effectively puts experience in the service of paranoid hostility through perceptions which confirm one's closest harbored suspicions.

Unmistakably paranoid, then, would be the mood and ambience of the story. The way it unfolds upon itself as a justification of Young Goodman Brown in his struggle against demonic forces offers itself as almost a classic psychiatric case history of paranoid delusional thinking.

But more important than symptoms alone would be the Freudian etiology of paranoia which is actually given its sequential explanation in being traced from its acute to its chronic stages as Young Goodman Brown's story advances from beginning to end. The source of Young Goodman Brown's paranoid circumstances through his unresolved Oedipal fixation is emphasized and reemphasized throughout the story of his ordeal. As maintained by Frederick Crews, the devil is clearly a father figure in the disguise he assumes as Young Goodman Brown's venerable grandfather who has long since been dead.[3] Together, Satan and Young Goodman Brown are described at one point as looking like father and son, and grandfather translates into father exactly as Goody Cloyse, Young Goodman Brown's satanic nurse, translates into bad or licentious mother, the willing mistress of his father's designs. Moreover, the celebration led by the father-figure at the witch's sabbath in the woods would simply consist of Young Goodman Brown's ultimate act of identifying with his father through his marriage with Faith according to patriarchal custom and expectations. They are newly-weds, and, as in the case of all marriages, church and civil rites must be completed by an act of intimacy which would impose upon Young Goodman Brown the role his father had once enjoyed with his mother. Of course it is specified in the story that he and Faith have been married for three months, ample time to have consummated their relationship much earlier, but whether they did or not, the forest ritual at least serves as its symbolic reenactment. Sexual consummation obviously seems to be what is meant by Satan, its patriarchal figure-head, when he refers to "the communion of your race," and all of those who can attend this communion seem to have lost their virginity in a comparable fashion.

Faith makes her conjugal demands explicit at the beginning of the story, "Pray tarry with me this night, of all nights in the year." Why of all nights in the year? Or of all nights in one's life? Chronological displacement would apparently be the answer—from the passage of a single day, when marriage is customarily both sealed and consummated, to a quarter year, the period of time which elapses between solstice and equinox. Whether conscious or unconscious, the effort seems plain to disguise the crisis faced by Young Goodman Brown, for the story's symbolism would be all too obvious if it were explicit that this ceremony takes place on his marriage night. So it becomes important to specify that the two are newly-weds, but with enough of an interim since their marriage to support the symbolic disguise which might let the story be told—exactly the same use of concealment as occurs in dream formation. Nevertheless, it remains obvious, as Crews insists, that sex is the issue and that what happens in the story is the rejection of sex except for the unpleasant necessity of bearing children.

Sexual temptation is also very likely suggested even at the story's beginning when it is said that Faith "thrusts her own pretty head into the street, letting the wind play with the pink ribbons of her cap ..." If head at all implies maidenhead, as can be the case in Shakespeare's plays, for example, the young wife displays a forwardness which demeans or "thrusts into the street" her chastity. That she does so by projecting her head from the open door of her house also suggests the cookbook (but not invalid) Freudian dream symbolism of houses as bodies and doors as apertures to these bodies. Through displacement, however, her door isn't penetrated inwards, but outwards, and this is done by herself, not Young Goodman Brown, courting shame and disgrace in her effort to induce him to remain with her in their house. Her words "Pray tarry with me" which are spoken at this point confirm the licentious implications of her gesture, and her fluttering pink ribbon, emphasized by its wayward personification as something "played with" by the wind, only begins to prepare Young Goodman Brown for the blood-filled basin he later sees into which one's hands might be dipped in the ritual of consummation. Young Goodman Brown's immediate departure despite Faith's seductive pleas expresses his preliminary rejection of this temptation, but without his fully understanding the implications of his action. Then when he passes behind the meeting house so their view of each other is obstructed, it seems as if this structure comes between them—as if the symbol of both community and bodily sharing must paradoxically separate the two in much the same way as his journey to consummate their relationship in a witch's sabbath is what in fact destroys it. Thus the first few lines of the story very likely offer a kind of initial epiphany to anticipate Young Goodman Brown's more explicit encounter with the ritual of sex in the forest's clearing. The way Faith is left behind, waving from her doorway, offers complex symbolization which explains his final abandonment of her on moral grounds at the story's end.

The supposedly dangerous temptation of conjugal love is also plain in the rampant symbolism of Satan's invocation at the forest ritual:

> By the sympathy of your human hearts for *sin* ye shall *scent* out all the places—whether in church, *bedchamber*, street, field, or forest—where crime has been committed, and shall exult to behold the whole earth one *stain of guilt*, one mighty *blood spot*. Far more than this. It shall be yours to *penetrate*, in every bosom, the *deep* mystery of sin, the *fountain* of all wicked arts ..." [italics added]

Here the satanic image of a body's penetration and its flow of blood is extended even to the feminine personification of earth, of course suggesting Gaeia, the earth goodness from whom humanity and the rest of the gods originally spring. Interestingly, the specific crimes next listed by Satan suggest sex and parenthood:

> ... how hoary-bearded elders of the church have whispered wanton words to the young maids of their households; how many a woman, eager for the widow's weeds, has given her husband a drink at bedtime and left him sleep his last sleep in her bosom; how beardless youths have made haste to inherit their father's wealth; and how fair maidens—blush not, sweet ones—have dug little graves in the garden, and bidden me, the sole guest, to an infant's funeral.

In other words, if Young Goodman Brown, a "beardless youth," can identify with his father as Satan (i.e., "inherit his father's wealth"), he would have no trouble in consummating his marriage to Faith by breaking the hymen and penetrating "the fountain of all wicked arts"—the drink which would "let him sleep his last sleep in her bosom." Moreover, his infancy would be given its funeral by Faith (his own "fair maiden") in her little garden grave, an overdetermined image of the womb which suggests both the homicidal rejection of adult responsibility by means of infanticide and a regressive fear of growing up, in this case through identification with the infant corpse. Maturity is simple but fearful. Young Goodman Brown need only divert his filial loyalty from his "good" mother, now little more than a half-recognized gesture of restraint, to his "bad" mother, Goody Cloyse ("good" becomes "goody," something entirely different), a witch who has lost her broom and is willing to accept in its place the father figure's serpentine staff. It is this staff, by the way, which Satan repeatedly tries to pass on to Young Goodman Brown as if it were his rightful inheritance, his initiation to the mysteries of adult experience. Once again the symbolism is not only obvious but crucial to the meaning of the story as a whole. Young Goodman Brown's infantile dependence upon a nurturing mother must be successfully displaced to phallic identification with his father in order to benefit from the mature recognition that women are sinners too, individuals with whom sexual companionship is possible. But he cannot complete this transition, and with the result that the parent figures who encourage his efforts to do so are rejected in their personifications as Satan and "Goody Cloyse" (or "delectable cloister"), a clutching and unpleasant witch.

As in the classic Freudian explanation of the origins of homosexuality, Young Goodman Brown's inability to identify with his father is indicated by his unwillingness to accept the ritual consummation of his marriage, and this very probably results from his uncertain sense of masculine identity which arises from his close affinity to his mother.[4] It is no accident that he rejects Satan's obviously phallic staff or that the single individual who tries to dissuade him from going through with consummation is probably his cherished "good" mother. It is she who offers the only resistance to the ceremony which would ritualize his communion, and in doing so she becomes his twisted conscience, the brief visual embodiment of his regressive and infantile strivings. This distinction is important: not his father but his mother dominates his conscience (or superego), and in fact her influence preserves him from excessive intimacy with her young surrogate, his bride, who could only disrupt the unbroken bond between the two of them, mother and son, on the basis of dependency rather than mature compatibility. Because Young Goodman Brown finds it easier to identify with his mother than with his father, he is willing to relinquish his patriarchal obligations as family head and respectable member of the community. He does not become an overt homosexual—this too would be evil, even unspeakable—but his confusion is externalized and brought under control by means of a delusional experience which carries out the double displacement of denial and projection typical of paranoid logic as explained by Freud: "Not that I cannot love Faith; rather, it is she who is involved in a universal plot to destroy my soul." In this manner Young Goodman Brown's insecure sexual identification can be justified by the ever-convenient religious choice between sin and virtue which puts all others at fault, not himself. He can be protected from the discovery of his personal difficulties (as can the reader who empathizes with him) simply by rejecting these others as probable agents of hell. They are plotting against him by trying to deprive him of his virtue, and their designs can only be thwarted through his hostility and vigilance for the rest of his life, "... for his dying hour was gloom." His single night's crisis thus suggests the "acute" stage of paranoia as triggered by unacceptable conjugal demands, and when it is resolved through his relentless struggle against the universal communion of mankind, his affliction has advanced to the so-called "chronic" stage of paranoia. There is modest relief in having at least identified his enemies, if not in having defeated them or successfully dealt with his own genuine problems.

Young Goodman Brown's infantile expectations in marrying Faith are obvious when he says, "I'll cling to her skirts and follow her to heaven," much as might have been demanded of his mother. But "good" Faith reveals "bad" faith (pun intended) when she makes physical demands exceeding those of his mother, as is divulged by her plea for him to "tarry" with her because of her uncontrollable feelings: "A lone woman is troubled with such dreams and such thoughts that she's afeard of herself sometimes." By implication Young Goodman Brown has even more to fear from her than she does herself, and he must somehow find an adequate defense acceptable to his conscience, one which would enable him, true to his name, to be "good" and "man" at the same time. His story tells how this is accomplished in two clearly defined stages: first when he leaves Faith to journey into the world of shadows where her demands might be disguised as satanic ritual, and then when this ritual is abruptly terminated because it is satanic. Of course, Young Goodman Brown begs the question by making his renunciation in this manner since it is he himself who raises the issue of sin, but the laws of deduction can be comfortably ignored through the primary process reasoning of delusional intensity which is dictated by his motives. Whether fallacious or not, a doubled withdrawal sequence from his wife—into the woods and out again—is successfully manipulated to be justified by Young Goodman Brown's suspicious and hostility for the rest of his life. Later he and Faith do have children and grandchildren, but their marriage is never really consummated as a union of two kindred souls since Young Goodman Brown cannot rely upon his wife to satisfy his innermost regressive needs. The story of his revelation thus embodies and carries out the denial-projective pattern of paranoid delusions as explained by Freudian theory. There is denial because of his inability to acknowledge the problem that lies within himself, and then there is projection in the moral repudiation of others as if it were they who cause the problem because of their conspiracy to thwart his salvation. Through a sequence of discoveries which obliges this understanding, the narrative of Young Goodman Brown's life shifts from his confused early expectations to a maturity which dispels this confusion, but at the sacrifice of being dominated by gloom and the necessity of ceaseless vigilance against others. As a documentation of this transition, plot itself becomes an elaborate *coitus interruptus* required by the bizarre ethical pretension of being engaged in a unique cosmic struggle against the devil. In the nick of time Young Goodman Brown is able to withdraw from consummating his marriage, and of course for reasons of profound religious significance.

Paradoxically, Young Goodman Brown first rejects his wife's overtures in order to make his symbolic journey into the woods (often pubic in dream formation) where these overtures might be disguised to be rejected one and for all as the symbolic ritual of consummation. But his reluctant quest is symbolic of both sexual penetration and the regressive withdrawal into his mother's womb. The choice represented by his passage into the thicket is entirely ambiguous and could have anatomical reference either to his mother or wife, and, as it were, with either a comic or tragic outcome. With a comic outcome Satan could serve as an accepted father figure comparable to Prospero, Theseus, Undershaft and others in presenting the hand of his son (if not his daughter) in marriage at the forest clearing. The warning gesture of the mother would not be seen, and the forest's ritual would end with consummation and the universal harmony to be expected of Menandrine comedy, for example with the concluding marriage ceremonies of *A Midsummer Night's Dream* and *As You Like It*. With a tragic outcome, in contrast, the Oedipal love of one's mother would oblige self-destructive aggression against a father figure comparable to Laius, Claudius, etc.—in this instance by engaging in a struggle of almost Miltonic proportions against the invidious powers of the devil. A young woman such as Faith would very likely not be involved, or, if she were, she too would probably be destroyed, like Ophelia, by the almost cosmic release of Oedipal violence to be expected of tragedy. But of course neither comedy nor tragedy takes place. The story of Young Goodman Brown, notable for its brevity, displays little more magnitude than a parable or bad dream, and what does prevail is a nightmarish enactment of the psychosexual ambivalence which obliges perpetual fear and uncertainty. The apparition of his mother gives Young Goodman Brown the courage to reject marriage as the "communion of your race," so he finds himself in limbo between two ego ideals, paternal and maternal, neither of which can be exactly appropriated. There is neither identification with this father through the act of consummation nor with his mother through overt homosexual identification. He consequently finds himself in a closet he doesn't understand and hostile toward the enemy voices which can be heard on the other side of the door. His story tells how and why he makes his decision not to come out of his closet, and once his choice is made his story has for all practical purposes been brought to its conclusion. An abortive transition has been made from a bridegroom's frightened expectancy to the resounding denial of a "stern, a sad, a darkly meditative, a distrustful, if not a desperate man." Nothing is left but gloom as Young Goodman Brown tries to live out his undeclared compact with his mother and no one else, one which falls short of homosexual identification through paranoid denial.

Most of this explication is of course an elaborate reconstruction, and it must be acknowledged that there is no single passage in the story which affords a single global explanation of Young Goodman Brown's problem. However, shades of paranoia, everything fits. Everywhere the story furnishes the necessary fragments of information to be combined and interpreted by anybody who seriously intends to give it the clinical evaluation which it deserves. Typical of paranoid behavior, the story doesn't take pains to spell out its inadequacies for all to recognize, but instead almost reluctantly discloses these in thorough if piecemeal fashion in the process of dealing with them. It is our task as readers and critics to be able to recognize the overall pattern of experience which emerges organized as fiction. Literary convention might somewhat disguise the syndrome for those who insist upon treating literature as being absolutely separate from personal experience, but for the rest of us the resemblance should really be too obvious to be ignored. If a distraught young gentlemen, Y.G. Brown, were to walk into a psychiatrist's office and confide that he had recently talked to the devil disguised as his grandfather, that this same devil had tried to steal his soul in a witch's sabbath, and that he knows from the voices he heard that everybody except his mother was involved in the conspiracy, even his bride—the diagnosis, I think, would be plain: a classic case of paranoia, almost too perfect to be true except in fiction.

Again it must be insisted that this doesn't mean that Hawthorne was paranoid or even that Young Goodman Brown, his fictive creation, suffers from this disorder. Often in this paper I have diagnosed his problems as if he were a flesh and blood human being with a personality which is complex enough to be fully evaluated in psychoanalytic terms. In fact he is a fictional character, not a real person, and his personality lacks the flexibility and polydimensional complexity to be expected of real people, even the most tortured victims of paranoia. He certainly exhibits some of the symptoms of paranoia, as I think has been amply demonstrated, but these are in large part dictated by his circumstances which are imposed, after all, by the delusional requirements of his story. It is his story as a whole which enacts the paranoid syndrome, and he himself remains mostly innocent of its delusional excesses despite the extent to which his life is dominated by them. Not he but his author and sympathetic readers resort to a demonic vision in order to reject patriarchal identification, and even these don't exactly commit themselves to such a fundamental decision. The most that can be claimed would be that they make a conscious and/or unconscious use of Young Goodman Brown's example to question, if not challenge, the often oppressive demands which confront them in their own lives. It is their freedom to indulge in this kind of tentative exploration confident that its harmful consequences will be kept pretty much the burden of Young Goodman Brown. So whether he himself projects his fantasies, as maintained by Crews, he certainly exists as the projection of fantasies by others, his audience, and for this reason he cannot be held fully responsible for being paranoid. Moreover, it is to be emphasized that what Young Goodman Brown suspects might well be true in the context of his story. A devil very probably does approach him disguised as his grandfather, and he very probably does allow himself to be led to a witch's sabbath, making paranoid delusion a reality at least as far as he, a fictional character, is concerned. Anybody who is really approached by the devil, as is not uncommon in literature, cannot be diagnosed as being psychotic for thinking so. What he sees he sees, and he must deal with this as best he can under the circumstances. He might live in a paranoid reality, but as a figment of this reality he can hardly be diagnosed as having been its author.[5] The victim of the imagination of others, he is ultimately innocent of the problems which have been bestowed upon him. This is of course the typical complaint of the paranoid individual, but in the case of a fictional character such as Young Goodman Brown it happens to be true, and he himself at least has no complaints about his mistreatment at the hands of his readers.

Does this mean that it is primarily Hawthorne and his readers who must be charged with being paranoid? Not necessarily. These too escape the diagnosis, but for entirely different reasons. To enjoy a work of fiction which manifests paranoid tendencies does not mean that readers and authors are paranoid or even pre-paranoid, for it is possible to benefit from this cathartic use of fiction without otherwise resorting to paranoia in the conduct of one's affairs. Disbelief can be suspended by readers without giving any credence whatsoever to the delusions they might temporarily entertain while engrossed in reading a story. The paranoid syndrome can be utilized on a provisional and "literary" basis, and with a pleasure and flexibility not to be enjoyed by the genuine victim of paranoia. Paranoia can be "tried on" for the occasion, and with the total confidence that it can just as easily be discarded once it has made its accounting of the eternal struggle between good and evil, happiness and despair, etc. To a certain extent it does provide the same battery of defenses to the reader as it does to the genuine paranoid individual, but with this important difference: the reader can always set it aside with the fullest confidence that it is fiction and that his life needn't be dominated by this fiction. Consequently, neither Hawthorne nor his readers, nor in fact his characters, are to be automatically diagnosed as being paranoid, not even for a story laden with as many paranoid symptoms as can be found in "Young Goodman Brown." As indicated earlier, what obviously *can* be described as being paranoid is simply the overall action of the story which pits characters against their circumstances in a paranoid fashion, i.e. in such a manner as to cause the paranoid response. It is the story itself which serves as a kind of free-floating multi-purpose delusional system, temporary and artificial, one in which a great variety of personal problems can be brought to allopathic focus upon an intense conflict against hostile forces of one sort or another. By exaggerating this conflict and then bringing it to its resolution, a story such as "Young Goodman Brown" shares the same purpose as the paranoid delusion in its reduction of anxiety levels, but unlike the paranoid delusion it makes itself accessible to balanced and healthy vicarious involvement. Such a story is organized in the same manner as the paranoid delusion, but for a larger audience and with the benign and "normal" intention of bringing confrontation to its satisfactory resolution. Like Pirandello's six characters in search of an author, it offers itself as an intact delusional system in search of whatever audience might find temporary pleasure in its manipulation of experience—unified, intensified, and, as it were, both purposeful and ethically determined.

The final and perhaps the most interesting question is whether the paranoid dynamics of "Young Goodman Brown" are peculiar to this single story or can be found elsewhere in literature. To what extent, if any, can "Young Goodman Brown" be taken as a paradigm of literary experience in general? Can it be used as a model to help explain and understand other works of fiction? And, more specifically, does it have any special relevance to the central tradition of American fiction? There doesn't seem to be any problem in making such a comparison with the rest of Hawthorne's works, since the Oedipal interpretations offered by Crews, Simon Lesser and others can easily be extended to take into account the paranoid traits which are obsessively reenacted from the stories of Ethan Brand and Rappacini to those of Hester and Zenobia. The vision of Hawthorne's fiction has enough guilt-ridden consistency (described by Crews as "underlying sameness") to make such an extension pretty much an exercise in belaboring the obvious.

Nor does there seem to be any difficulty in finding parallels with the mature fiction of Melville, especially *Moby Dick*, which was both written under Hawthorne's influence and dedicated to him. In fact, there are bizarre resemblances and implied interactions which can and ought to be explored in greater depth in order to demonstrate the full precariousness of Young Goodman Brown's desperate choice in life. As Leslie Fiedler has amply demonstrated, *Moby Dick* displays considerable evidence of latent homosexual tendencies, suggesting that it exceeds Hawthorne's fiction in its resistance to patriarchal identification, and with hostility intense enough to be brought to its culmination in tragic self-destruction. Ahab's obsessive pursuit of Moby Dick leads to his doubly phallic destruction impaled to it wherever it penetrates the seas. More fortunate is Ishmael, who very probably survives because he can lovingly handle sperm (i.e. the flesh of whale) and consummate his brotherhood with Queequeg to deserve the coffin which symbolically buoys him to the surface when the Pequod is drawn into its thalassic vortex of destruction. If Melville's symbolism has enough schematic consistency for the ocean to symbolize the womb and Moby Dick the phallus, denizen of the womb, Ahab's obsession forces his self-sacrifice to heterosexual demands—exactly the martyrdom repugnant to Young Goodman Brown. In contrast, Ishmael, like Young Goodman Brown, is repelled by this fate—and in fact, one step better, he can reject it by acknowledging the homosexual affinities which presumably afford him the possibility of salvation. Melville thus seems to resolve Young Goodman Brown's paranoid ambivalence through the polar distinction between these two figures, Ahab and Ishmael, whose respective fates demonstrate the inverted *carpe diem* theme that homophobic repression can only bear self-destructive consequences. If a novel could offer itself as an exemplum to a short-story character, the message of *Moby Dick* to Young Goodman Brown would very probably be that he remove himself from his closet by similarly purging himself of the potentially tragic homophobic impediments which still clutter his imagination. But of course such a recommendation would be particularly repulsive to Young Goodman Brown, even more so than the witch's sabbath he declines.

It is obvious that Melville identifies with Ishmael (he begins *Moby Dick* by telling the reader, "Call me Ishmael"), and, interestingly enough, there is a close resemblance between Ahab and Hawthorne as described by Melville in his correspondence with Hawthorne and in his laudatory review "Hawthorne and his Mosses," where his praise is clearly suggestive of the portrait of Ahab in Chapter XVI. Melville likewise describes Hawthorne in one of his letters with almost exactly the same words as he uses to describe Ahab: "There is a grand truth about Nathaniel Hawthorne. He says No! in thunder; but the devil himself cannot make him say yes." This, we recall, is also suggestive of Young Goodman Brown's rejection of Satan at the forest ceremony. In another of his letters to Hawthorne, Melville also consecrates his novel with Ahab's baptism of the harpoon in the name of the devil, " Ego no baptizo te in nomine patris, sed in nomine diaboli!" But in doing so he truncates his sentence, "This is the book's motto (the secret one), Ego non baptiso te in nomine—but make out the rest for yourself," suggesting that Hawthorne, like Ahab (and Young Goodman Brown too), could be expected to know the temptations of the devil. In "Hawthorne and his Mosses" Melville even makes a direct comparison between Hawthorne and "Young Goodman Brown" by paraphrasing one of its sentences, "It is yours to penetrate in every bosom the deep mystery of sin."[7] But of course the ability to make such a penetration does not mean it is exercised, so the ambiguity of "penetrate" (either to "perceive" or "thrust into") puts Hawthorne in the same difficult circumstances as Young Goodman Brown, torn between the examples of Ahab and Ishmael. If there is any resemblance at all between Hawthorne and Ahab, or between Ahab and Young Goodman Brown, it might indeed result from comparable biographical and autobiographical intentions (contrary to my earlier precautions in this paper), but Hawthorne would have been far less fervid in his satanic obsession than Ahab—much closer, in fact, to the example he himself proposed in Young Goodman Brown, and even here the resemblance was probably slight. Melville's implied equation nevertheless stands. If Ishmael could have stepped across the boundaries of fiction to suggest that Young Goodman Brown might "tarry" with him, the latter could be expected to have become instantly transmogrified into another Captain Ahab, peg leg and all. "No, in thunder," he too would have cried, but without plunging to tragic destruction into his own ocean's vortex, mother of life itself. Nor could he even have drunk the more modest glass of poison suggested by Hawthorne's Satan. It was his fate to remain torn between the examples of Ahab and Ishmael, unable to deal with the choice except as a devilish temptation. Extravagant these parallels might seem, but they are too persistent to be overlooked.

What relevance is there beyond Melville of the paranoid example offered by Young Goodman Brown to the continuity of the American literacy imagination? Are there any other connections besides this one brief and remarkable instance of personal friendship which seems to have been documented and thereby terminated through the agency of fiction? More, I think, than might be immediately recognized, for Young Goodman Brown epitomizes our national rejection of patriarchal responsibility by means of a regressive dedication to frontier conflict which has been insightfully explored by Fiedler and others in their studies of American fiction. Like Young

Goodman Brown, the typical frontier hero offers the reader his escape from domestic priorities through a wilderness quest in which Oedipal difficulties can be projected as if these were an external crisis to be brought to its satisfactory resolution. Young Goodman Brown is perhaps unique as a "negative" example since he confronts the wilderness just once, and very briefly, before returning home to the obligations he must fulfill but cannot entirely accept. As opposed to the seasoned frontiersman, he makes what amounts to a one-night stand, and the farthest he penetrates (both bodily and conceptually) is the clearing where ritual hell-fire provides the turning point in his life. For these others much longer journeys can be undertaken precisely because their Oedipal crisis has been better disguised, more effectively rendered as an issue of frontier survival. As a result, story becomes more optimistic as a repetitive-compulsive pursuit of victory against enemies, personal weakness, and a variety of bigger forces to be encountered under western skies. Moreover, the charming but vacuous integrity of the frontiersman can be repeatedly proved as he challenges and extends the unique boundaries of our national consciousness exactly as predicted by Frederick Jackson Turner, if in strictly psychosexual terms with the fruits of emotional paucity absorbed through paranoid frontier victory. In popular culture this frontiersman later becomes the detective whose innocent sophistication at last prevails against sinister schemes to make a "fall guy" of him, then an equally innocent Joe Citizen who is caught in the struggle against communism, international conspiracy, or even a berserk CIA, but who is likewise protected from destruction by his almost regressive integrity. Whatever his persona, he resembles Young Goodman Brown in being saved by his innocence from destructive powers he cannot fully understand— powers which in fact embody and epitomize the latent tendencies his readers must reject in themselves through their compensatory dedication to virtue, justice, and cosmic righteousness.

     If such a hero seems to be more capable of spectacular accomplishments than Young Goodman Brown, he nevertheless suffers from the same deficiency in self-awareness and personal integration. Equally important, he almost inevitably falls victim to the same inability to form mature emotional attachments with women, and with little talent for coping with this inadequacy except through profligacy or Platonic admiration—or, in extreme cases, through his sublimation of sexual confusion into a compensatory dedication to violence. This is true of Natty Bummpo, Huck Finn, and all the rest of the pantheon of American heroes in both the high and low media—even Gatsby and Jake Barnes, Rabbit Angstrom and Augie March, Benny Profane and Humbert Humbert. Like Young Goodman Brown, each seems to be dominated by the regressive search for a Faith too elusive to be put (or kept) on her pedestal. Without skirts to cling to or anybody to follow to heaven, they can only pursue an impotent wilderness quest whose unconscious intentions cannot possibly be accomplished, let alone recognized. Excitement usurps the responsibility incurred by patriarchal identification, a substitution that seems entirely justified by the unhappy example of Young Goodman Brown. The emotional deadlock is perhaps broken which reduces Hawthorne's to chronic anger and suspicion, but vestigial paranoid defenses do remain which are just as much an avoidance of Satan's blood covenant. For this reason Young Goodman Brown should be recognized (at least by psycho-analytic critics) as perhaps the most remarkable of the "negative" archetypes which define the American vision. Hundreds of years before its mythic frontier finally closes in upon itself, he tests its perimeter, judges possibilities, and finds it a "dream of evil omen," one which must bring him to his dying hour a distrustful, if not a desperate man.

NOTES

1. The paranoid organization of narrative structure is more thoroughly discussed in my articles, "Defense of the Homophobic Imagination," *College English*, vol. 37, no. 1 (Sept., 1975), pp. 62–67a, and "The Dialectics of Paranoid Form," *Genre*, 11 (spring, 1978), pp. 131–157. A roughly comparable application to poetry is made in my earlier article, "Up against the 'Mending Wall': The Psychoanalysis of a Poem by Frost," *College English*, vol. 34, no. 7 (April, 1973), pp. 934–951.

2. Norman Cameron, "The Paranoid Pseudo-Community," *American Journal of Sociology*, 49:32, 1943; "The Paranoid Pseudo-Community Revisited," *American Journal of Sociology*, 64:52, 1959. Also useful as introductory references are Norman Cameron's "Paranoid Conditions and Paranoia," in *American Handbook of Psychiatry*, ed. by Silvano Arieti, vol. I (New York, 1959), pp. 508–539; and *The Paranoid*, by David Swanson, Philip Bohnert, and Jackson Smith (Boston, 1970).

3. *The Sins of the Fathers: Hawthorne's Psychological Themes* (Oxford, 1966), pp. 98–106.

4. Young Goodman Brown's characterization effectively meshes Freud's explanation of homosexuality in *Leonardo da Vinci: A Psychosexual Study of an Infantile Reminiscence* and his explanation of paranoia as repressed homosexuality in his study of Schreber, *Psycho-analytic Notes on an Autobiographical Account of a Case of Paranoia (Dementia Paranoides)*. Seldom is the connection quite so plain either in fiction or the personality of genuine victims of paranoia.

5. It would be tempting to suggest that Young Goodman Brown's most natural response to his difficulties would have been to try his hand at fiction, concocting the life and works of Nathaniel Hawthorne.

6. Leslie Fiedler, *Love and Death in the American Novel* (New York, 1960, 1966), pp. 369–388.

7. Herman Melville, "Hawthorne and his Mosses, by a Virginian Spending a July in Vermont," *Literary World*, August 17. August 24, 1850—in *Billy Budd and Other Prose Pieces by Herman Melville*, ed. by Raymond W. Weaver, from *The Works of Herman Melville* (London, 1924), vol. XIII, p. 140. Also ref. Merrell R. Davis and William H. Gilman, *The Letters of Herman Melville* (New Haven, 1960), pp. 124, 125, 133, 140, etc.

DAVID BROMWICH

The American Psychosis

If you have ever looked into the psychologists who wrote a generation before Freud, you will know that psychosis did not always mean a state of clinical derangement. In the writings of William James and others, it often denoted an intense or a crystallized mood, a mental state that defines a character or that just takes hold of the mind for a time. The quality of this mood or state or moral cocoon is to be impervious and self-contained. That is the connection with our later meaning. I cannot remember where I found the phrase "the American psychosis"—probably in the work of a social critic of the twenties or thirties. The writer, whoever it was, left a certain mystery about the term. As my examples will show, I use it here to describe an idealism that I take to be primitive and incorrigible. D.H. Lawrence spoke with precision on the subject when he said that the hero of Cooper's frontier novels was "hard, isolate, stoic, and a killer." This is a famous judgment now, usually read with a narrower sense than Lawrence intended. But he had another shot at the analysis of Americans in *St. Mawr*, and another in the essay that appears as his introduction to Edward Dahlberg's novel *Bottom Dogs*. It is the last of these pieces that interests me. Other people must have seen what he saw there, but nobody else has put it into words.

What Lawrence finds ingrained in Americans is something life-hardened, yet untouchable by life. Their experience does not finally get to

From *Raritan* 21, no. 4 (Spring 2002). © 2002 by *Raritan: A Quarterly Review*.

them. This is true not only of people who have had the luck to know the rewards of ego; it is also true in America, most surprisingly, of the very young and the very poor. Go a little under the surface, says Lawrence, and "you begin to see how terrible and brutal is the mass of failure that nourishes the roots of the gigantic tree of dollars." America has produced a sparse and almost totally neglected pioneer literature that is a chronicle of failures. It tells of "hard first-comers" who "fought like devils against their difficulties" but who "have been defeated, broken, their efforts and their amazing hard work lost, as it were, on the face of the wilderness." Americans, says Lawrence, will only hear these reports in small and sentimental doses, because, "they know too well the grimness of it, the savage fight and the savage failure which broke the back of the country but also broke something in the human soul. The spirit and the will survived: but something in the soul perished: the softness, the floweriness, the natural tenderness." This breaking of the heart of a generation, in every pioneer generation, brought a peculiar and detached result. "The will-to-success and the will-to-produce became clean and indomitable once the sympathetic heart was broken." Thus was secreted in the American mind a belief so profound it need never be articulated. "It is not God's business to be good and kind…. God's business is to be indomitable. And man's business is essentially the same."

Familiarity with people and "friendliness"—an American word for an American idea—are encouraged and grow easier in the after-years of the frontier. But Lawrence thinks that these are surface effects.

> Of course the white American believes that man should behave in a kind and benevolent manner. But this is a social belief and a social gesture, rather than an individual flow. The flow from the heart, the warmth of fellow-feeling which has animated Europe and been the best of her humanity, individual, spontaneous, flowing in thousands of little passionate currents often conflicting, this seems unable to persists on the American soil. Instead you get the social creed of benevolence and uniformity, a mass *will*, and an inward individual retraction, an isolation, an amorphous separateness like grains of sand, each grain isolated upon its own will, its own indomitableness, its own implacability, its own unyielding, yet heaped together with all the other grains.

The mass of individuals that Lawrence is talking about have the property of being each finished, each constructed to shut things out and reduce consciousness to a necessary minimum beyond the needs of the self.

This imperviousness is a human possibility that first took root in

America. It has not flourished anywhere else; maybe it cannot be exported—though the global market presumes it is the form of morale that people would choose, if they could choose, everywhere. Anyway the people who live in the antinomian way I am speaking of, the larger and the smaller grains of sand, agree in supposing that the self is real and society a bondage. Jonathan Swift could think he was describing an admirable social capacity when he devoted a sermon to "mutual subjection." None of these American believers would grasp his point. The only relevant mutual subjection, for them, is between consciousness and itself or between an isolated man and God. This assertion and this negation mark a normal self-imagining only for Americans. Still, how can it seem warped or perverse when it thrives so heartily? Self-subjection and mutual resistance are the native turn given to the older virtues of self-sufficiency and fortitude.

Like Lawrence, I am talking mainly about white people. Or, rather, initially them. But the ways in which the mood was transmitted to European immigrants will be plain to anyone who has used the opportunity to observe America for more than office space. Many later immigrants and many black Americans have absorbed it through the theology of money. I have a word to say at the end about money. I have nothing to say about the "ideology of the nation," which the field of American Studies, for a generation now, has treated as the master clue to the American idea of the self. This seems to me an intellectualist fallacy, but it is pointless to look for a knockdown argument on either side, and where you come out probably depends on intuition and prejudice. Scholars like Sacvan Bercovitch, who find traces everywhere in American thought and writing of a national ideology, aim to convey a sentiment of deep futility about the American project. They have it sewn up—and the sense of a finished interpretation leaves very little room for wonder, for admiration, or even for salutary fear. The state of mind I am speaking of has the quality of accident not design, and there is reason to believe that it made the nation far more that the nation made it.

* * *

The leading exhibit of course is Emerson's "Self-Reliance"—a work so definitive of the psychosis that it hardly matters who read the essay, who heard reports of it, and who assimilated the doctrine through its lay-apostles among popular lecturers and the authors of self-help tracts. But to realize the strange compactness of Emerson's teaching, you have to go back before him to the thinkers who acted as his ultimate sponsors. These were, as Perry Miller saw, the radical Separatists who broke away from the Congregationalism of Massachusetts Bay Colony in the early seventeenth century. The church of those first New Englanders was nonseparating: that is, it chose not to defy the Church of England openly, and aimed otherwise to hold itself together in a wilderness, where unity of some sort was a condition of survival. For the sake of survival too, members of the colony would eventually relax the demand for a conversion in each believer, and would adopt the expedient custom of baptizing every adult who merely assented to the faith. Yet these nonseparating Congregationalists had all but nominally separated from the Church of England. Those in England who most nearly correspond to them would come to be called Independents: a name that cannot mislead. Meanwhile, those destined to be the peculiar heroes of the colony, the purifiers of conscience who threw the community back upon first principles, were themselves, once more, separatists.

Everyone has a rough idea of this atmosphere of belief. Let me sharpen the impression by quoting some lines from a modern poet, John Brooks Wheelwright. Politically, Wheelwright was a Trotskyist of the thirties, and aesthetically a separatist of the invisible avant-garde. "Bread-Word Giver" (dedicated to "John, Unborn") is meant to be chanted as a prayer for strength and sustenance; and it begins by invoking the poet's ancestor John Wheelwright, one of the most contentious, eloquent, and disturbing preachers in the colony's first generation.

> John, founder of towns,—dweller in none;
> Wheelwright, schismatic,—schismatic from schismatics;
> friend of great men whom these great feared greatly;
> Saint, whose name and business I bear with me;
> rebel New England's rebel against dominion;
> who made bread-giving words for bread-makers;
> whose blood floods me with purgatorial fire;
> I, and my unliving son, adjure you:
> keep us alive with your ghostly disputation
> make our renunciation of dominion
> mark not the escape, but the permanent of rebellion.

John Wheelwright, the ancestor, was the brother-in-law of Anne Hutchinson, who would be tried as an Antinomian by the General Court of the colony and expelled when she claimed as the source of her doctrine *immediate revelation from God*. John Wheelwright was one of only two preachers whom Mrs. Hutchinson acknowledged to be "under a covenant of grace," that is, justified to God, as distinct from the mass of His servants "under a covenant of works," who were sanctified by men only and preoccupied with the forms of worldly preparation. The small band of separatists were fractious, and their influence worked against the perpetuation of the society. Some men in Boston, for example, had refused to fight against the Pequods because their chaplain, John Wilson, was declared to be under a covenant of works. To be thus preoccupied by works, to hope illicitly by a record of positive deeds to improve one's odds at heaven, was a version of an older heresy that the Puritans knew as Arminianism; and nobody ever denounced that heresy more stirringly than Wheelwright, who rose once at the end of another minister's sermon to warn against the seeming goodness of those who trust their standing in the church as evidence of justification. "The more holy they are," said Wheelwright, "the greater enemies they are to Christ.

Edmund Morgan, whose history of the colony, *The Puritan Dilemma*, I have been drawing on, says that Wheelwright meant those words figuratively. But Morgan's book shows that to refuse such testimony from the inspired among the community of saints always looked like defending the lukewarm, while to follow the schismatic inspiration of Wheelwright and Hutchinson would have been fatal to the colony as a political entity. This was the constant though hidden version of the Puritan dilemma experienced by such believers: not only the necessity of both living for God and living in the world, but the impossibility of rejecting those who reject the world without thereby endangering the germ of what is most godlike in yourself. The leading doctrine of Anne Hutchinson, namely that "the person of the Holy Ghost dwells in a justified person," meant that the outward sanctification of the church member offered no clue whatever to his or her state of inward justification. It also meant that any interposition of ministerial helps, or any other external guide to conduct, was potentially a trespass against the indwelling spirit of God in those who were truly saved. Hutchison crossed the line that separated the doctrinally controversial from the politically intolerable—and thereby forsook command of a strong countertendency within the colony—only when she asserted under questioning by the court that she knew it was God who urged her to act as she did. She knew this not, she said, by a personal interpretation of the Bible, which would have been allowed, but rather as Abraham had known that it was God who urged him to offer his son—"By an immediate revelation.... By the voice of his own spirit to my soul."

Mrs. Hutchinson's excommunication in March 1637 was not the first and would not be the last such result of the contest between Puritan expedience regarding the world and the soul's imperative of self-justification. Scarcely a year before, the greatest of the separatists, Roger Williams, had passed from Salem and Plymouth to Narragansett Bay, where he would found the new colony of Rhode Island. An entirely coherent progress of convictions led Williams to declare his break. Soon after arriving in Boston in 1631, he avowed that he could not join in worship with those who, having founded a new Congregational church, would not repent their former impurity in having had communion with the churches in England. Unless they would change and repent, he could never foresee joining them. Williams declined to officiate during the absence of another minister of Boston ("I durst not officiate to an unseparated people, as upon examination and conference I found them to be"), and he went on to Salem, where again a certain native sweetness of temper won him a following, so that he was offered a ministry. The offer was withdrawn after reconsideration of his doctrines, and he moved once more to Plymouth, where it is reported that he objected to the application to the unregenerate of the name "Goodman"; and where, as Morgan impartially says, he "raised the question whether the colonists had any right to the land they occupied." Williams thought the land belonged to the Indians. The accepted legal understanding, namely that the Massachusetts Bay Company had acquired the land by a patent from the king, did not impress him. The presumption that the king had the power to make such a grant Williams called "a solemn public lie."

And so his fortunes turned, as he wished them to turn, against the worldly success that his attainments and character had made available to him. In April 1635 he was brought before the colony's court of assistants for his refusal to take on oath of loyalty against the enemies of the colony. The very word *oath*, like the ceremony itself, betokened a mixing of the act of worship with affairs of state, and it was Williams's firm conviction that government had no authority to encroach on matters of belief, any more than believers could with impunity transfer the objects of their interest from conscience to dominion. In the end he took the advice of his friend John Winthrop, and fled before he could be arrested; he would write soon after of Winthrop, in the hope of gaining his companionship: "Abstract yourselfe with a holy violence from the Dung Heape of this Earth." The followers who came with him to Providence were soon rebaptized, but Williams was already losing his assurance that there could be, in Morgan's words again, "a proper church at all until God raised up some new apostolic power." He felt at last that he could have communion only with his wife, and passed to the final implications of his own position when, denying the state all authority over private belief, he recognized that churches themselves, being placed in the world, were by that fact rendered irremediably impure.

Obedient to this logic, as John Winthrop observed of Williams drily, "having, a little before, refused communion with all, save his own wife, now he would preach and pray with all comers." Yet Winthrop's comment speaks in the voice of a worldly irony and from a point of view informed by the necessity of worldly compromise, whereas the ideals of Puritanism had been unworldly from the first. The question, even before departure from England, had been whether one could somehow reduce to a practice a principled refusal of accommodation. How far, given the need of political as well as ecclesiastical authority, should one "render unto Caesar the things which are Caesar's"? There is no single answer to this question that both preserves the integrity of conscience and can serve as an earnest of social stability among neighbors. Read in this light, Williams's stance and his transformation have a consistency denied to Winthrop. Of the two great men, the preserver of a society and the discoverer of a conscience to which all society is an encroachment, it is the latter who vividly exemplifies the American psychosis. Winthrop helped America to become a live option. He helped indeed to preserve it against dangers like Williams himself. But America did not have to be invented for his sake.

* * *

The conversion of private experience to general amenability comes always in America at the cost of an original vigor of separatism. On the other hand, the germ of separatism is compelled again and again, in order to refresh and prove its faith, to withdraw from a deep to a still deeper solitude. As for the tolerance that the separatist may concede by a tactical submission to authority, this seems a way of saying that in pragmatic terms the claims of all are equally real because they are equally unreal. What could be the grounds for Williams's refusing to worship with anyone, once he had seen that he could only worship in himself? This would be the advice of Emerson too, in his essay "Montaigne; or, the Skeptic": "Let us treat the men and women well; treat them as if they were real; perhaps they are." But is that all? To the ear of a secular observer of morals, say a reader familiar with Jane Austen, George Eliot, and other nineteenth-century writers famous for treating the men and women well, the equability of Emerson's statement is wild, wild to the point of hilarity, and not least for the air of unassuming kindliness with which the injunction is uttered. Can it be so hedged a bet that the men and women *will* turn out to be real? But Emerson is speaking the sober truth of a "schismatic from schismatics." More than this, in sincerity, he cannot say.

There is little difference between what Anne Hutchinson meant by *soul* and what Emerson will come to mean by *self*. The latter word is charged with similar implications in a changed climate of belief; one needs to bear this in mind in order to avoid some common mistakes about Emerson's essay "Self-Reliance." If you fail to see, at the bottom of this "self," the spirit of God addressing the enraptured soul, you are liable to exaggerate his kinship with an optimistic and property-loving individualist like Henry Ford. The puzzle about the great essay is that it does initially seem addressed to healthy young democratic citizens, as a recipe for getting along without too much chafing insincerity. Yet the self that Emerson describes is not in the smallest degree a social creature. Its abiding sense of identity comes from awareness of its difference from others. But that is too mild a paraphrase: the self portrayed in "Self-Reliance" subsists by virtue of its defection from society. I am permitted to assume obligations as the lightest of burdens only after I have recognized that they can do nothing for me. They cannot even do much harm.

Emerson has a word for the process of becoming certain that society does not participate in conscience. He calls it "absolution." The self is the entity that gives and receives absolution.

> Absolve you to yourself, and you shall have the suffrage of the world. I remember an answer which when quite young I was prompted to make to a valued adviser, who was wont to importune me with the dear old doctrines of the church. On my saying, "What have I to do with the sacredness of traditions, if I live wholly from within?" my friend suggested,—"But these impulses may be from below, not from above." I replied, "They do not seem to me to be such; but if I am the Devil's child, I will live then from the Devil." No law can be sacred to me but that of my nature. Good and bad are but names very readily transferable to that or this; the only right is what is after my constitution; the only wrong what is against it. A man is to carry himself in the presence of all opposition, as if everything were titular and ephemeral but he.

The doctrine is religious in one important sense. It is concerned with, and wants to change our minds about, the nature of first and final things. That the phrase *absolve you to yourself* is no casual paradox may be judged by the antinomian sentiment that Emerson soon after candidly affirms. "If I am the Devil's child, I will live then from the Devil."

Enlightenment polemicists against institutional religion would never have ventured such an assertion. The rational doubts they did express, they would shelter rhetorically by placing them in the mouth of a friend, a professed skeptic, or an "infidel." Emerson, by contrast, claims the words for himself as a child or as a young man. It will be part of the teaching of "Self-Reliance" that the child is wiser and stronger than the man precisely because he is more self-willed. About the child in general, and especially the boy-child, Emerson says admiringly "you must court him; he does not court you. But the man is as it were clapped into jail by his consciousness. As soon as he has once acted or spoken with eclat he is a committed man, watched by the sympathy or the hatred of hundreds, whose affections must now enter into his account." Evidently, the sympathy of others is as much to be shunned as their hatred. It, too, becomes an accessory to yourself, which you may easily and falsely reckon part of yourself; and by thus falling in with other people's opinion, unavoidably you enter those people into your "account"—a kind of moral bookkeeping that is death to conscience. In this way you commence to treat yourself as property and yourself as the proprietor: the sort of inert property that Emerson deplored as a dead weight on society. But there follows a sharper provocation. Emerson goes on to deride philanthropy—that benign and regular expression of a covenant of works, the pride of New England's seventh generation—as nothing but canting hypocrisy. The cheat of philanthropy is that it cements a passive relationship between oneself and one's acts. It corrupts all the more spontaneous affections.

Not only in this essay but in his Divinity School Address and elsewhere, Emerson goes out of his way to associate his own teaching with that of Jesus. "I shun father and mother," he says, "and wife and brother when my genius calls me." The relevant text is Matt. 10:34–38, after Jesus' raising of the dead and curing of the blind: "Think not that I am come to send peace on earth; I came not to send peace, but a sword. For I am come to set a man at variance against his father, and the daughter against her mother, and the daughter in law against her mother in law. And a man's foes shall be they of his own household. He that loveth father or mother more than me is not worthy of me: and he that loveth son or daughter more than me is not worthy of me. And he that taketh not his cross, and followeth after me, is not worthy of me." This is meant to shape our response to the apparently trite and unremarkable statement that "the only right is what is after my constitution; the only wrong what is against it." Emerson means the constitution of his own nature, of which his physical illness and health are a fair index. But he also means the constitution of his faith, which has its own communion of one, with a reflex understanding of absolution. May not the same test then be applied to state and society? One always has the right to appeal from a political to a personal constitution. History and politics, Emerson says, are merely extensions of this singular and exclusive principle of the self. "An institution is the lengthened shadow of one man…and all history resolves itself very easily into the biography of a few stout and earnest persons."

Where Roger Williams and Anne Hutchinson had set themselves

against all acquiescence in other people's doctrines, Emerson makes it clear that his enemy is fashion, and perhaps above all the currency of political and morel *opinions*. In this, he speaks as a man of the nineteenth century. At the same time he is translating to a later idiom an inveterate motive of suspicion. The danger once lay in a servile obedience to theological precepts, a docility not easily to be distinguished from fear of one's neighbors; now, the menace comes instead from a timid identification with the mass of people, which may extend to a craving for uniformity. By means of such unconscious and external identification, people are encouraged actually to feel better about themselves from knowing that a great many others feel the way they do. Against the tranquilizing faith of this settlement, Emerson directs all the eloquence of his power of hatred ("the doctrine of hatred must be preached, as the counteraction of the doctrine of love, when that pules and whines"). So he urges the upright man's "conviction that envy is ignorance; that imitation is suicide; that he must take himself for better or worse as his portion ... We but half express ourselves, and are ashamed of that divine idea which each of us represents." He regrets even the necessity of using language—a medium of expression that, just because it is shared, conforms one person's meaning with another's simply as the price of being understood. We but half express ourselves, but we do in this way, at least, impress some meaning on our hearers. Emerson's sorrow at the pervasiveness of half-expression has something of the programmatic inutility of all consistent idealism. Yet a psychological perception informs his judgment. We come to be wrongly ashamed of something unexpressed in ourselves when we are taught to value in ourselves chiefly the part that is well understood.

The self-reliance of Emerson hates the very idea of utility, as it hates every demand on behalf of the common good. Accordingly, the essay concentrates some of its energy into an attack on the realist premise that society is prior to the individual. "Society is a wave," begins a passage in a mock-clinical idiom that Emerson could not always keep under control, though here he does. "Its unity is only phenomenal. The persons who make up a nation today, next year die, and their experience dies with them." These neutral-sounding axioms carry the afterglow of a blast earlier in the essay, where Emerson has deployed his favorite mode of paradox to invert the usual Whig defense of compromise for the public good.

> Society everywhere is in conspiracy against the manhood of every one of its members. Society is a joint-stock company, in which the members agree, for the better securing of his bread to each shareholder, to surrender the liberty and culture of the eater.

This reverses the classical fable of the revolt of the organs of the body against the head. The organs are wrong not because the head should be obeyed but because there should be no body at all.

"The virtue most in request is conformity." Well, but society only exists (it might be said) to achieve a decent conformity of parts in a total design. This much would not have been denied by republican theorists like Milton and Harrington, whose stock among American readers was always high. Emerson, however, is denying that there can ever be a gain for the soul in the barter of mutual advantage that is the reason-for-being of organized society. He will say unforgettably about those who define themselves by this working of an artful prudence against the ends of character, "Their every truth is not quite true. Their two is not the real two, their four is not the real four; so that every word they say chagrins us and we know not where to begin to set them right." *Chagrins us,* because we see in ourselves the traces of a conformity that, if we did not feel the shame of it acutely enough, would land us in the position of those weak and wasted souls, and how plausibly then we might arrive at arguments explaining our two which is not the real two. The subject of this essay on self-reliance has turned out to be the dignity of separatism.

It is worth pausing a moment longer at the anti-Whig undercurrent of "Self-Reliance," not only because its details are clearly accented and yet easy to miss the drift of, but also because the whole performance says something about Emerson's broader attitude toward politics. At least until 1850, when Daniel Webster threw all his weight behind the sectional compromise that contained the Fugitive Slave Act, Emerson was himself a sympathizer with the Whig party and a strong admirer of Webster in particular. Webster was a pure Whig, if such a thing is possible, Emerson a very impure one, but both would have traced their lineage to Burke, and one may gauge how far Emerson's morality runs ahead of his politics by comparing some well-known sentences from Burke's *Reflections on the Revolution in France* with the answers to them in "Self-Reliance." Emerson's words appear below in italics:

Our political system is placed in a just correspondence and symmetry with the order of the world and with the mode of existence decreed to a permanent body composed of transitory parts, wherein, by the disposition of a stupendous wisdom, molding together the great mysterious incorporation of the human race, the whole, at one time is never old or middle-aged or young, but, in a condition of unchangeable constancy, moves on through the various tenor of perpetual decay, fall, renovation, and progression. *Society is a wave.... Its unity is only phenomenal. The persons who make up a nation today, next year die, and their experience dies with them.*

One of the first motives to civil society, and which becomes one of its fundamental rules, is that no man should be judge in his own cause. *Absolve you to yourself, and you shall have the suffrage of the world.* He abdicates all right to be his own governor. He inclusively, in a great measure, abandons the right of self-defense, the first law of nature. Men cannot enjoy the rights of an uncivil and of a civil state together. That he may obtain justice, he gives up the right of determining what it is in points most essential to him. That he may secure some liberty, he makes a surrender in trust of the whole of it. *Society is joint-stock company, in which the members agree, for the better securing of his bread to each shareholder, to surrender the liberty and culture of the eater.*

Notice that Emerson point by point confronts the case for a liberty founded on restraint and a nature given plasticity by the slow accretions of habit. If the public trust is to be replaced by self-trust, then man must become his own governor. He *ought* to be the judge in his own cause and will rightly view any proposed surrender of his liberty as a conspiracy against body and soul.

In order to recover an idea of self-reliance severe enough to have pleased the first-generation Separatists, it was necessary for Emerson to establish not just the lesser reality but the unreality of society. In front of every advantage of the social state, which Burke had greeted as a softening of manners and an amelioration of life, Emerson therefore simply puts a minus sign. He transfers all the sociable virtues into the column of vices for the self. The real test of his argument comes in what he has to say about the calculable benefits to be derived from common enterprises. These may be thought of broadly as the benefits of promise-keeping, also a familiar topic in political thought. Locke, who cast doubt on the *"double conformity"* of words and things by means of ideas, treated the good word of the promise-maker as a uniquely apt index of personal eligibility for citizenship. Promises are secured by conscience—a judge, according to Locke, incapable of acting selfishly. Indeed, it is partly for the sake of assuring sincere promises that one must refrain from tampering with the privacy of conscience. It followed for Locke that a regime of liberty and toleration was practically suitable to a race of reasonable and promise-keeping beings. It likewise followed that people such as Catholics, unable to secure their promises with a conscience separate from the church hierarchy, were properly to be excluded from religious toleration. Emerson was well aware of this history of disputation, which laid the groundwork for the creation of the political rights of individuals under the American Constitution. And yet, speaking again for "*my* constitution," he elects to give up the game of promise-making and promise-keeping. "Suppose you should contradict yourself; what then? It seems to be a rule of wisdom never to rely on your memory alone, scarcely even in acts of pure memory, but to bring the past for judgment into the thousand-eyed present, and live for ever in a new day."

In this way the individual promise is summoned before the tribunal of the present self, to be kept or broken according to its value at the present moment. A more regular and binding procedure may be "adored by little statesmen and philosophers and divines"; but "with consistency a great soul simply has nothing to do. He may as well concern himself with his shadow on the wall." On the face of things, it would seem that the genius of self-trust who attempted to follow this advice could not be easily discriminated from the opportunist, the dandy, or the slave of caprice. But this challenge is anticipated by Emerson's words about the integrity of the speaker who dares to contradict himself. "Speak what you think now in hard words and tomorrow speak what tomorrow thinks in hard words again, though it contradict every word you said today." Of course, not everyone has hard words to speak, or will venture to speak them even once. It is not clear what to make of the endorsement of contradiction as applied to feebler spirits.

Rhetorically, Emerson knew that with consistency denied as a value, something else was needed to give miraculous justification to a self whose reliance is revealed with every new posture. Though he says the relying matters more than what is relied on, he does also seek to offer one substantial point of anchorage. He calls it by other names in other places—"principles" is one such name, perhaps the most available one. But here he asks "Who is the Trustee?" and the answer is "the aboriginal Self." This "shoots a ray of beauty even into trivial and impure actions, if the least mark of independence appear." The power of self-reliance, then, is such as to transform any act or word, or any contradiction between acts or words, into an occasion of beauty, provided it show some mark of independence. Emerson probably knew and certainly suspected that John Brown was a deranged and murderous enthusiast, but the least ray of independence had shone in his actions at Harper's Ferry and in the speech he made at his trial. It is entirely in keeping with the plan of "Self-Reliance" that its author should later have treated Brown as a prophetic hero worthy of the company of Copernicus, Galileo, Newton, Luther, and Jesus. We read the signs of independence in the self-trusting person just as we read the glories of nature. After all, we are mainly in the world for the sake of these. "It is only in isolate flecks," as William Carlos Williams would write, "that something is given off."

* * *

I have read Emerson on and off for years and have never been sure how to describe the effect he carried into the work of later writers. Plainly, his individualism conferred a self-recognition on American literature, to the extent that our literature is anything but an epithet to augment the dignity of a geographic entity or a mixed ethnic constitution. Maybe rightly a literature *should* be no more than those things; but ours does sometimes seem to be more or other; and Emerson is the reason why it seems so. One hesitates to call his usual subject psychological, because psychology, as the word is commonly used, involves the mind's operations and an interest in the reciprocal relations of the self and a world of other people. One of the odd things about the Emersonian self is how it floats free of such concerns. His subject matter is inward but not in any ordinary sense psychological. Yet I agree with Barbara Packer, Stanley Cavell, George Kateb, and other recent commentators that Emerson is to be read as a moral psychologist. The appropriateness of seeing him that way is justified in his descriptions of such feelings as pride, shame, chagrin, exhilaration.

The moral relation that counts for Emerson, the only one, is set in motion when, by accident, something in me responds to something in the world, as if it were part of me already, a part I needed to come to know again. He took what he liked from Romantic and Puritan writers to assert "that matter is the shadow and spirit the substance—that man acts by an influx of power" (the paraphrase is Perry Miller's). Emerson in this sense shared with minds as diverse as Wordsworth and Jonathan Edwards an intimation of a distance that separates the visible from the invisible. But though in "Self-Reliance" he might speak of "the sense of being which in calm hours rises" in the soul, the source of his sentiment had become, more strictly than in any earlier writer, the soul's peculiar testimony of being steeped in its own ecstasy. The space that seems to widen from such self-discoveries is often described by Emerson as if it were the physical space of landscape. And he knew of course and mainly spoke about the soul's testimony from pleasure alone. Yet his aesthetic was always inclusive. In such a place and gifted with such freedom, why should the soul not testify also of its pain?

Here is a characteristic landscape by Emily Dickinson.

> There's a certain Slant of light
> Winter Afternoons—

That oppresses, like the Heft
Of Cathedral Tunes—

Heavenly Hurt, it gives us—
We can find no scar,
But internal difference,
Where the Meanings, are —

None may teach it—Any—
'Tis the Seal Despair—
An imperial affliction
Sent us of the Air—

When it comes, the Landscape listens—
Shadows—hold their breath—
When it goes, 'tis like the Distance
On the look of Death—

The poem, notwithstanding the mention of death, despair, affliction, and hurt, is not particularly elegiac. I do not think it is about the death of anyone. Nor does it show us the poet saying an unwilling farewell to a hidden aspect of herself. The mood it embodies and means to evoke in the reader is, instead, a mood of attention, the prayer of a soul. The emotion for which the outward correlatives are all picked out with sublime accuracy is the emotion that Dickinson calls despair, but she gives the word its neutral sense of hopelessness, or an absence of hope. This was a mood encouraged by Emerson: "There is somewhat low even in hope" (ambition is as much of a drag as "this corpse of your memory") but despair may be imperial. As it took Dickinson to see, the tuning of the soul's attention to a pitch of clarity not burdened by any desire calls for a preternatural suspense of habit, a suspense even of nature itself. So her poem dwells in a moment when "Shadows—hold their breath"—a line that by itself would declare the presence of a great poet. An implication of the metaphor is that the physical world has turned ghostly, in sympathy with a poet who is neither one of the living nor one of the dead. A ghost may walk without casting a shadow, which is like speaking while holding your breath.

The critics of poetry, by now a majority, who think it is shallow and needless to connect poetry with the natural world, are taking away our rights. There is a certain slant of light you find peculiarly in New England on autumn and winter afternoons. It deepens the red of brick and stone, and darkens the green of lawns. It brings every blue closer to purple and sharpens the edges of shadows. Church and Inness and Martin Johnson Heade all painted it, this light that feels as if it came after something, a light before a sunset that will come on quickly and unremarkably. It is made by Dickinson the clue to a certain quality of the poet's soul. Maybe the light would take on a different enchantment if it were glimpsed streaming through the high window of a cathedral; but though it is tempting to chase "Cathedral Tunes" to funeral music, "affliction" to a fatal disease, and "the look of Death" to a corpse turned face up in a coffin, these suggestions are muted because the figure is meant to stay figurative. The poet speaks of "the Distance/On the look of Death"—nothing is more fixed and endless or more indefinite than that look. Searchers after types in old New England looked for images and shadows of divine things, and Dickinson finds here in actual things images and shadows of herself. It is true the metaphysical poets also did this, especially Vaughan and Herbert, who from traits of idiom and sensuous texture have some affinity with Dickinson. But the metaphors of self and world explored by these poets link the self and the world more firmly by means of their resemblances to God. The metaphors of Dickinson do not work like that. They yield a record of herself alone, and her difference from herself, "internal difference/Where the Meanings, are." This mood in Dickinson is strangely to be cherished.

I do not find in her work, what many readers say they have found, the presence of a character whom I can know. "Success is counted sweetest" does not do it—does not carry the note of interested invitation—much less "Because I could not stop for Death" or "I'm Nobody! Who are you" or any of the obvious candidates. She is not, like Whitman, "Both in and out of the game, and watching and wondering at it." She is out and out. Her great subject is the affliction, or exhilaration, of continuing the game within herself. She sets any possible companion at a distance, often with stock effects of deliberate absurdity, as in the ingenious metaphysical antierotic courtship poem that begins "I cannot live with You." Nevertheless, there are a few poems in which Dickinson allows us to watch her as she looks at herself, the way a novelist may regard a created character.

> A loss of something ever felt I—
> The first that I could recollect
> Bereft I was—of what I knew not
> Too young that any should suspect
>
> A Mourner walked among the children
> I notwithstanding went about

As one bemoaning a Dominion
Itself the only Prince cast out—

Elder, Today, a session wiser
And fainter, too, as Wiseness is
I find myself still softly searching
For my Delinquent Palaces—

And a Suspicion, like a Finger
Touches my Forehead now and then
That I am looking oppositely
For the site of the Kingdom of Heaven—

The last stanza confessed that though once she was punished for living as the devil's child, today she continues still to live from the devil. This is said without Emerson's boyish assurance of maintaining his credit with upright natures. It is more like a sigh of self-exasperation—I still have not got it right. She is restless for satisfactions not of this world, which she has known in herself since childhood, when she was a solitary mourner among the children. She looks on these postures now with a sense of their comedy, but without condescension toward her earlier self. To grow older is to become what they call wise, but this maturity is a weakening of the soul's thirst, a kind of faintness. And so her search has continued. The speaker might be Cathy in *Wuthering Heights*, grown old, except that Dickinson sees herself from outside, and what she looks to recover is not another person. That is one sense in which her palaces are "delinquent." Nature, taken as an end, is as opposite as can be to the kingdom of heaven. But Dickinson abides by her nature without compliant. The poem affords a sociable imagining of the aboriginal self, and it shows that self as gregarious as it ever becomes. How many of the heroes of American fiction are, like the speaker of this poem, daydreamers? Or, if not dreamers, people who, when they avoid thinking of themselves, commence to see spectral characters, animated shadows, ghosts?

* * *

Goodman Brown is a young and susceptible and credulous member of the church in Salem, who goes walking in the woods one night, away from his wife Faith, to meet a gentleman who has lured him on this errand with a vague promise of a spectacle of unsanctified doings. The gentleman, who is the devil, performs what he promised. Several members of the congregation are disclosed to Brown in the commission of lust and other sins. Finally, he is given to witness them gathered in a clearing, in rapt attention at a devil's mass. The consequence, for the rest of his life, as Hawthorne tells us, is Goodman Brown's withdrawal into a profound melancholy. We may understand it as cynicism or disillusionment, but, to him, it is something darker, a loss of faith that can barely be concealed. Brown was a man of the crowd left suddenly alone with his knowledge of the crowd. His self-distrust is unspeakable—figuratively so in the course of the story, literally so by the end.

"Young Goodman Brown" has been interpreted as an ironic record of a delusion, or as a drab commentary, in Hawthorne's plain historical mode, on the fanaticism of Puritan belief. Yet there are clues planted in the story that indicate a quite different intent. The names that pass in review in Brown's consciousness, Sarah Cloyse, Martha Cory, and others, members of the congregation about whom he may or may not be learning the truth on his unseemly errand, include among them actual persons caught up in the witchcraft trials of 1692. Historically, what clinched the cases against those sentenced to death was evidence of a new and dubious kind, "spectral evidence." This meant eyewitness reports of the doings of the spectral shapes of actual people. Such evidence, when admitted to a court of law, as the Salem judges soon determined that it should be admitted, would count against the persons whom a witness could testify to having spectrally seen. It was hearsay evidence raised to a supernatural power. That an accused person had been observed to act in a way that suspended the laws of nature, even though one admitted the laws of nature could never be suspended—this, in Salem, long after the witch-craze had died out in Europe, was permitted to contribute to a proof that the accused was performing acts of wickedness. The process of secularization was far advanced in the laws of Massachusetts in the 1690s, but it made this stop on its way. One of the hanging judges was Judge Hathorne, the ancestor of Nathaniel.

Of the story's commentators, Michael Colacurcio has done justice to the psychological realism of Hawthorne's portrait, and to the relevance of spectral evidence to Brown's real or imagined terrors. But what happens if we read it as a story about the fate of the self in the nineteenth century as much as the fate of the soul in the seventeenth? I believe the writing of "Young Goodman Brown" served Hawthorne as a delayed penitential exercise, but it was also in its time an ironic work of social commentary. We are invited to treat Brown as typical of the pathology of the civic life at Salem, a life that allowed the accusations to go forward because self-trust and social trust had been vexed against each other beyond the breaking point. On the one hand, it is understood by those who seek justification that all social intercourse is a secondary fact of experience; one who judges by such evidence is exposing his crooked assurance regarding the authority of a covenant of works. On the other hand, how shall we judge our experience otherwise? How, given that we are judging in society? A covenant of grace, by definition, is inscrutable to any eye but God's. The covenant of works brings anyway the amenity that it can be known by visible goods. The crudeness and ingenuity of Salem had been to ask whether corruption, wickedness, a secret turning of the heart, could not also be known by visible signs. The trouble is that to believe this requires a translation of grace into a palpable and calculable good. Faith does naturally crave some token of reward. Yet once allow the proof of faith to rest in sensible form and you have confessed your faithlessness. Goodman Brown is caught in this trap. A conformist to the core, a citizen and member-in-good-standing, it does not occur to him to question how sincere his faith can be if it depends on his knowledge of the constancy of his neighbors. So he becomes an unhappy doubter for life, under cover in his place in church.

The story dramatizes an unspoken dialogue that must have passed in the minds of many believers.

Q: What holds you back from sin?
A: Nothing in myself.
QED: This knowledge is so dreadful that you will do anything to evade it. Thus you will put off on your neighbors the terror of your own disobedience.

The more Goodman Brown loses his faith—literally, according to the allegory, the farther he walks from home—the thicker the spectral terrors crowd upon his consciousness. By the end of the story he is ready to testify against them or to withdraw into melancholy. It is a matter of whim or chance which of these endings will befall an individual like Brown. But the whole story is cast as a contrary-to-fact experiment of thought: this apparently is a Salem in which the trials did not happen. No mention is made of them in the denouement recounting the rest of Brown's life; and, to give point to Hawthorne's fable, the trials did not have to happen. They have taken place with sufficient finality in one haunted mind.

Like much of Hawthorne's fiction, "Young Goodman Brown" embodies a thought. It is a diagnosis of why radical Protestantism, with its idea of an aboriginal soul, was destined to be extinguished. Any man whose faith is constituted by his fear of the eyes of other men, and whose sense of *their* faith is constituted by an intuition of their fear of seeing him—such a man will take this journey in his mind, if not in the physical world, and the result will always be the same. To be inquisitive about other people's faith is already to have lost your own. Note that though Hawthorne is not an

Emersonian, he accepts the Emersonian *either/or* regarding the self and society. An incorrigibility that may look like indifference lies at the heart of Protestant justification. Yet an eager interest in the condition of other people's faith is necessary to the regulative function of all religion. How then can a mind dwell separately in its neighborhood—sufficiently attentive to others, but still living in the light of conscience? The ideal citizen, in this way of life, was supposed to resemble Anne Hutchinson and Roger Williams in independence of spirit, and yet to resemble Young Goodman Brown in anxiety of concern with actions of others. The society chose Brown as its model; how could it have done otherwise? Society was the chooser, and the person is a social creature. And so the faith died out. Or, rather, Hawthorne seems to say, it changed its identity without a change of name. He knows because he is living among the wreckage.

* * *

Two centuries later, in the New York society that Henry James describes in "The Jolly Corner," the conflict between the private and the social self has moved to a field of action where commerce calls the tune. It does so without embarrassment, in every walk of life. The question asked by the novice has ceased to be, Shall I be known under a covenant of grace or a covenant of works? It is now, rather, Shall I be free to study myself or shall I make a lot of money? A choice like this, between spiritual and financial profit, has determined the mature life of the hero of James's story. The action turns on a visit he makes to the scene of his departure for that life, to look back on it and to wonder whether his imaginable other self, who would have devoted a career to money-making, could have had as strong a claim as the self that he became instead. About the previous actions of this hero, Spencer Brydon, there hovers the faintest hint of scandal and immoralism: this is the part of his life that he cannot speak of to his confidante, Alice Staverton; we are told it has had to do with "the freedom of a wanderer, overlaid by pleasure, by infidelity." Yet Brydon's has been on the whole a passive life, given to a generous fetching of impressions—a life, in short, a good deal like that of Henry James and not much like that of the grandfather who gave the James family its tremendous fortune. One might say that Brydon has chosen a path of grace; but grace is defined now entirely in aesthetic terms.

He plots and at last achieves an encounter with the ghostly version of himself. And the ghost is terrifying. It has a hunted look: the face appears damaged somehow beyond reentry into humanity; the creature seems to know this and to feel a speechless chagrin. It says nothing at all when discovered, its only gesture being to shield the face from view. The double trick of the revelation is that Brydon, as we gradually come to know him, seems himself to have had an unsatisfactory life, in his withdrawal from the active and commercial world. Now it appears the self he would have turned into, in the course of enterprise and assimilation, was to have suffered a far worse deformity, to be physically and spiritually maimed, an object equally of horror and pity. We are meant to take the ghost simply as a given. But to take it that way means not to credit the eulogistic self-deception by which Brydon allows himself to believe that it was not really the ghost of his own other life. This is the comfort that he coaxes at last from Alice Staverton: "He isn't— no, he isn't—*you!*" Yet the ghost has been memorable enough to show what the story wants it to show.

The salvation or the fall of a self cannot be decided by a right choice of withdrawal from the world of action. That is what Brydon's hunt and his discovery and his self-deception prove, if they prove anything. He has indeed withdrawn, and yet he is among the fallen, and, as the presence of the ghost suggests by indirection, he was always secretly among the fallen. It is this that the ghost has come to tell him. He was fit to live under a covenant of works, instead of which he became a collector of works, and the result has left him bewildered. What he thinks of the new face of the city, which has changed so ominously in his absence, is true also of what he detects about himself on the track of the ghost: "he missed what he would have been sure of finding, he found what he would never have imagined." His other self has had a prosperous career as a monster in the business of building "monstrosities." This is one of several such floating expressions in the story, which test with startling results the power of near puns to construct more than verbal ambiguities. "The ghost of a reason" is another; much play is made with what life may have "made for me"; and James lavishes all his skill of echo and suggestion at the edges of the word "value." This last the story has caught on the point of a larger change of signification, and James uses Brydon's predicament to comment on the traces of cash value in the general theory of value.

On the must optimistic reading, one can take the allegory to suggest that the good man buys a facade of goodness at the price of paralysis and inhibition. Yet it may be a price worth paying. Behind that facade lies a world of action that turns people into ruins, or at best "a tall mass of flats," like the buildings that the new-money men of the city thoughtlessly make and unmake. As an account of the utter contrariety of grace and works, or beauty and utility, "The Jolly Corner" has a companion nearby in James's oeuvre, "The Beast in the Jungle." There the hero is a man waiting for the romantic action or passion that will give his life a meaning, or rather fill it with the one meaning that was to have been its glory. He recognizes too late that this life of waiting has only assured that experience itself should pass him by; the thing, if anything, that was to have happened was a love with the woman beside whom he has stood apprehensively watching. Both of these heroes exemplify an aporia (to borrow Adorno's term): an insoluble complication that reveals a thing at once central and unspeakable about a society and its language. The standoff between will and thought that confronts Brydon—that they should be mutually definitive and mutually exclusive—is a necessary effect of his acceptance of an aboriginal self. Yet grace, if that is the name for the election Brydon seeks for himself—grace that does not aim to produce its own reflection in works or buildings—now more than ever stands in need of external justification. By contrast, in an America frankly dominated by a commercial morality, works are seen as carrying their justification with themselves.

"The Jolly Corner" is written from the conviction that life is a progress or a regress from myself to something deeper in myself. If this lower layer should turn out to disclose another and alien self—an "*alter ego*" as James puts it in an early use of that phrase—I have a preternatural duty to confront it and return with news of the meaning this alter ego discerns in me. When James describes the shiver of pleasure with which his hero bathes in the first glory of his hunt for the ghost, Brydon's sensations uncannily share the emotional pitch of "Self-Reliance"—of "a sense of things which rises, we know not how, in the soul," a sense that is "not diverse from things ... but one with them and proceeds obviously from the same source." What Emerson asserted of the self's relation to the phenomena of life, James will say instead of the self's relation to a ghost that has lived its other life in an unknown possible world. The knowledge that this was therefore a possibility in oneself, that it perhaps remains a part of oneself, has been so forgotten or repressed that it can only be encountered in this shadowy form. "We first share the life by which things exist and afterwards see them as appearances in nature and forget that we have shared their cause." This sentiment, from Emerson on the self's surprise at finding evidence in nature of its own alienated majesty, might well have come from James instead, writing about Spencer Brydon. On the other hand, James on Brydon's intuition of the ghost sounds very like Emerson on the self:

> He was a dim secondary social success—and all with people who had not truly an idea of him. It was all mere surface sound, this murmur of their welcome, this popping of their corks, just as his gestures of response were the extravagant shadows, emphatic in proportion as they meant little, of some game of *ombres chinoises*. He projected himself all day, in thought, straight over the

bristling line of hard unconscious heads and into the other, the real, the waiting life; the life that, as soon as he had heard behind him the click of his great house-door, began for him, on the jolly corner, as beguilingly as the slow opening bars of some rich music follows the tap of the conductor's wand.

He always caught the first effect of the steel point of his stick on the old marble of the hall pavement, large black-and-white squares that he remembered as the admiration of his childhood and that had then made in him, as he now saw, for the growth of an early conception of style. This effect was the dim reverberating tinkle as of some far-off bell hung who should say where?—in the depths of the house, of the past, of that mystical other world that might have flourished for him had he not, for weal or woe, abandoned it. On this impression he did ever the same thing; he put his stick noiselessly away in a corner—feeling the place once more in the likeness of some great glass bowl, all precious concave crystal, set delicately humming by the play of a moist finger round its edge. The concave crystal held, as it were, this mystical other world, and the indescribably fine murmur of its rim was the sigh there, the scarce audible pathetic wail to his strained ear, of all the old baffled foresworn possibilities.

This is the incitement to the hunt—a motive equally aesthetic and autoerotic. "You don't care for anything but yourself," Alice Staverton says to Brydon. Whether one takes her judgment as praise, or a signal of benign complicity, or an accusation, depends on one's reading of James's complex relationship to Protestant antinomianism. At any rate this is not an innocent remark, in the tradition I have been sketching. Brydon for his part might reply—there are Jamesian characters who do almost reply—"How could I care for anything else?" To the extent that this is so, it follows that the object he *has* been caring for, the ghost, must in some way be himself. That is the hardest vein of irony in the happy ending of the story.

If one asks why Brydon should carry his quest to so absurd a length, for he faints and nearly dies at the encounter, the reason can only be that he is hoping to learn definitively that he is absolved. Most of all, perhaps, absolved for not having worked at business, for having had his inconclusive life of freedom and of pleasure touched by infidelity. Whom can he rely on to absolve him, if not himself? Nietzsche in *Beyond Good and Evil* has an aphorism in the form of dialogue: "'I have done that,' says my memory. 'I cannot have done that,' says my pride, and remains inexorable. Eventually—memory yields." James's story is this aphorism, with the interest shifted from action to identity: "I am that"; "I could not be that." Eventually, self-knowledge yields. Farther under, it is one of the unhappiest endings in all of fiction. No hero's marriage to a spouse in whose company he or she is bound to prosper and suffocate has ever produced so despondent a feeling as Brydon's supposed certainty of his innocence. We are left to speculate what the ghost, were the story told from its point of view, would contrive to make of this hero—passive, self-pitying, comfortable, blood-thirsty in his pursuit of curiosities. It could hardly be less terrified by Brydon than he by it.

* * *

"For example," it has been said, "is not an argument." But in criticism sometimes it is the least false thing we can offer. If proof were wanted of the ascendancy of an intractable protestant spirit centered in the self, the control for the experiment would have to come from witnessing the same principle at work in a religious writer of an apparently opposite sort. Say a Catholic writer, in the line of Mauriac and the Graham Greene of *Brighton Rock*, for whom God's justice is absolute and separate from man and the patterns resembling faith in the soul are never what they seem. Flannery O'Connor's story "A Good Man Is Hard to Find" is a drama of recognition between two unbelievers. A normally disagreeable family, husband and wife and excitable children and a baby, are on a car trip with the husband's mother and the cat Pitty Sing. They hear of The Misfit and his gang along the way, and the meddling grandmother, sure of herself and every wrong, leads them on a picturesque side trip down an unfamiliar country road. They go off the road into a ditch, and The Misfit is the one who finds them. He has a theory that Christian revelation only matters if it was divulged to him directly, a theory in which there are strange echoes of the high-minded Antinomians.

> "Jesus was the only One that ever raised the dead," The Misfit continued, "and He shouldn't have done it. He thown everything off balance. If He did what He said, then it's nothing for you to do but thow away everything and follow Him, and if He didn't then it's nothing for you to do but enjoy the few minutes you go left the best way you can—by killing somebody or burning down his house or doing some other meanness to him. No pleasure but meanness," he said and his voice had become almost a snarl.
> "Maybe He didn't raise the dead," the old lady mumbled, not knowing what she was saying and feeling so dizzy that she sank down in the ditch with her legs twisted under her.
> "I wasn't there so I can't say He didn't," The Misfit said. "I

wisht I had of been there," he said, hitting the ground with his fist. "It ain't right I wasn't there, because if I had of been there I would of known."

A grotesque flicker of charity comes through the grandmother's answering gesture of extending her arms to embrace the man: "You're one of my own children!" That is when he shoots her.

"She would have been a good woman," The Misfit will say later, "if it had been somebody there to shoot her every minute of her life." This is a boisterous joke but is also speaks the literal truth of his relation to the grandmother. The menace of violent death alone could precipitate the freely given act of love by which at last we know that she is prepared. "The least ray of independence" came to be visible in the most impure and confused of her moments. Flannery O'Connor, when she commented on this story, was at pains to stress an orthodox reading of the moment when the grandmother beckons in a Christ-like posture. In the same lecture, O'Connor directed some well-chosen words of derision against the sophisticates who make The Misfit into a kind of hero. But though her portrait of The Misfit is indeed penetrable as that of a "prophet gone wrong," to use O'Connor's description of him outside the story, his actions are so stark in their self-reliance as to eclipse the grandmother's change of heart among the motives of the story. The Misfit has performed a gratuitous act obedient to the law of his constitution. The obstacle that all institutions are to the Emersonian believer, Jesus Christ and the reports of His divinity are to him. The only way to right the things that Jesus set wrong—the only way not to shrivel and wither in His shadow—is to act regardless of any previous law or custom. In O'Connor's novel *The Violent Bear It Away*, and in other characteristic stories such as "The Life You Save May Be Your Own," no alternative ever arises to counter the dominant type she aimed to satirize, the misfit who can absolve himself. These stories are one of the great things in American literature of the twentieth century: impartial, fearless, disciplined yet utterly wild. O'Connor believed that her work was misunderstood, but did she not also misunderstand her self? She returns again and again to characters like The Misfit, not to damn them, since that would be redundant, but chiefly to watch and listen. She was a Catholic in the grace she asserted, but her particular subject, and the knowledge of America it reflects, are antinomian with a ferocity the author may judge but cannot shed.

The analysis might go on. The American psychosis has not yet come to anything like a provisional end. One sign of its prevalence is the way the myth is assumed as a challenge even by gifted writers who are not quite possessed by it—Mailer in *An American Dream*, Bellow in *Henderson the Rain*

King. Through all the testimony, one fact anyway stands out with distinctness. This is the growing importance of money as a dissolvent of manners and customs, money as an image of something deeper than experience, money as a power that converts every rival symbolism to a language of its own. In every period of our history, but never more so than today, money has been the leveler by which self-engrossment is made to adapt to a surface ideal of gregarious practicality. Money has taken increasingly to itself the obscure and compelling charge that Emerson assigned to the hidden self. It has the right kind of abstraction, and the right kind of opacity. It is at once an embodiment and a creator of value: the farther from any produced object, the better. It is the thing, more convenient than a person, that absolves you to yourself. By comparison with money, the soul has lapsed to the inferior reality of an entity that cannot be modified or exchange. It would take a novelist of James's powers to focus "the thousand-eyed present" on a communion so purified of people that even the self has become a name for a thing.

Chronology

1804	Nathaniel Hawthorne born on July 4 in Salem, Massachusetts, the second of three children of Elizabeth (neé Manning) and Nathaniel Hathorne, a ship's captain.
1808	Nathaniel Hathorne dies of yellow fever at Suriname (Dutch Guiana). The Hathornes move to the Manning family home on 12 Herbert Street, Salem.
1813	In November, a foot injury causes lameness and keeps Nathaniel from school for fourteen months. He is tutored at home by Joseph Worcester, who will later become the noted lexicographer.
1814	At mid-year, a new physician, Dr. Smith of Hanover, prescribes a new form of hydrotherapy and by late August there is some improvement.
1818	In the fall, the Hathorne family moves to Raymond, Maine, which is still a wilderness area. Nathaniel will later idealize his life in Maine, where he hunted, fished, and roamed through the woods at will. During the winter of 1818–1819, he attends school at nearby Stroudwater, under the direction of Reverend Caleb Bradley, a Harvard graduate. He is restless and unhappy here. Nevertheless, he reads a good deal during this time, his two favorite books being Spenser's *Faerie Queene* and Bunyan's *Pilgrim's Progress*.
1819	In the summer, Nathaniel returns to Salem to live with his

mother's family, under the guardianship of his uncle Robert Manning. His mother stays in Maine. Here he will attend Samuel Archer's school on Marlborough Street. During this time, Nathaniel reads a great deal, including *Waverley*, *The Mysteries of Udolpho*, *Roderick Random*, *The Adventures of Count Fathom*, and the first volume of *The Arabian Nights*.

1820   Prepares for college under Benjamin L. Oliver in Salem, and works part-time as secretary and bookkeeper for his Uncle William in the stagecoach office. Also embarks on a short-lived project as publisher, editor and author of a newspaper, *The Spectator*, patterned after the famous journal of Addison and Steele. The issues, which are carefully written out by hand, include such essays as "On Wealth," "On Benevolence," and "On Industry." The first issue is dated August 21, 1820 and the last, September 25, 1820.

1821   Writes to his mother informing her that he does not want to become a minister, lawyer, or physician, but, rather, an author. In October, Nathaniel enters Bowdoin College, New Brunswick, Maine. Decides to take his meals at the home of Samuel Newman, a young and competent professor of Greek and Latin. The bane of his college days, in addition to compulsory religious services, is the required weekly declamation. At Bowdoin, he befriends Horatio Bridge, Franklin Pierce, Jonathan Cilley, and Henry Wadsworth Longfellow.

1825   In September, Nathaniel graduates from Bowdoin, 18th in a class of 38. Returns to live with his family in Salem.

1828   Nathaniel adds the "w" to his family name. In October, *Fanshawe* is published anonymously by the Boston publisher, Marsh and Capen. Hawthorne soon realizes that publishing this apprentice work is a mistake, and disposes of as many copies as he can locate.

1829   Plans a second collection of stories, to be called *Provincial Tales*, and submits manuscript to S.G. Goodrich, editor of *The Token*.

1830   From this year forward, Hawthorne's stories and sketches begin appearing anonymously in gift-annuals, newspapers and magazines—*The Token*, the *Salem Gazette*, the *New-England Magazine*, the *American Monthly Magazine*, *Youth's Keepsake*.

1831   A fire at the Marsh and Capen store destroys all the unsold
          copies of *Fanshawe*. Hawthorne releases some tales
          intended for publication in *The Token*: "The Gentle Boy,"
          "The Wives of the Dead," "Roger Malvin's Burial," and
          "My Kinsman, Major Molineux." Hawthorne visits the
          Shaker community in Canterbury, New Hampshire, where
          he develops a keen interest in their way of life and its
          literary possibilities.

1832   Hawthorne plans a third collection, to be called "The Story
          Teller." During September–October he makes extensive
          journeys in northern New York State, visits Niagara Falls
          and travels through the heart of the White Mountains of
          New Hampshire, Vermont, and Montreal.

1834   During November–December, "The Story Teller, Nos. I
          and II," is published in *New-England Magazine*.

1835   "Young Goodman Brown" is published in *New-England
          Magazine*. "The Minister's Black Veil," "The Maypole of
          Merrymount," and "The Wedding-Knell" are accepted for
          publication in *The Token*.

1836   In January, Hawthorne makes his entry into the
          professional literary world when he moves to Boston to edit
          American Magazine of Useful and Entertaining Knowledge. In
          March, the first issue with Hawthorne's name as editor
          appears. His salary is not paid. In May, the magazine goes
          bankrupt. From May to September, Hawthorne, with the
          help of Elizabeth Palmer Peabody, writes *Peter Parley's
          Universal History, on the Basis of Geography*.

1837   *Twice-Told Tales* is published in March. Unbeknownst to
          Hawthorne, Horatio Bridge has given his financial
          guarantee to publisher. In July, Longfellow's highly
          favorable review of *Twice-Told Tales* appears in the *North
          American Review*, declaring Hawthorne to be "a new star ...
          in the heaven of poetry." In the fall, Hawthorne begins his
          association with John L. O'Sullivan's *Democratic Review*.
          Eight Hawthorne pieces appear there in fifteen months. In
          November, he meets Sophia Amelia Peabody.

1838   From July to September, Hawthorne lives in North Adams,
          Massachusetts, where he enjoys observing small-town rural
          life, and makes trips to the Berkshires, upstate New York,
          Vermont, and Connecticut.

1839	In January, with the help of Sophia's sister, Elizabeth, and as a result of insufficient earnings as a writer, Hawthorne takes on appointment as measurer in the Boston Custom House, a position he will hold for two years. On March 6, he writes the first surviving love letter to Sophia Peabody.
1840	In November, Hawthorne resigns from the Custom House, effective as of January 1, 1841. In December, he publishes *Grandfather's Chair*, a children's history of New England, dated 1841. Late in the year, Hawthorne invests in George Ripley's Brook Farm, an experiment in communal living in West Roxbury, Massachusetts, with the hope that he would find a situation that would support his writing.
1841	During the winter, Hawthorne returns to Salem and publishes *Famous Old People*. In March, *The Liberty Tree* is published. For several months, Hawthorne labors among the transcendental community before giving up his plan of bringing Sophia there after their marriage. In October, he leaves the community for Boston, forfeiting his financial investment. Nevertheless, his experience at Brook Farm will provide the basis for *The Blithedale Romance*.
1842	In January, the second edition of *Twice-Told Tales* is published, with an additional volume containing sixteen more recent tales and sketches together with five that antedate the 1837 collection. On July 9, Hawthorne and Sophia Peabody are married. They move to Concord, Massachusetts and rent the Old Manse, where they will live until October 1845. Hawthorne completes another children's book, *Biographical Stories for Children*.
1844	On March 3, their daughter Una, named after Spenser's heroine, is born at the Old Manse. From October 1844 to October 1845, Hawthorne lives in Concord. Ralph Waldo Emerson, Henry David Thoreau, and Louisa Alcott are resident in Concord as well.
1845	From January to April, Hawthorne edits Horatio Bridge's *Journal of an African Cruiser*. In October, the Hawthornes move to his mother's house in Salem, as Nathaniel seeks a political appointment to supplement his meager income from writing. It is not until 1847 that the Hawthornes find their own house in Salem.
1846	On April 9, Hawthorne is sworn in as surveyor at Salem

Custom House on Derby Street, having been nominated by President Polk. The first two years in the position are not a productive literary period. In June, *Mosses from an Old Manse* is published in two volumes. It is a critical, albeit not a financial, success. On June 22, Julian Hawthorne is born.

1847   *Mosses from an Old Manse* inspires Poe's review "Tale Writing—Nathaniel Hawthorne," published in *Godey's Lady's Book* in November in which he complains of Hawthorne's monotony of style and penchant for allegory.

1848   In November, Hawthorne becomes manager and corresponding secretary of Salem Lyceum, engaging lecturers for the organization's regular programs. He invites Emerson, Thoreau, Theodore Parker, Horace Mann, Charles Sumner, Daniel Webster and Louis Agassiz to lecture.

1849   On June 8, Hawthorne, a Democrat, is removed from office at the Custom House, following the election of Whig President, Zachary Taylor, in 1848. On July 31, his mother dies. In September, he begins writing *The Scarlet Letter*, which he originally planned as a long short story, and "The Custom House."

1850   In March, *The Scarlet Letter* is published in an edition of 2,500 copies. This is followed by a second edition of 2,500 in April, followed by a third edition of 1,000 copies in September. In June, the Hawthornes move to a small red farmhouse, "Red Cottage," in Lenox, Massachusetts. On August 5, Hawthorne meets Herman Melville at a literary picnic in the Berkshires. In August, he also begins *The House of the Seven Gables*. On August 17 and 24, Melville's flattering and effusive essay, "Hawthorne and His Mosses" appears anonymously in *The Literary World*. In November, *True Stories from History and Biography* (a reissue of *Grandfather's Chair* and *Biographical Stories*) is published, dated 1851.

1851   In March, a third edition of *Twice-Told Tales* is published, with a preface. In April, two printings of *The House of the Seven Gables* are issued, followed by one in May and one in September. On May 20, Rose Hawthorne is born. In November, *A Wonder Book for Girls and Boys* is published, dated 1852. In December, *The Snow-Image* is published, dated 1852. Melville dedicates *Moby Dick* to Hawthorne, "In token for my admiration of his genius."

1852   In May, Hawthorne buys the Alcott House in Concord, naming it "The Wayside." In July, *The Blithedale Romance* is published. In September, Hawthorne publishes *Life of Franklin Pierce*, a campaign biography of the presidential candidate. In November, Franklin Pierce is elected president.

1853   In March, Hawthorne is nominated for the lucrative consulship at Liverpool and Manchester by President Pierce. In July, he embarks on an eleven-day voyage for England with his family aboard the paddle-wheel steamer, the *Niagara*. In September, *Tanglewood Tales*, a volume of children's stories, is published.

1853–57   While working as consul, Hawthorne keeps notebooks in which he records his English experiences and impressions.

1854   Revised edition of *Mosses* is published.

1856   In November, Melville visits Hawthorne in Liverpool on way to Holy Land. He also meets Hawthorne briefly on return journey in May 1857.

1857   In October, Hawthorne gives up his consulship.

1858   In January, Hawthorne travels to Italy by way of France and takes up residence in Rome. He keeps notebooks on his Italian experiences and begins work on an English romance, never to be completed, but published posthumously as *The Ancestral Footstep*. From May to October, the Hawthornes live in a villa in Florence. He begins work on a romance with an Italian theme.

1859   In June, Hawthorne returns to England, where he rewrites the Italian romance.

1860   In February, *The Transformation* is published in England; in March the romance is published in America with the title *The Marble Faun*. In June, Hawthorne returns to America and settles at "The Wayside," in Concord, where he begins work on a second version of his English romance.

1861   Hawthorne abandons the romance, after making seven studies for the story. The fragment is published as *Dr. Grimshawe's Secret*. In autumn, Hawthorne begins work on a series of English essays. He begins a new romance on theme of elixir of life, but abandons this in 1862. Set at the time of the Revolution, the fragment is published posthumously as *Septimius Felton*.

1862   Hawthorne's health declines and he is deeply troubled by the Civil War. He travels to Washington, D.C., where he meets President Lincoln and tours the battlefields at Manassas and Harpers Ferry, Virginia. Upon his return home, he writes "Chiefly About War Matters," which appears in the *Atlantic Monthly* in July.

1863   In September, *Our Old Home* is published, the collected essays on England, most of which had appeared separately in *Atlantic Monthly*.

1864   On May 19, while on a tour of New England with Franklin Pierce, Hawthorne dies quietly in his sleep in Plymouth, New Hampshire, having written three chapters of another romance about the elixir of life, posthumously published as *The Dolliver Romance*.

Contributors

HAROLD BLOOM is Sterling Professor of the Humanities at Yale University. He is the author of over 20 books, including *Shelley's Mythmaking* (1959), *The Visionary Company* (1961), *Blake's Apocalypse* (1963), *Yeats* (1970), *A Map of Misreading* (1975), *Kabbalah and Criticism* (1975), *Agon: Toward a Theory of Revisionism* (1982), *The American Religion* (1992), *The Western Canon* (1994), and *Omens of Millennium: The Gnosis of Angels, Dreams, and Resurrection* (1996). *The Anxiety of Influence* (1973) sets forth Professor Bloom's provocative theory of the literary relationships between the great writers and their predecessors. His most recent books include *Shakespeare: The Invention of the Human* (1998), a 1998 National Book Award finalist, *How to Read and Why* (2000), *Genius: A Mosaic of One Hundred Exemplary Creative Minds* (2002), and *Hamlet: Poem Unlimited* (2003). In 1999, Professor Bloom received the prestigious American Academy of Arts and Letters Gold Medal for Criticism, and in 2002 he received the Catalonia International Prize.

HAROLD F. MOSHER, JR. has been Associate Professor of English at Northern Illinois University. He is an editor of *ReJoycing: New Readings of Dubliners* (1998). and the author of "Greimas, Bremond, and the Miller's Tale" (1997) and "Ambiguity in the Reading Process: Narrative Mode in 'After the Race'" (1986).

JANE DONAHUE EBERWEIN has been a Professor of English at Oakland University. She is the editor of *An Emily Dickinson Encyclopedia* (1998), and author of "New Perspectives on the American Rhetoric of

Conversion" (1999) and "Dickinson's Local, Global, and Cosmic Perspectives" (1998).

JOHN S. HARDT has been Associate Professor of English and Chair of the Language and Literature Division at Ferrum College in Virginia. He is co-author of "James Studies 1978–1979: An Analytic Bibliographical Essay" (1981) and "And Faulkner Nodded: Calvin Coolidge in Sanctuary" (1979).

JULES ZANGER has been Professor of English at Southern Illinois University at Edwardsville. He is the author of "Poetry and Political Rhetoric: Bryant's 'The Prairies'" (2000), "Cold Pastoral: Sherwood Anderson's 'Death in the Woods'" (1990), and "The Disenchantment of Magic" (1986).

JOAN ELIZABETH EASTERLY has been Associate Professor of English and Foreign Languages at Pellissipi State Technical Community College in Knoxville.

WALTER SHEAR has been a Professor of English at Pittsburgh (KS) State University. He is the author of "Bellow's Fictional Rhetoric: The Voice of the Other" (1996) and "Generation Differences and the Diaspora in *The Joy Luck Club*" (1993).

BENJAMIN FRANKLIN V has been a Professor of English at the University of South Carolina. He is the author of *Boston Printers, Publishers and Booksellers: 1640–1800*, "The Selling of *A Spy in the House of Love*" (1997) and "Advertisements for Herself: The Anaïs Nin Press" (1997), and served as editor for *Recollections of Anaïs Nin* (1996).

JAMES C. KEIL has been Assistant Professor of English at Howard University. He is the author of "Reading, Writing, and Recycling: Literary Archaeology and the Shape of Hawthorne's Career" (1992) and "Theories, Concepts, and the Acquisition of Word Meaning" (1991).

DEBRA JOHANYAK has been Assistant Professor of English at the University of Akron-Wayne College, Orville, Ohio. She is the author of "William Gilmore Sims: Deviant Paradigms of Southern Womanhood?" (1993) and "James Fenimore Cooper: The Maternal Heritage of Sex and Sin in the Leatherstocking Dark Ladies" (1995).

EDWARD JAYNE has served as a professor of English lecturing on American literature. He is the author of *Negative Poetics* (1992) and "Metaphoric Hypersignification, Metonymic Designification" (1994).

DAVID BROMWICH is the Bird White Housum Professor of English and a lecturer at the Law School at Yale University. He is the author of *Skeptical Music: Essays on Modern Poetry* (2001), *Disowned by Memory: Wordsworth's Poetry of the 1790s* (1998), and *A Choice of Inheritance: Self and Community from Edmund Burke to Robert Frost* (1989).

Bibliography

Benoit, Raymond. "'Young Goodman Brown:' The Second Time Around." *Nathaniel Hawthorne Review* 19, no. 2 (Spring 1993): 18–21.

Berkove, Lawrence I. "'Reasoning as We Go': The Flawed Logic of Young Goodman Brown." *Nathaniel Hawthorne Review* 24, no. 1 (1998 Spring): 46–52.

Boudreau, Gordon V. "The Summons of Young Goodman Brown." *Greyfriar* 13 (1972): 15–24.

Brown, Dennis. "Literature and Existential Psychoanalysis: 'My Kinsman, Major Molineux' and 'Young Goodman Brown.'" *Canadian Review of American Studies* 4 (1973): 65–73.

Burleson, Donald R. "Sabbats: Hawthorne/Wharton." *Studies in Weird Fiction* 12 (Spring 1993): 12–16.

Cherry, Fannye N. "The Sources of Hawthorne's 'Young Goodman Brown.'" *American Literature* 5 (1934): 342–48.

Clark, James W., Jr. "Hawthorne's Use of Evidence in 'Young Goodman Brown.'" *Essex Institute Historical Collections* 104 (1968): 12–34.

Clark, James W., Jr. "Hawthorne's Use of Evidence in 'Young Goodman Brown.'" *Essex Institute Historical Collections* 111 (1975): 12–34.

Cohen, B. Bernard. "Deodat Lawson's Christ's Fidelity and Hawthorne's 'Young Goodman Brown.'" *Essex Institute Historical Collections* 104 (1968): 349–70.

Colacurcio, Michael J. "Visible Sanctity and Specter Evidence: The Moral World of Hawthorne's 'Young Goodman Brown.'" *Essex Institute Historical Collections* 110 (1974): 259–99.

Connolly, Thomas E., ed. Introduction to *Nathaniel Hawthorne: "Young Goodman Brown."* Columbus, Ohio: C.E. Merrill (1968).

Cook, Reginald. "The Forest of Goodman Brown's Night: A Reading of Hawthorne's 'Young Goodman Brown.'" *New England Quarterly* 43 (1970): 473–81.

Harding, Brian, ed. Introduction to *Young Goodman Brown and Other Tales.* New York: Oxford University Press (1998): vii–xxx.

Humma, John B. "'Young Goodman Brown' and the Failure of Hawthorne's Ambiguity." *Colby Library Quarterly* 9 (1971): 425–31.

Kesterson, David B. "Nature and Theme in 'Young Goodman Brown.'" *Dickinson Review* 2 (1970): 42–46.

Kim, Ji-Won. "Text Edifies Its Reader: A Reading of N. Hawthorne's 'Young Goodman Brown.'" *The Journal of English Language and Literature* 42, no. 1 (1996): 141–58.

Levin, David. "Shadows of Doubt: Specter Evidence in Hawthorne's 'Young Goodman Brown.'" *American Literature* 34 (1962): 344–52.

Levy, Leo B. "The Problem of Faith in 'Young Goodman Brown.'" *Journal of English and Germanic Philology* 74 (1975): 375–87.

Liebman, Sheldon W. "The Reader in 'Young Goodman Brown.'" *Nathaniel Hawthorne Journal* 5 (1975): 156–67.

Martin, Terry. "Anti-Allegory and the Reader in 'Young Goodman Brown.'" *Mid-Hudson Language Studies* 11 (1988): 31–40.

Matheson, Terence J. "'Young Goodman Brown': Hawthorne's Condemnation of Conformity." *Nathaniel Hawthorne Journal* 8 (1978): 137–145.

Mathews, James W. "Antinomianism in 'Young Goodman Brown.'" *Studies in Short Fiction* 3 (1965): 73–5.

McKeithan, D.M. "Hawthorne's 'Young Goodman Brown': An Interpretation." *Modern Language Notes* 67 (1952): 93–6.

Morris, Christopher. "Deconstructing 'Young Goodman Brown.'" *American Transcendental Quarterly* 2, no. 1 (March 1988): 23–33.

Park, Yangkeun. "Application of Discourse Analysis to Literature: Reinterpretation of Hawthorne's 'Young Goodman Brown.'" *The Journal of English Language and Literature* 37, no. 4 (Winter 1991): 901–19.

Robinson, E. Arthur. "The Vision of Goodman Brown: A Source and Interpretation." *American Literature* 35 (1963): 218–25.

Shuffleton, Frank. "Nathaniel Hawthorne and the Revival Movement." *American Transcendental Quarterly* 44 (Fall 1979): 311–323.

St. Armand, Barton L. "'Young Goodman Brown' as Historical Allegory." *Nathaniel Hawthorne Journal* (1973): 183–97.

Stoehr, Taylor. "'Young Goodman Brown' and Hawthorne's Theory of Mimesis." *Nineteenth-Century Fiction* 23 (1969): 393–412.

Tritt, Michael. "'Young Goodman Brown' and the Psychology of Projection." *Studies in Short Fiction* 23, no. 1 (Winter 1986): 113–117.

Walsh, Thomas F., Jr. "The Bedeviling of Young Goodman Brown." *Modern Language Quarterly* 19 (1958): 331–6.

Wilczynski, Marek. "Nathaniel Hawthorne's 'Young Goodman Brown': An Attempt at Deconstruction." *Studia Anglica Posnaniensia* 20 (1987): 227–39.

Williamson, James L. "'Young Goodman Brown': Hawthorne's 'Devil in Manuscript.'" *Studies in Short Fiction* 18, no. 2 (Spring 1981): 155–162.

Wright, Elizabeth. "The New Psychoanalysis and Literary Criticism: A Reading of Hawthorne and Melville." *Poetics Today* 3, no. 2 (1982 Spring): p. 89–105.

Acknowledgments

"The Sources of Ambiguity in Hawthorne's "Young Goodman Brown": A Structuralist Approach" by Harold F. Mosher, Jr., from *ESQ* 26, 1st quarter (1980): 16–25. © 1980 by *ESQ: A Journal of the American Renaissance*. Reprinted by permission.

"My Faith is Gone! 'Young Goodman Brown' and Puritan Conversion" by Jane Donahue Eberwein. From *Christianity and Literature* 32, no. 1 (Fall 1982): 23–32. © 1982 by CCL. Reprinted by permission.

"Doubts in the American Garden: Three Cases of Paradisal Skepticism" by John S. Hardt. From *Studies in Short Fiction* 25, no. 3 (Summer 1988): 249–59. © 1989 by *Studies in Short Fiction*, Inc. Reprinted by permission.

"'Young Goodman Brown' and 'A White Heron': Correspondences and Illuminations" by Jules Zanger. From *Papers on Language and Literature* 26, no. 3 (Summer 1990): 346–57. © 1990 by The Board of Trustees, Southern Illinois University. Reprinted by permission.

"Lachrymal Imagery in Hawthorne's 'Young Goodman Brown'" by Joan Elizabeth Easterly. From *Studies in Short Fiction* 28, no. 3 (Summer 1991): 339–43. © 1991 by *Studies in Short Fiction*, Inc. Reprinted by permission.

"Cultural Fate and Social Freedom in Three American Short Stories" by Walter Shear. From *Studies in Short Fiction* 29, no. 4 (Fall 1992): 543–49. © 1992 by *Studies in Short Fiction*, Inc. Reprinted by permission.

"Goodman Brown and the Puritan Catechism" by Benjamin Franklin V. From *ESQ* 40, no. 1 (1994): 66–88. © 1994 by *ESQ*. Reprinted by permission.

"Hawthorne's 'Young Goodman Brown': Early Nineteenth-Century and Puritan Constructions of Gender" by James C. Keil. From *New England Quarterly* 69, no. 1 (March 1996): 33–55. © 1996 by *The New England Quarterly*. Reprinted by permission of the publisher and the author.

"Romanticism's Fallen Edens: The Malignant Contribution of Hawthorne's Literary Landscapes" by Debra Johanyak. From *CLA Journal* 42, no. 3 (March 1999): 353–63. © 1999 by the College Language Association. Reprinted by permission of the College Language Association.

"Pray Tarry With Me Young Goodman Brown" by Edward Jayne. From *Literature and Psychology*, vol. 29, no. 3 (1979): 100–13. © 1979 by *Literature and Psychology*. Reprinted by permission.

"The American Psychosis" by David Bromwich. From *Raritan* vol. 21, no. 4 (Spring 2002): 33–63. © 2002 by *Raritan: A Quarterly Review*. Reprinted by permission.

Index